The Best of COUNTRY COOKING 2002

Editor: Jean Steiner
Art Director: Kristin Bork
Food Editor: Janaan Cunningham
Associate Editors: Julie Schnittka, Susan Uphill, Heidi Reuter Lloyd
Food Photography Artists: Stephanie Marchese, Vicky Marie Moseley
Food Photography: Dan Roberts, Rob Hagen
Photo Studio Manager: Anne Schimmel
Production: Ellen Lloyd, Catherine Fletcher
Publisher: Roy Reiman

©2002 Reiman Publications, LLC
5400 S. 60th St., Greendale WI 53129
International Standard Book Number: 0-89821-340-1
International Standard Serial Number: 1097-8321

For additional copies of this book or information on other books, write *Taste of Home* Books, P.O. Box 908, Greendale WI 53129, call toll-free 1-800/344-2560 to order with a credit card or visit our Web site at **www.reimanpub.com**.

PICTURED ON COVER. From the top: Sweet 'n' Sour Tossed Salad (p. 61), Pretty Plum Parfaits (p. 118) and Pineapple Ham Loaf (p. 18).

PICTURED ABOVE. Clockwise from top right: Macaroni and Cheese Casserole (p. 79), Poached Salmon (p. 44) and Coconut Cream Meringue Pie (p. 122).

Treat Your Family to the Best Cooking in the Country!

WELCOME TO *The Best of Country Cooking 2002*. If you and your family love down-home food, you'll savor the 366 home-style recipes in this just-published book—the fifth in our popular cookbook series.

This giant collection includes the very best recipes from recent issues of *Country Woman*, *Country*, *Country EXTRA*, *Reminisce* and *Reminisce EXTRA* magazines. All are hearty, wholesome and proven favorites of a family just like yours.

You see, these recipes weren't developed in some high-tech industrial "kitchen". Instead, they're from the personal recipe files of hundreds of everyday cooks across the country. Each and every dish has been sampled and approved by the toughest critic around—a hungry family!

What's more, every recipe in this book was tested—many of them twice—by us as well. So you can be doubly confident each and every dish is a "keeper" that doesn't require a tryout first.

So go ahead *today* and take your pick of this beautiful book's 93 Main Dishes, including Stovetop Pot Roast (a twice-a-month "must" in Mary Lou Chernik's Taos, New Mexico home), Southern Fried Chicken (Amherst, Virginia cook Patricia Gowen's tasty twist on the traditional recipe) and Pineapple Ham Loaf (a proven potluck pleaser for Aleatha Smith of Billings, Montana).

There's also a Side Dishes & Condiments chapter filled with 30 country-style complements like Crumb-Topped Broccoli Bake from Hope Huggins of Santa Cruz, California. And turn to Breads & Rolls for a basketful of fresh-baked goodies such as Butter-Dipped Biscuit Squares shared by Rebekah DeWitt of Star City, Arkansas—they go great with any meal.

Everyone will save room for dessert when any of this book's 57 scrumptious cakes, pies, cookies and more will be the sweet conclusion. Beverly, West Virginia baker Lori Daniels likes to serve Macaroon Cherry Pie on Presidents' Day or Valentine's Day, but it's popular with her family in any season. And Erna Madsen's Holiday Brownies are so chocolaty, she can't wait until Christmas to make them in her Bothell, Washington kitchen.

In addition, this tried-and-true treasury contains a savory selection of 54 Soups & Salads, and an appealing assortment of Snacks & Beverages. You'll also enjoy some extra-special features most other cookbooks overlook:

Thirty-Minute Meals—Six complete meals (18 recipes in all) that are ready to eat in *less than half an hour*.

Memorable Meals—Six complete meals featuring 24 favorite recipes from home cooks.

Cooking for Two—A separate chapter with 48 recipes all properly proportioned to serve two people.

Want more? *The Best of Country Cooking 2002* offers individual sections on cooking quick-and-easy fare that you can whip up for your hungry family with little effort.

As you page through *The Best of Country Cooking 2002*, watch for the special symbol at right. It signifies a "best of the best" recipe—a winner of a coast-to-coast cooking contest one of our magazines sponsored.

Finally, throughout this colorful collection are lots of helpful kitchen tips from everyday cooks plus dozens of "restricted diet" recipes marked with this check ✓ that use less fat, sugar or salt.

See why we call this book "The Best"? Now, wait 'til you and your family *taste* why!

CONTENTS

GET READY to gather compliments when you serve any of these super snacks and refreshing beverages at your next get-together.

PERFECT FOR PARTIES. From top: Taco Joe Dip (p. 6), Summertime Strawberry Punch (p. 5), Cucumber Canapes (p. 5) and Marinated Shrimp (p. 5).

Snacks & Beverages

MARINATED SHRIMP

(Pictured at left)

Margaret DeLong, Gainesville, Florida

Seafood is a staple here in Florida. This recipe is quick and easy to make and can be prepared well in advance. I always seem to get a lot of requests for the recipe when I make it for a party.

- 2 pounds cooked medium shrimp, peeled and deveined
- 1 medium red onion, cut into rings
- 2 medium lemons, cut into slices
- 1 cup pitted ripe olives
- 1/2 cup olive *or* vegetable oil
- 1/3 cup minced fresh parsley
- 3 tablespoons red wine vinegar *or* cider vinegar
- 3 tablespoons lemon juice
- 1 garlic clove, minced
- 1 bay leaf
- 1 tablespoon minced fresh basil *or* 1 teaspoon dried basil
- 1 teaspoon salt
- 1 teaspoon ground mustard
- 1/4 teaspoon pepper

In a 3-qt. glass serving bowl, combine shrimp, onion, lemons and olives. In a jar with a tight-fitting lid, combine remaining ingredients; shake well. Pour over shrimp mixture and stir gently to coat. Cover and refrigerate for 24 hours, stirring occasionally. Discard bay leaf before serving. **Yield:** 14 servings.

SUMMERTIME STRAWBERRY PUNCH

(Pictured at left)

Mary McQueen, Woodstock, Ontario

This drink is perfect for a summer picnic or family get-together. When I serve it in a punch bowl, I'll often make an ice ring of ginger ale with a few berries in it to float on top instead of using ice cubes.

- 1 can (12 ounces) frozen pink lemonade concentrate, thawed, undiluted
- 1 package (20 ounces) frozen unsweetened strawberries, partially thawed
- 1/4 cup sugar
- 2 cups cold brewed strong tea
- 2 liters ginger ale, chilled

Ice cubes

In a food processor or blender, combine lemonade concentrate, strawberries and sugar. Cover and process until smooth. Transfer to a large pitcher or punch bowl; stir in tea. Add the ginger ale and ice cubes. Serve immediately. **Yield:** 3-1/2 quarts.

CUCUMBER CANAPES

(Pictured at left)

Nadine Whittaker, South Plymouth, Massachusetts

Folks always ask me for the recipe whenever I serve these delicate finger sandwiches with a creamy herb spread and festive red and green garnishes.

- 1 cup mayonnaise (no substitutes)
- 1 package (3 ounces) cream cheese, softened
- 1 tablespoon grated onion
- 1 tablespoon minced chives
- 1/2 teaspoon cider vinegar
- 1/2 teaspoon Worcestershire sauce
- 1 garlic clove, minced
- 1/4 teaspoon paprika
- 1/8 teaspoon curry powder
- 1/8 teaspoon *each* dried oregano, thyme, basil, parsley flakes and dill weed
- 1 loaf (1 pound) white *or* rye bread
- 2 medium cucumbers, scored and thinly sliced

Diced pimientos and additional dill weed

In a food processor or blender, combine the mayonnaise, cream cheese, onion, chives, vinegar, Worcestershire sauce and seasonings. Cover and process until blended. Cover and refrigerate for 24 hours. Using a 2-1/2-in. biscuit cutter, cut out circles from bread slices. Spread mayonnaise mixture over bread; top with cucumber slices. Garnish with pimientos and dill. **Yield:** 2 dozen.

corner with water; roll up tightly to seal.

In an electric skillet, heat 1 in. of oil to 375°. Fry egg rolls for 2 minutes on each side or until golden brown. Drain on paper towels. Serve with sweet-sour sauce. **Yield:** 7 egg rolls.

TACO JOE DIP

(Pictured on page 4)

Lang Secrest, Sierra Vista, Arizona

This recipe was given to us by our daughter. My husband and I love it. Because it's made in a slow cooker, it's great for parties or busy days.

    1 can (16 ounces) kidney beans, rinsed and drained
    1 can (15-1/4 ounces) whole kernel corn, drained
    1 can (15 ounces) black beans, rinsed and drained
    1 can (14-1/2 ounces) stewed tomatoes
    1 can (8 ounces) tomato sauce
    1 can (4 ounces) chopped green chilies, drained
    1 envelope taco seasoning
  1/2 cup chopped onion
Tortilla chips

In a slow cooker, combine the first eight ingredients. Cover and cook on low for 5-7 hours. Serve dip with tortilla chips. **Yield:** about 7 cups.

Editor's Note: To make Taco Joe Soup, add a 29-ounce can of tomato sauce to the slow cooker. It will serve 6-8.

SPEEDY PIZZA RINGS

Karen Hope, Miller, Missouri

If your family likes pizza, they're going to love these pizza-flavored rings featuring zucchini.

    2 medium zucchini (about 2-inch diameter), cut into 1/4-inch slices
    1 can (8 ounces) pizza sauce
    1 package (3 ounces) sliced pepperoni
    1 cup (4 ounces) shredded mozzarella cheese
Sliced jalapeno peppers* and ripe olives, optional

Arrange zucchini in a single layer on a large microwave-safe plate coated with nonstick cooking spray. Microwave, uncovered, on high for 3 minutes. Spread 1 teaspoon pizza sauce on each zucchini round; top each with a slice of pepperoni.

HAWAIIAN EGG ROLLS

(Pictured above)

Terri Wheeler, Vadnais Heights, Minnesota

An avid cook, I am constantly trying to come up with recipes for leftovers. This one gives a whole new twist to extra ham.

  10 fresh spinach leaves, julienned
  1/2 teaspoon ground ginger
    2 tablespoons olive or vegetable oil
  1/2 pound fully cooked ham, coarsely ground (2 cups)
    4 water chestnuts, chopped
  1/4 cup undrained crushed pineapple
    2 tablespoons chopped green onions
    1 tablespoon soy sauce
    7 egg roll wrappers
Vegetable oil for frying
Sweet-sour sauce

In a saucepan, saute spinach and ginger in oil for 1-2 minutes. In a bowl, combine the ham, water chestnuts, pineapple, onions and soy sauce. Stir in the spinach mixture. Place 3 tablespoons of the ham mixture in the center of each egg roll wrapper. Fold the bottom corner over filling; fold sides over filling toward center. Moisten the remaining

Heat, uncovered, for 2 minutes. Sprinkle each with cheese, jalapenos and olives if desired. Microwave 40-60 seconds longer or until cheese is melted. **Yield:** 10-12 servings.

*Editor's Note: When cutting or seeding hot peppers, use rubber or plastic gloves to protect your hands. Avoid touching your face. This recipe was tested in an 850-watt microwave.

****

HALLOWEEN PUNCH

Sue Thomas, Casa Grande, Arizona

Fitting right into October fun is this suitably orange-colored sipper. I'll often put the punch bowl inside a hollowed-out pumpkin to make it extra festive.

- 1 can (46 ounces) pineapple juice, *divided*
- 1 package (3 ounces) orange gelatin
- 1 carton (64 ounces) orange juice
- 1 liter ginger ale, chilled
- 1 quart orange sherbet

In a saucepan, bring 1 cup of pineapple juice to a boil. Stir in gelatin until dissolved. Cool; transfer to a large pitcher or container. Add orange juice and remaining pineapple juice. Chill. Just before serving, pour into a punch bowl; add ginger ale and mix well. Top with scoops of sherbet. **Yield:** 20-24 servings.

****

ALMOND TEA

Cheryl Dillon, Fort Collins, Colorado

My favorite part of the day is sitting down in a comfortable chair with a glass of this tasty tea.

- 1 can (12 ounces) frozen lemonade concentrate, thawed
- 1 cup sugar

- 3 to 4 tablespoons unsweetened instant tea
- 1 tablespoon almond extract
- 1 tablespoon vanilla extract
- 14 cups water

In a 1-gal. container, combine the first five ingredients; mix well. Add 8 cups water; stir to blend. Add the remaining water. Serve over ice. **Yield:** 16 servings (4 quarts).

****

SHRIMP APPETIZER SPREAD

(Pictured below)

Brenda Buhler, Abbotsford, British Columbia

There's no secret to this creamy seafood appetizer—it's simply delicious! I first tasted it at a friend's house and liked it so much, I requested the recipe. It's since become a family favorite.

- 1 package (8 ounces) cream cheese, softened
- 1/2 cup sour cream
- 1/4 cup mayonnaise
- 3 packages (5 ounces *each*) frozen cooked salad shrimp, thawed
- 1 cup seafood sauce
- 2 cups (8 ounces) shredded mozzarella cheese
- 1 medium green pepper, chopped
- 1 small tomato, chopped
- 3 green onions with tops, sliced

Assorted crackers

In a mixing bowl, beat cream cheese until smooth. Add sour cream and mayonnaise; mix well. Spread mixture on a round 12-in. serving platter. Sprinkle with shrimp. Top with seafood sauce. Sprinkle with mozzarella cheese, green pepper, tomato and onions. Cover and refrigerate. Serve with crackers. **Yield:** 20 servings.

CATCH SOME "Z'S"

(Pictured on page 10)

Moms won't lose sleep preparing this savory finger food for a get-together. That's because our Test Kitchen staff kept the goodies simple—by cutting "Z" shapes from refrigerated crescent rolls and seasoning them before baking. If you like, provide a bowl of warmed pizza sauce on the side...then watch kids start dipping!

  1 tube (8 ounces) refrigerated crescent rolls
  1 tablespoon butter *or* margarine, melted
  2 tablespoons grated Parmesan cheese
  1/4 teaspoon garlic salt
Pizza sauce, warmed, optional

Unroll crescent roll dough; press seams and perforations to seal. Cut dough with a 2-in. "Z" cookie cutter; place on ungreased baking sheets. Brush with butter. Combine Parmesan cheese and garlic salt; sprinkle over dough. Bake at 375° for 5-6 minutes or until golden brown. Serve warm with pizza sauce if desired. **Yield:** 2 dozen.

HAM 'N' CHEESE TORTILLAS

(Pictured below)

Jamie Whitaker, Aurora, Missouri

My family eats these tasty tortillas as fast as I can make them. Good thing they can be made in a hurry! They're a new and flavorful way to serve traditional ham and cheese.

Vegetable oil for frying
  6 flour tortillas (10 inches), quartered

  3 packages (6 ounces *each*) boiled ham (24 slices)
4-1/2 cups shredded cheddar cheese
  1 cup picante sauce *or* salsa
Garlic salt
Sour cream and minced chives, optional

In an electric skillet, heat 2 in. of oil to 375°. Fry tortillas wedges, a few at a time, until lightly browned and crispy. Drain on paper towels. Place wedges in a single layer on baking sheets.

Top each with a folded ham slice, 3 tablespoons cheese and 2 teaspoons picante sauce. Sprinkle with garlic salt. Broil 4-6 in. from the heat until cheese is melted, about 2 minutes. Serve warm. If desired, top with a dollop of sour cream and sprinkle with chives. **Yield:** 2 dozen.

SLEEPY-TIME SHAKES

(Pictured on page 11)

Dixie Terry, Marion, Illinois

Besides the tangy pineapple juice kids will savor, milk makes this creamy beverage perfect to pour at a slumber party. Since drinking milk at bedtime can have a tiring effect, what could be better to give a group of energetic youngsters? Just make sure the tea you add to this punch is decaffeinated!

1/2 gallon vanilla ice cream, softened
  1 cup pineapple juice
1/2 cup milk
1/2 cup sweetened instant iced tea
1/2 cup sugar
  2 star fruit, cut into 1/2-inch slices

In a mixing bowl, combine the ice cream, pineapple juice, milk, tea and sugar. Mix until smooth. Pour into chilled glasses; garnish with star fruit. Serve immediately. **Yield:** 7 servings.

STARRY NIGHT TACO CUPS

(Pictured on page 11)

These Mexican-style snacks will surely add sparkle to a slumber party spread! To make them, our home economists lined muffin cups with tortilla shells, then filled each with a not-too-spicy beef mixture kids can garnish with cheese, lettuce and other toppings. For tasty dippers besides, you could serve the cutout stars with salsa.

  1 pound ground beef
1/2 cup chopped onion

1/4 cup salsa
1/4 cup ketchup
1 tablespoon chili powder
1 teaspoon salt
16 flour tortillas (7 inches)
Toppings: shredded lettuce, chopped tomato,
shredded cheddar cheese *and/or* sour cream

In a skillet, cook beef and onion over medium heat until meat is no longer pink; drain. Add salsa, ketchup, chili powder and salt; heat through. Cut each tortilla into a 4-in. square; set scraps aside. Microwave eight squares at a time for 20 seconds. Press onto the bottom and up the sides of greased muffin cups; set aside.

Cut tortilla scraps into stars with a 1-in. cookie cutter; place on a greased baking sheet. Bake at 350° for 6 minutes or until golden brown; set aside. Fill each tortilla cup with 2 tablespoons meat mixture. Bake for 12-15 minutes longer or until tortillas are golden brown. Serve with toppings of your choice; garnish with toasted stars. **Yield:** 16 servings.

▰▰▰▰▰▰▰▰▰▰

SLUMBER PARTY COOKIE PIZZA

(Pictured on page 10)

Shirley Petryk, Redmond, Washington

I bake this chewy cookie in a pizza pan, add convenient canned frosting for the "sauce" and slice gumdrops to look like pepperoni, mushrooms and more on top. I'm always making this recipe for my 12 grandchildren. Presented to them in a pizza box, the treat gets rave reviews every time.

1/2 cup butter *or* margarine, softened
1/2 cup peanut butter
1/2 cup sugar
1/2 cup packed brown sugar
1 egg
1/2 teaspoon vanilla extract
1-1/4 cups all-purpose flour
1/2 teaspoon baking soda
1/4 teaspoon salt
1/2 cup semisweet chocolate chips
1 can (16 ounces) vanilla frosting *or* 2
cups frosting of your choice
Red, black, white, green and yellow gumdrops
1/4 cup white *or* vanilla chips

In a mixing bowl, cream butter, peanut butter and sugars. Beat in egg and vanilla. Combine flour, baking soda and salt; gradually add to the creamed mixture. Stir in chocolate chips. Pat onto a greased 14-in. pizza pan. Bake at 350° for 20-25 minutes or until golden brown; cool. Spread frosting to within 1 in. of edge.

Using a sharp knife, cut red gumdrops into 1/4-in. slices. Cut black gumdrops into slices and cut a hole in the center. Cut white gumdrops lengthwise, then into mushroom shapes. Cut green gumdrops into slices and place a small piece of red gumdrop in the center. Dice yellow and more green gumdrops. Arrange all gumdrop shapes over frosting. Melt white chips; place in a pastry or plastic bag. Cut a small hole in the corner; drizzle over pizza. **Yield:** 8-10 servings.

▰▰▰▰▰▰▰▰▰▰

PEACH SMOOTHIES

(Pictured above)

Dana Tittle, Forrest City, Arkansas

Nothing could be sweeter than starting the day off with this refreshing beverage. But I enjoy the smoothies so much, I make them throughout the day.

2 cups milk
2 cups frozen unsweetened sliced peaches
1/4 cup orange juice concentrate
2 tablespoons sugar
5 ice cubes

In a blender, combine all ingredients; cover and process until smooth. Pour into glasses; serve immediately. **Yield:** 4 servings.

SLEEP will be the furthest thing from youngsters' minds when you set out these late-night snacks at a slumber party.

NIGHTTIME NIBBLING. Clockwise from top left: Catch Some "Z's" (p. 8), Confetti Caramel Corn (p. 12), Sleepy-Time Shakes (p. 8), Starry Night Taco Cups (p. 8) and Slumber Party Cookie Pizza (p. 9).

CONFETTI CARAMEL CORN

(Pictured on page 11)

Dorothy Smith, El Dorado, Arkansas

When throwing a party, you'll want to include handfuls of these sweet bits and pieces. Made with bright fruit-flavored breakfast cereal, it's a fun variation on ordinary caramel corn.

    7 cups Trix cereal
    2/3 cup butter *or* margarine
    2/3 cup sugar
    1/4 cup light corn syrup
      2 teaspoons vanilla extract
    1/2 teaspoon baking soda

Place cereal in a large bowl. In a saucepan, combine the butter, sugar and corn syrup. Bring to a boil over medium heat; cook and stir for 5 minutes. Remove from the heat. Stir in vanilla and baking soda. Pour over cereal and stir to coat. Transfer to greased baking sheets. Bake at 300° for 25 minutes, stirring after 15 minutes. Break apart while warm. Cool completely. Store in an airtight container. **Yield:** 10 cups.

SWEET-SOUR DEVILED EGGS

(Pictured below)

Claudia Millhouse, Myersville, Maryland

Folks will be sweet on these appetizers when they try them. My family doesn't like traditional deviled eggs—

but they gobble these sweet-sour versions right up. The eggs have also proven popular with our friends.

    12 hard-cooked eggs
    1/3 cup plus 1 tablespoon mayonnaise
      5 teaspoons sugar
      5 teaspoons cider vinegar
      1 teaspoon prepared mustard
    1/2 teaspoon salt
    1/4 teaspoon pepper
Paprika and minced fresh parsley

Slice eggs in half lengthwise; remove yolks and set whites aside. In a small bowl, mash yolks with a fork. Add mayonnaise, sugar, vinegar, mustard, salt and pepper. Stuff or pipe into egg whites. Garnish with paprika and parsley. **Yield:** 24 servings.

CHICKEN SALAD PUFFS

Lola Pullen, Lakeland, Florida

Stuffed with a chunky chicken salad, these pretty golden puffs are perfect for a holiday buffet. Everyone seems to enjoy the subtle sweetness from the pineapple and the crunch of the celery and pecans.

      1 cup water
    1/2 cup butter (no substitutes)
    1/2 teaspoon salt
      1 cup all-purpose flour
      4 eggs
FILLING:
      2 cups finely chopped cooked
        chicken

1 can (8 ounces) crushed
    pineapple, drained
1/2 cup mayonnaise
1/4 cup chopped celery
1/4 cup thinly sliced green onions
1/4 cup chopped pecans
  2 tablespoons sweet pickle relish
1/4 teaspoon onion salt
1/4 teaspoon garlic salt
1/4 teaspoon paprika
Salt and pepper to taste

In a saucepan, bring water, butter and salt to a boil. Add flour all at once and stir until a smooth ball forms. Remove from the heat; let stand for 5 minutes. Add eggs, one at a time, beating well after each addition. Continue beating until smooth and shiny. Drop by rounded teaspoonfuls 2 in. apart onto greased baking sheets.

Bake at 400° for 15-20 minutes or until golden brown. Remove to wire racks. Immediately cut a slit in each puff to allow steam to escape; cool completely. Split puffs and set tops aside; remove soft dough from inside. In a bowl, combine all of the filling ingredients; mix well. Fill puffs with chicken salad mixture and replace the tops. Refrigerate until serving. Refrigerate leftovers. **Yield:** about 3-1/2 dozen.

APRICOT BURRITOS

Charl Sanchez, Roseville, California

These apricot-filled burritos are popular with my son and his friends. I usually have a plateful ready for them as a sweet after-school snack. It's easy since they can be put together in minutes.

1 cup chopped dried apricots
1 cup water
1/4 cup sugar
1/4 cup packed brown sugar
1/4 teaspoon ground cinnamon
1/4 teaspoon ground nutmeg
8 flour tortillas (6 inches)
Oil for frying
Cinnamon-sugar

In a saucepan, combine the first six ingredients. Bring to a boil; reduce heat. Simmer, uncovered, for 10 minutes or until thickened. Place 1 tablespoon on each tortilla. Fold sides and ends over filling; roll up. In an electric skillet, heat 1 in. of oil to 375°. Fry burritos, in batches, for 1 minute on each side or until golden brown. Drain on paper towels. Sprinkle with cinnamon-sugar. **Yield:** 8 burritos.

FRIED JALAPENOS

(Pictured above)

DeLea Lonadier, Montgomery, Louisiana

Here's an appetizer that will heat up any gathering. Family and friends often request that I make these zesty jalapenos.

2 jars (12 ounces *each*) whole jalapeno
    peppers*, drained
1 jar (5 ounces) olive-pimiento cheese
    spread
3/4 cup all-purpose flour, *divided*
6 tablespoons cornmeal, *divided*
1/4 teaspoon salt
1/4 teaspoon pepper
1 cup buttermilk
Vegetable oil

Cut off stems and remove seeds from peppers. Stuff with cheese spread. Refrigerate for at least 2 hours. In a small bowl, combine 1/4 cup flour, 2 tablespoons cornmeal, salt, pepper and buttermilk until smooth; set aside. In another bowl, combine remaining flour and cornmeal.

Dip stuffed peppers into buttermilk batter, then dredge in flour mixture. In an electric skillet or deep-fat fryer, heat oil to 375°. Fry peppers, two or three at a time, until golden brown. Drain on paper towels. **Yield:** 2 dozen.

*****Editor's Note:** When cutting and seeding hot peppers, use rubber or plastic gloves to protect your hands. Avoid touching your face.

cover and refrigerate for 4 hours or until firm. Serve with crackers, breadsticks or vegetables. **Yield:** about 3 cups.

*Editor's Note: When cutting or seeding hot peppers, use rubber or plastic gloves to protect your hands. Avoid touching your face.

ONIONS AND CREAM APPETIZER

Joy Collins, Vestavia Hills, Alabama

Need a deliciously different snack for a holiday gathering? I've fixed this recipe countless times, and even those who don't generally care for onions like them in this sweet creamy blend.

> 2 cups water
> 1 cup sugar
> 1/4 cup vinegar
> 1 teaspoon celery seed
> 6 cups sliced sweet onions, separated
>   into rings
> 1 cup mayonnaise
Assorted crackers

In a large saucepan, combine the first four ingredients; bring to a boil. Drop onion rings into boiling mixture; cook for 5 minutes. Cover and remove from the heat. Let stand for 20-30 minutes or until onions are transparent; drain. Cool. In a bowl, whisk the mayonnaise until smooth; stir in onions. Cover and refrigerate overnight. Serve with crackers. **Yield:** 3 cups.

SWEET POTATO CHEESE BALL

(Pictured above)

Edwina Harper, Bastrop, Louisiana

My husband and I farm 300 acres of sweet potatoes. I promote our product at fairs, agriculture expos and school functions. I pass out recipes and this is one of the favorites.

> 1 package (8 ounces) cream cheese,
>   softened
> 2 cups cold mashed sweet potatoes
> 1/4 cup finely chopped onion
> 2 tablespoons finely chopped jalapeno
>   pepper*
> 1 teaspoon seasoned salt
> 1 teaspoon Worcestershire sauce
> 1 teaspoon Louisiana hot sauce
> 1/2 to 1 teaspoon hot pepper sauce
> 1/4 cup chopped pecans
Assorted crackers, breadsticks *or*
   raw vegetables

In a mixing bowl, beat cream cheese and sweet potatoes until smooth. Add the next seven ingredients; mix well. Cover and refrigerate for 4 hours or until easy to handle. Shape into a ball;

HAM PICKLE PINWHEELS

Gloria Jarrett, Loveland, Ohio

My mom introduced me to these appetizers a number of years ago, and I've been making them for parties ever since. They're easy to make and are always well received by guests.

> 1 package (8 ounces) cream cheese, cubed
> 1/4 pound sliced Genoa salami
> 1 tablespoon prepared horseradish
> 7 slices deli ham
> 14 to 21 okra pickles *or* dill pickle spears

Place cream cheese, salami and horseradish in a blender or food processor; cover and process until smooth. Spread over ham slices. Remove stems and ends of okra pickles. Place two or three okra pickles or one dill pickle down the center of each ham slice. Roll up tightly and wrap in plastic wrap. Refrigerate for at least 2 hours. Cut into 1-in. slices. **Yield:** about 3-1/2 dozen.

Hot Raspberry-Lemonade Drink Mix

To accompany the warm wishes you send in a gift basket, include this fruity blend from our Test Kitchen staff. The combination of powdered mixes is one folks can enjoy anytime by simply stirring in hot water.

1-1/2 cups powdered lemonade mix with sugar
   1 carton (1.3 ounces) raspberry soft drink mix*
   1 cup instant tea mix
Boiling water

In a bowl, combine the first three ingredients. Store in an airtight container. To prepare one serving, dissolve 1 teaspoon of mix in 1 cup of boiling water. **Yield:** 3 cups mix.

*Editor's Note: This recipe was tested with Crystal Light Raspberry Ice soft drink mix.

Party Franks

(Pictured below)

Lucille Howell, Portland, Oregon

These tiny tangy appetizers have such broad appeal. I prepare them often for holiday gatherings, weddings and family reunions. They're convenient to serve at parties since the sauce can be made ahead, then just reheated with the franks before serving.

3/4 cup chopped onion
   2 tablespoons vegetable oil
   1 cup ketchup
1/2 cup water
1/2 cup cider vinegar
   2 tablespoons sugar
   2 tablespoons Worcestershire sauce
   2 tablespoons honey
   2 teaspoons ground mustard
   2 teaspoons paprika
3/4 teaspoon salt
1/4 teaspoon pepper
1/8 teaspoon hot pepper sauce
   1 large lemon, sliced
2-1/2 to 3 pounds miniature hot dogs *or* smoked sausage links

In a large saucepan, saute the onion in oil until tender. Stir in the next 11 ingredients. Add sliced lemon. Bring to a boil. Reduce heat; simmer, uncovered, for 20-25 minutes or until slightly thickened, stirring occasionally. Discard the lemon slices.

Place hot dogs or sausage links in a 13-in. x 9-in. x 2-in. baking dish. Top with the sauce. Bake, uncovered, at 350° for 18-20 minutes or until heated through. Keep warm; serve with toothpicks. **Yield:** 25-30 servings.

STIR UP *some mealtime excitement with these hearty skillet suppers, oven entrees, microwave dishes and grilled specialties.*

SKILLET SENSATIONS. Clockwise from top left: Stovetop Pot Roast (p. 18), Au Gratin Peas and Potatoes (p. 17), Sweet 'n' Sour Meatballs (p. 17) and Italian Sausage Stew (p. 19).

Main Dishes

AU GRATIN PEAS AND POTATOES

(Pictured at left)

Marie Peterson, De Forest, Wisconsin

While this delicious potato skillet is a wonderful side dish, we find it a satisfying main course, too. The skillet preparation takes less time than it does to bake an au gratin casserole or scalloped potatoes.

    6 bacon strips, diced
    1 medium onion, chopped
    4 cups sliced peeled cooked potatoes
1/2 teaspoon salt
    1 package (10 ounces) frozen peas,
       cooked and drained
    2 cups (8 ounces) shredded sharp
       cheddar cheese, *divided*
1/2 cup mayonnaise
1/2 cup milk

In a skillet, cook bacon until crisp. Remove with a slotted spoon to paper towels. Drain, reserving 1 tablespoon drippings. In the drippings, saute onion until tender. Layer with potatoes, salt, peas, 1 cup of cheese and bacon. Reduce heat; cover and simmer for 10 minutes or until heated through. Combine mayonnaise and milk until smooth; pour over bacon. Sprinkle with the remaining cheese. Remove from the heat; let stand for 5 minutes before serving. **Yield:** 4 servings.

SWEET 'N' SOUR MEATBALLS

(Pictured at left)

Andrea Busch, Brackenridge, Pennsylvania

When I fixed this flavorful recipe for the first time, it was a welcome change from some of our regular ho-hum dinners. It still is every time I serve it.

    1 egg
1/4 cup seasoned bread crumbs
1/2 teaspoon salt
1/4 teaspoon ground ginger
Dash pepper
    1 pound ground beef
    1 can (20 ounces) pineapple chunks

1/4 cup cider vinegar
1/4 cup packed brown sugar
    2 tablespoons soy sauce
    1 cup sliced carrots
    1 medium green pepper, julienned
    1 tablespoon cornstarch
    2 tablespoons cold water
Hot cooked rice

In a bowl, combine the first five ingredients. Add beef and mix well. Shape into 1-in. balls. In a skillet over medium heat, brown meatballs until no longer pink; drain. Drain pineapple, reserving juice; set pineapple aside. Add water to juice to measure 1 cup. Stir in vinegar, brown sugar and soy sauce; pour over meatballs. Add carrots.

Bring to a boil. Reduce heat; cover and simmer for 5-8 minutes or until carrots are crisp-tender. Stir in green pepper and pineapple; cover and simmer 5 minutes longer or until pepper is crisp-tender. Combine cornstarch and water until smooth; stir into meatball mixture. Bring to a boil; cook and stir for 2 minutes or until thickened. Serve over rice. **Yield:** 4-6 servings.

SPICY STEW

Sandra Bradley, Floydada, Texas

Unlike other stew recipes, this zesty version is ready in just over 30 minutes.

    1 pound ground beef
    3 medium green peppers, chopped
    1 medium onion, chopped
    1 can (28 ounces) diced tomatoes,
       undrained
    1 can (15-1/4 ounces) peas, drained
    3 cans (16 ounces *each*) kidney beans,
       rinsed and drained
    1 tablespoon sugar
    2 teaspoons chili powder
    1 teaspoon garlic powder
    1 teaspoon ground cumin
1/2 teaspoon *each* salt and pepper

In a Dutch oven, cook beef, peppers and onion until meat is browned; drain. Stir in remaining ingredients; bring to a boil. Reduce heat; cover and simmer for 30 minutes. **Yield:** 6-8 servings.

Roast Is Scent-sational

MOUTHS start to water whenever Mary Lou Chernik of Taos, New Mexico simmers her Stovetop Pot Roast—and that's often.

Confides Mary Lou, "This roast is a twice-a-month 'must' for my husband, Jim, and me. And if the kids are dropping by—we have a grown son and daughter and a toddler grandson—I just add more vegetables to the pot."

Chock-full of colorful carrots, potatoes, turnips, celery and green beans, Mary Lou's pot roast is as eye-catching as it is palate-pleasing. And it's no flash in the pan, either!

"It's just as flavorful the second time around as the base for a savory stew served with hot buttered biscuits," she says.

"To stretch it even further, I often roll out a few pie crusts, fill them with stew and freeze for speedy potpies.

"I vary the vegetables, too, using whatever's available in the garden. To dress up the roast, I'll sprinkle on fresh chives or parsley, garnish with red or yellow sweet pepper strips and mix in corn for more color."

During times when Mary Lou has something cooking on all burners, she'll slide her skillet pot roast from the stovetop into the oven. "Once I get it started, there's little more to do than lift the lid and check the water level," she says.

"A word of advice though," Mary Lou cautions. "Once this pot roast starts filling the house with its comforting aroma, it's hard to concentrate on anything else!"

STOVETOP POT ROAST
(Pictured on page 16)

- 1 boneless chuck roast (3 to 4 pounds)
- 2 to 3 garlic cloves, halved lengthwise
- 2 tablespoons olive *or* vegetable oil
- 1 large onion, cut into 1/2-inch slices
- 3 celery ribs, cut into 1/2-inch slices
- 2 medium turnips, peeled and cut into chunks
- 4 cups water
- 2 beef bouillon cubes
- 4 medium potatoes, peeled and quartered
- 1 pound carrots, cut into chunks
- 1/2 pound fresh *or* frozen green beans, partially thawed
- 1/2 pound fresh mushrooms, sliced
- 3 tablespoons cornstarch
- 1/4 cup cold water
- Salt and pepper to taste

Cut slits in roast; insert garlic slivers into the slits. In a large deep skillet, brown roast on all sides in oil. Remove roast. Add onion, celery and turnips to skillet. Place roast over vegetables; add water and bouillon cubes. Bring to a boil. Reduce heat; cover and simmer for 2 hours.

Add the potatoes, carrots and green beans; cover and cook for 45 minutes. Add mushrooms; cover and cook 15 minutes longer or until meat and vegetables are tender.

Remove to a serving platter and keep warm. Skim fat from pan juices. Combine cornstarch and cold water until smooth; stir into pan juices. Bring to a boil; cook and stir for 2 minutes. Season with salt and pepper. Slice roast; serve with vegetables and gravy. **Yield:** 8-10 servings.

PINEAPPLE HAM LOAF
(Pictured on front cover)

Aleatha Smith, Billings, Montana

My cousin served this tender ham loaf at a family get-together, and I eagerly asked her for the recipe. Since then, I've often taken it to church functions and served it when friends come over for dinner. It's always well received.

- 2 eggs
- 1/2 cup milk
- 1 teaspoon Worcestershire sauce
- 3/4 cup dry bread crumbs
- 1-1/2 teaspoons ground mustard, *divided*
- 1/4 teaspoon salt
- 1/4 teaspoon pepper
- 1 pound fully cooked ham, ground (4 cups)
- 1 pound ground pork
- 1 can (20 ounces) sliced pineapple
- 1/2 cup packed brown sugar

In a bowl, combine eggs, milk, Worcestershire sauce, bread crumbs, 1 teaspoon mustard, salt and pepper. Add ham and pork; mix well. Shape into eight oval patties; set aside. Drain pineapple, reserving 1/2 cup juice. Place a pineapple slice between each ham patty. (Refrigerate remaining pineapple and juice for another use.) Carefully place in an ungreased 9-in. x 5-in. x 3-in. loaf pan.

Pat patties around pineapple to form a loaf. Combine brown sugar, remaining mustard and reserved juice; pour a small amount over loaf. Bake, uncovered, at 350° for 1-1/4 hours or until lightly browned and a meat thermometer reads 160°, basting occasionally with remaining juice mixture. **Yield:** 8 servings.

ITALIAN SAUSAGE STEW
(Pictured on page 16)

Ann Erney, Middlebury Center, Pennsylvania

One day when I was preparing Italian sausages, I decided to do something different. After browning them, I put the sausages in a pot and added other ingredients, ending up with this stew. My husband and I like it very much.

1-1/2 pounds Italian sausage links, cut into
    1-inch pieces
  3 cups water
  4 medium potatoes, peeled and cut into
    chunks
  2 medium carrots, cut into chunks
  2 celery ribs, cut into chunks
  2 small onions, cut into wedges
1/4 cup Worcestershire sauce
  1 teaspoon dried oregano
1/2 teaspoon *each* dried basil, thyme and
    rosemary, crushed
  1 bay leaf
Salt and pepper to taste
3/4 cup ketchup
1/2 large green *or* sweet red pepper, cut into
    chunks
  1 tablespoon minced fresh parsley
  1 tablespoon cornstarch
  1 tablespoon cold water

In a soup kettle or Dutch oven over medium heat, brown sausage; drain. Add water, potatoes, carrots, celery, onions, Worcestershire sauce and seasonings. Bring to a boil. Reduce heat; cover and cook over low heat for 1 hour or until sausage is no longer pink and vegetables are tender.

Add the ketchup, green pepper and parsley; cook 12-15 minutes longer or until pepper is tender. Discard bay leaf. Combine cornstarch and cold water until smooth; stir into stew. Bring to a boil; cook and stir for 2 minutes or until thickened. **Yield:** 6 servings.

SKILLET ENCHILADAS
(Pictured below)

Cathie Beard, Philomath, Oregon

This stovetop Mexican-style dish disappears fast when our two grown children and three grandchildren visit. They love the flavorful ingredients rolled up in crispy corn tortillas.

  1 pound ground beef
  1 medium onion, chopped
  1 can (10-3/4 ounces) condensed cream
    of mushroom soup, undiluted
  1 can (10 ounces) enchilada sauce
1/3 cup milk
  1 to 2 tablespoons canned chopped
    green chilies
Vegetable oil
  8 corn tortillas
2-1/2 cups (10 ounces) finely shredded
    cheddar cheese, *divided*
1/2 cup chopped ripe olives

In a large skillet, cook beef and onion over medium heat until meat is no longer pink; drain. Stir in the soup, enchilada sauce, milk and chilies. Bring to a boil. Reduce heat; cover and simmer for 20 minutes, stirring occasionally. Meanwhile, in another skillet, heat 1/4 in. of oil. Dip each tortilla in hot oil for 3 seconds on each side or just until limp; drain on paper towels.

Top each tortilla with 1/4 cup cheese and 1 tablespoon olives. Roll up and place over beef mixture, spooning some of mixture over the enchiladas. Cover and cook until heated through, about 5 minutes. Sprinkle with remaining cheese; cover and cook until cheese is melted. **Yield:** 8 enchiladas.

CRANBERRY PORK CHOPS
(Pictured below)

Joan Dobbs, Evansville, Illinois

This pork chop meal is a proven winner to fix for family and friends. I never have leftovers.

1-1/2 cups sugar
1-3/4 cups water, *divided*
1 package (12 ounces) fresh *or* frozen cranberries
1/2 cup barbecue sauce
8 bone-in pork chops (1/2 to 3/4 inch thick)
Salt and pepper to taste
2 tablespoons vegetable oil
2 tablespoons cornstarch
1/4 cup cold water

In a saucepan, combine sugar and 1-1/2 cups water. Cook and stir over medium heat until the sugar is dissolved. Bring to a boil; boil, uncovered, for 5 minutes. Add the cranberries; cook 5 minutes longer or until the berries pop. Skim off foam if necessary. Stir in barbecue sauce and remaining water. Mix well; set aside.

Season pork chops with salt and pepper. In a large skillet over medium heat, brown chops on both sides in oil; drain. Pour cranberry sauce over chops. Cover and simmer for 35-40 minutes or until meat juices run clear. Remove chops and keep warm. Combine cornstarch and cold water until smooth; add to skillet. Bring to a boil; cook and stir for 2 minutes or until thickened. Spoon over pork chops. **Yield:** 8 servings.

Editor's Note: One 16-ounce can of whole-berry cranberry sauce may be substituted for the sugar, cranberries and 1-1/2 cups water. Combine cranberry sauce with the barbecue sauce and 1/4 cup water; use as directed in recipe.

ANTIPASTO SUB

Jeanette Hios, Brooklyn, New York

This zesty sandwich is piled high with flavor. One night instead of setting out sandwiches with antipasto on the side, I combined the two. It was a big hit with all of my friends.

1 unsliced loaf (1 pound) Italian bread
3 cans (2-1/2 ounces *each*) sliced ripe olives, drained
3 jars (6-1/2 ounces *each*) marinated artichoke hearts, drained and sliced
2 jars (7 ounces *each*) roasted red peppers, drained
1/2 pound thinly sliced provolone cheese
3/4 pound thinly sliced salami
3 tablespoons olive *or* vegetable oil
3 tablespoons cider *or* red wine vinegar
1/2 teaspoon garlic powder
1/2 teaspoon Italian seasoning
1/4 teaspoon salt
1/4 teaspoon pepper

Cut bread in half lengthwise; hollow out top, leaving a 1-1/2-in. shell. (Discard removed bread or save for another use.) Invert bread top; layer with olives, artichokes, red peppers, cheese and salami. Replace bread bottom. Wrap tightly in plastic wrap; refrigerate. In a jar with a tight-fitting lid, combine the remaining ingredients; shake well. Refrigerate. Cut sub into slices; serve with the dressing. **Yield:** 10-12 servings.

SESAME FLANK STEAK

Karen Bouton, Kent, Washington

I can't remember where I got this recipe, but I've modified it over the years to suit my family's tastes.

✓ Uses less fat, sugar or salt. Includes Nutritional Analysis and Diabetic Exchanges.

1-1/2 pounds flank steak
1/4 cup sesame seeds, toasted
1/4 cup thinly sliced green onions
3 tablespoons reduced-sodium soy sauce
2 tablespoons vegetable oil
1 tablespoon brown sugar
1 tablespoon ground ginger
3 garlic cloves, minced
1 teaspoon ground mustard
1 teaspoon Worcestershire sauce

Score steak and place in a large shallow glass container or resealable plastic bag. Combine the remaining ingredients; pour over meat. Cover or

seal and refrigerate for 4 hours or overnight. Drain and discard marinade. Grill steak, covered, over medium heat until the meat reaches desired doneness (for rare, a meat thermometer should read 140°; medium, 160°; well-done, 170°). Thinly slice across the grain. **Yield:** 8 servings.

Nutritional Analysis: One serving equals 172 calories, 169 mg sodium, 44 mg cholesterol, 2 gm carbohydrate, 19 gm protein, 10 gm fat, trace fiber. **Diabetic Exchange:** 3 lean meat.

POTATO HAM BAKE

Arthur Heidorn, Hillside, Illinois

I like to make this casserole with the leftovers from a baked ham. It's a great meal all by itself.

> 3 medium potatoes, peeled and thinly sliced
> 2 cups cubed fully cooked ham
> 1 medium onion, sliced and separated into rings
> 8 slices process American cheese
> 1 can (10-3/4 ounces) condensed cream of mushroom soup, undiluted
> 1/2 cup frozen peas, thawed

In a greased 3-qt. baking dish, layer half of the potatoes, ham, onion, cheese and soup. Repeat layers. Cover and bake at 350° for 1-1/4 hours or until potatoes are almost tender. Sprinkle with peas. Bake, uncovered, for 10 minutes or until heated through. **Yield:** 6 servings.

ZUCCHINI FRITTATA

Mildred Fox, Fostoria, Ohio

This easy egg dish is too pretty and tasty to serve just for breakfast. It's great any time of day.

> 4 cups diced zucchini
> 1 small onion, chopped
> 4 eggs
> 1 cup (4 ounces) shredded cheddar cheese
> 1 cup cubed fully cooked ham
> 3/4 teaspoon salt
> 1/8 teaspoon pepper

In a 9-in. microwave-safe pie plate, combine the zucchini and onion. Cover and microwave on high for 5 minutes or until tender; drain. In a bowl, combine the eggs, cheese, ham, salt and pepper. Carefully pour over zucchini mixture. Microwave at 70% power for 11-12 minutes or until

a knife inserted near the center comes out clean. **Yield:** 6 servings.

Editor's Note: This recipe was tested in an 850-watt microwave.

CREAMY MUSHROOM CHICKEN
(Pictured above)

Sharmon McMillen, Park City, Montana

I call this meal "the easy chicken fixin'". I love it that the leftovers are equally delicious heated up in the microwave.

> 6 boneless skinless chicken breast halves
> 1/4 teaspoon pepper
> 2 tablespoons vegetable oil
> 1 cup sliced fresh mushrooms
> 1/4 cup butter *or* margarine
> 4-1/2 teaspoons all-purpose flour
> 1 cup milk
> 3/4 cup grated Parmesan cheese, *divided*
> Minced fresh parsley
> Hot cooked pasta

Sprinkle chicken with pepper. In a large skillet over medium heat, brown chicken in oil until juices run clear. Remove to a serving platter and keep warm. In same skillet, saute mushrooms in butter until tender. Sprinkle with flour; stir until coated. Gradually add milk. Bring to a boil; cook and stir for 2 minutes or until thickened. Remove from heat; stir in 1/2 cup Parmesan cheese. Pour over chicken. Sprinkle with parsley and remaining cheese. Serve with pasta. **Yield:** 6 servings.

PORK CHOPS OVER RICE

Nancy Christenberry, Ortonville, Michigan

If you asked my husband to name his favorite foods, he'd likely mention these chops. I've also served this appealing skillet supper to company. Ever since I clipped the recipe out of the paper many years ago, it's become a standard in my kitchen.

      8 boneless pork chops (3/4 inch thick)
      1 tablespoon vegetable oil
      1 cup uncooked long grain rice
      1 can (14-1/2 ounces) chicken broth
    1/2 cup water
      1 small onion, chopped
      1 package (10 ounces) frozen peas
    1/2 teaspoon salt
    1/2 teaspoon dried thyme

In a large skillet over medium heat, brown pork chops in oil; remove. Drain. Add the rice, broth, water, onion, peas, salt and thyme to skillet. Place pork chops over the rice mixture. Bring to a boil. Reduce heat; cover and simmer for 20-25 minutes or until rice is tender. **Yield:** 8 servings.

MEAT LOAF WELLINGTON
(Pictured above)

Wanda Orton, Emporia, Kansas

My family would rather have this than plain meat loaf. It's a good way to dress up an ordinary dish for company. Many people have asked for the recipe.

          1 can (10-1/2 ounces) beef gravy, *divided*
    1-1/2 cups cubed day-old bread
        1/4 cup chopped onion
          1 egg
          1 teaspoon salt
          2 pounds ground beef
          1 tube (8 ounces) refrigerated crescent rolls

In a bowl, combine 1/4 cup gravy, bread cubes, onion, egg and salt. Crumble beef over mixture and mix well. Press into a greased 9-in. x 5-in. x 3-in. loaf pan. Bake, uncovered, at 375° for 1 hour or until meat is no longer pink and a meat thermometer reads 160°. Remove loaf from pan; drain on paper towels.

   Place on a greased 13-in. x 9-in. x 2-in. baking pan. Unroll crescent roll dough; seal perforations. Cover the top and sides of meat loaf with dough; trim excess. Bake 10-15 minutes longer or until pastry is golden brown. Heat the remaining gravy; serve with meat loaf. **Yield:** 6-8 servings.

MEATY BEAN CASSEROLE

"Bean" in the mood for some filling fare to serve your family? Nothing fits the bill quite like this recipe brought to you by the folks at the Bean Education and Awareness Network. Two kinds of meat make it doubly delicious.

    1-1/4 pounds boneless skinless chicken
           breasts *or* pork tenderloin, cut into
           3/4-inch pieces
       12 to 16 ounces smoked sausage links,
           halved and cut into 1/2-inch slices
        1 tablespoon olive *or* vegetable oil
    1-1/2 cups chopped onion
        1 cup chopped sweet red pepper
        4 to 6 garlic cloves, minced
        4 cans (15 ounces *each*) great northern
           beans, rinsed and drained
        1 can (14-1/2 ounces) Italian diced
           tomatoes, undrained
        1 can (14-1/2 ounces) chicken broth
        1 teaspoon dried thyme
Pepper to taste
        2 to 2-1/2 cups soft bread crumbs

In a Dutch oven, cook the chicken and sausage in oil until lightly browned, about 10 minutes. Remove with a slotted spoon and keep warm. In the drippings, saute onion, red pepper and garlic for 5 minutes. Stir in beans, tomatoes, broth, thyme, pepper, chicken and sausage. Bake, uncovered, at 350° for 45 minutes. Sprinkle with bread crumbs. Bake 45 minutes longer or until golden brown. **Yield:** 8 servings.

CHICKEN BEAN STEW

Tired of more traditional beef stews? Give this recipe from the Bean Education and Awareness Network a try. Featuring chicken and beans, it's tasty, unique and chock-full of goodness, too.

 1 cup chopped onion
 1 cup chopped green pepper
 1 garlic clove, minced
 1 tablespoon vegetable oil
3/4 pound boneless skinless chicken breasts,
  cut into 1/2-inch cubes
 2 cans (16 ounces *each*) baked beans
 1 can (15 ounces) garbanzo beans, rinsed
  and drained
 1 can (14-1/2 ounces) diced tomatoes,
  undrained
3/4 teaspoon rubbed sage
1/2 teaspoon ground cumin
Salt and pepper to taste

In a Dutch oven or soup kettle, saute onion, green pepper and garlic in oil until tender. Add the chicken; cook and stir over medium heat until juices run clear, about 5 minutes. Stir in the remaining ingredients. Reduce heat; simmer, uncovered, for 8-10 minutes. **Yield:** 7 servings.

SOUTHERN FRIED CHICKEN
(Pictured below)

Patricia Gowen, Amherst, Virginia

This recipe was a happy accident. I discovered at the last minute that I didn't have enough all-purpose flour for coating the chicken, so I used pancake mix instead. It did taste different—but everyone at our house really liked it.

 1 cup pancake mix
 2 to 3 teaspoons salt
1/4 teaspoon pepper
1/4 teaspoon paprika
 1 broiler/fryer chicken (3 to 4 pounds),
  cut up
Oil for deep-fat frying

In a large resealable plastic bag, combine the pancake mix, salt, pepper and paprika. Add chicken, a few pieces at a time; shake to coat. Heat 2 in. of oil in an electric skillet or deep-fat fryer to 375°. Fry chicken, a few pieces at a time, for 6 minutes; turn and cook 6 minutes longer or until golden brown and juices run clear. **Yield:** 4-6 servings.

TEMPERATURE TEST

If your deep-fat fryer doesn't have a temperature indicator, you can test if the oil has reached 375° by dropping in a cube of crustless white bread. It should be golden brown in about 40 seconds.

SLICED HAM WITH ROASTED VEGETABLES

(Pictured below)

Margaret Pache, Mesa, Arizona

To prepare this colorful, zesty oven meal, I "shop" in my backyard for the fresh garden vegetables and oranges (we have our own tree) that spark the ham's hearty flavor. It's my family's favorite main dish.

- 6 medium potatoes, peeled and cubed
- 5 medium carrots, julienned
- 1 medium turnip, peeled and cubed
- 1 large onion, cut into thin wedges
- 6 slices (4 to 6 ounces *each*) fully cooked ham, halved
- 1/4 cup orange juice concentrate
- 2 tablespoons brown sugar
- 1 teaspoon prepared horseradish
- 1 teaspoon grated orange peel

Line two 15-in. x 10-in. x 1-in. baking pans with foil and coat with nonstick cooking spray. Add potatoes, carrots, turnip and onion; generously coat with nonstick cooking spray. Bake, uncovered, at 425° for 25-30 minutes or until tender. Arrange ham slices over the vegetables. In a bowl, combine remaining ingredients. Spoon over ham and vegetables. Cover and bake 10 minutes longer or until the ham is heated through. **Yield:** 6 servings.

SUNFLOWER CHICKEN

Lori Daniels, Beverly, West Virginia

This chicken stir-fry gets a nice crunch from sunflower kernels, carrots, celery and broccoli. It's full of color and flavor.

> ✓ Uses less fat, sugar or salt. Includes Nutritional Analysis and Diabetic Exchanges.

- 1 pound boneless skinless chicken breasts, cut into strips
- 3 medium carrots, sliced
- 2 celery ribs, sliced
- 1 medium onion, chopped
- 1 can (4 ounces) mushroom stems and pieces, drained
- 1 medium sweet red pepper, julienned
- 4 cups broccoli florets
- 1/4 cup sunflower kernels, toasted
- 1/4 teaspoon salt-free seasoning blend
- 1/4 teaspoon garlic powder
- 3 tablespoons cornstarch
- 1 can (14-1/2 ounces) reduced-sodium chicken broth

Hot cooked rice

In a skillet coated with nonstick cooking spray, stir-fry the chicken until no longer pink. Add vegetables, sunflower kernels, seasoning blend and garlic powder; stir-fry for 5-6 minutes or until vegetables are tender. Combine cornstarch and broth until smooth; add to skillet. Bring to a boil; cook and stir for 2 minutes or until thickened. Serve over rice. **Yield:** 6 servings.

Nutritional Analysis: One serving (calculated without rice) equals 190 calories, 183 mg sodium, 43 mg cholesterol, 16 gm carbohydrate, 20 gm protein, 5 gm fat. **Diabetic Exchanges:** 3 very lean meat, 1 starch, 1/2 fat.

BLACK BEAN RICE BAKE

The Bean Education and Awareness Network shared the recipe for this comforting casserole. The combination of chicken, rice and beans can't be beat.

- 1 package (6 ounces) long grain and wild rice mix
- 1-1/2 cups sliced fresh mushrooms
- 1/2 cup chopped onion
- 1/2 cup chopped green pepper
- 1/2 cup chopped sweet red pepper
- 1 tablespoon vegetable oil
- 2-1/2 cups cubed cooked chicken
- 1 can (15 ounces) black beans, rinsed and drained

1-1/2 cups sour cream
1-3/4 cups shredded cheddar cheese, *divided*
1/2 cup frozen corn
1/2 cup frozen peas
2 teaspoons Italian seasoning
Salt and pepper to taste

Cook the rice according to package directions. Meanwhile, in a skillet, saute mushrooms, onion and peppers in oil until crisp-tender. Add the chicken, beans, sour cream, 1 cup of cheese, corn, peas, Italian seasoning, salt and pepper. Stir in rice. Transfer to a 3-qt. baking dish. Sprinkle with the remaining cheese. Bake, uncovered, at 350° for 30-35 minutes or until heated through. **Yield:** 6-8 servings.

WHERE'S THE SQUASH LASAGNA

Norma Brinson, Greenville, North Carolina

I devised this recipe to hide zucchini from my unsuspecting grandchildren and any others who think they don't like it. It's always a hit at our house.

1 pound ground beef
2 large zucchini (about 1 pound), shredded
3/4 cup chopped onion
2 garlic cloves, minced
1 can (14-1/2 ounces) stewed tomatoes
2 cups water
1 can (12 ounces) tomato paste
1 tablespoon minced fresh parsley
1-1/2 teaspoons salt
1 teaspoon sugar
1/2 teaspoon dried oregano
1/2 teaspoon pepper
9 lasagna noodles, cooked, rinsed and drained
1 carton (15 ounces) ricotta cheese
2 cups (8 ounces) shredded mozzarella cheese
1 cup grated Parmesan cheese

In a skillet, cook beef, zucchini, onion and garlic over medium heat until meat is no longer pink; drain. Place tomatoes in a food processor or blender; cover and process until smooth. Stir into beef mixture. Add the water, tomato paste, parsley and seasonings. Bring to a boil. Reduce heat; simmer, uncovered, for 30 minutes, stirring occasionally. Spread 1 cup meat sauce in a greased 13-in. x 9-in. x 2-in. baking dish. Arrange three noodles over sauce.

Spread with a third of the meat sauce; top with half of the ricotta. Sprinkle with a third of the mozzarella and Parmesan. Repeat. Top with remaining noodles, meat sauce and cheeses. Cover and bake at 350° for 45 minutes. Uncover; bake 15 minutes longer or until bubbly. Let stand for 15 minutes before cutting. **Yield:** 12 servings.

TURKEY SCALLOPINI

(Pictured above)

Karen Adams, Seymour, Indiana

Quick-cooking turkey breast slices make this recipe a winner when you only have a few minutes to fix a satisfying meal. I've also used flattened boneless skinless chicken breast halves in place of the turkey for this entree.

6 turkey breast slices (about 1-1/2 pounds)
1/4 cup all-purpose flour
1/8 teaspoon salt
1/8 teaspoon pepper
1 egg
2 tablespoons water
1 cup soft bread crumbs
1/2 cup grated Parmesan cheese
1/4 cup butter *or* margarine
Minced fresh parsley

Pound turkey to 1/4-in. thickness. In a shallow bowl, combine flour, salt and pepper. In another bowl, beat egg and water. On a plate, combine the bread crumbs and Parmesan cheese. Dredge turkey in flour mixture, then dip in egg mixture and coat with crumbs. Melt butter in a skillet over medium-high heat; cook turkey for 2-3 minutes on each side or until meat juices run clear and coating is golden brown. Sprinkle with parsley. **Yield:** 6 servings.

FRUIT CREPES

(Pictured above)

Jean Murtagh, Solon, Ohio

These fruit-topped crepes are a great way to start the day. They taste so yummy, it's hard to believe they're good for you!

✓ Uses less fat, sugar or salt. Includes Nutritional Analysis and Diabetic Exchanges.

      2 egg whites
   2/3 cup fat-free milk
      2 teaspoons vegetable oil
   1/2 cup all-purpose flour
   1/4 teaspoon salt
   1/4 cup reduced-sugar orange marmalade
      1 cup unsweetened raspberries,
          blackberries *or* blueberries
Sugar substitute equivalent to 8
      teaspoons sugar
   1/2 cup fat-free sour cream
   1/8 teaspoon ground cinnamon

In a mixing bowl, combine egg whites, milk and oil. Combine flour and salt; add to milk mixture and mix well. In a saucepan, heat marmalade until melted; remove from the heat. Fold in berries and sugar substitute; set aside. In a small bowl, combine sour cream and cinnamon; set aside.

Heat an 8-in. nonstick skillet coated with non-stick cooking spray; add 2 tablespoons batter. Lift and tilt pan to evenly coat bottom. Cook until top appears dry and bottom is light brown. Remove to a wire rack. Repeat with remaining batter. Spread each crepe with 1 tablespoon sour cream mixture; roll up and place in an ungreased

11-in. x 7-in. x 2-in. baking dish. Spoon fruit mixture over top. Bake, uncovered, at 375° for 15 minutes. **Yield:** 4 servings.

Nutritional Analysis: One serving (2 crepes) equals 173 calories, 231 mg sodium, 1 mg cholesterol, 32 gm carbohydrate, 7 gm protein, 3 gm fat, 2 gm fiber. **Diabetic Exchanges:** 1-1/2 starch, 1/2 fat, 1/2 skim milk.

MAPLE-GLAZED PORK CHOPS

Cheryl Miller, Fort Collins, Colorado

Everyone cleaned their plates when my mother made these succulent tangy-sweet pork chops when I was growing up.

   1/2 cup all-purpose flour
Salt and pepper to taste
      4 bone-in pork loin chops (1 inch thick)
      2 tablespoons butter *or* margarine
   1/4 cup cider vinegar
   1/3 cup maple syrup
      1 tablespoon cornstarch
      3 tablespoons water
   2/3 cup packed brown sugar

In a large resealable plastic bag, combine flour, salt and pepper. Add pork chops and shake to coat. In a skillet, brown chops on both sides in butter. Place in an ungreased 13-in. x 9-in. x 2-in. baking pan. Bake, uncovered, at 450° for 20-25 minutes or until juices run clear.

Meanwhile, in a skillet, bring the vinegar to a boil. Reduce heat; add maple syrup. Cover and cook for 10 minutes. Combine cornstarch and water until smooth; add to the maple mixture. Bring to a boil; cook and stir for 2 minutes or until thickened. Place chops on a broiler pan; sprinkle with brown sugar. Broil 4 in. from the heat for 2-3 minutes or until sugar is melted. Drizzle with maple glaze. **Yield:** 4 servings.

SKILLET SPAGHETTI

Sr. Mary Maurice, Murphysboro, Illinois

This has always been a favorite dish of our Sisters who work in a hospital. When we get back to the convent, it's a quick and easy recipe.

  1 pound ground beef
  3 cups water
  2 cans (11-1/2 ounces *each*) tomato juice
    (about 2-3/4 cups)
  1 can (6 ounces) tomato paste
  2 tablespoons dried minced onion
  1 to 2 tablespoons chili powder
1-1/2 teaspoons dried oregano
  1 teaspoon sugar
  1 teaspoon salt
  1 teaspoon garlic salt
  1 package (7 ounces) spaghetti
Grated Parmesan cheese, optional

In a skillet, cook beef over medium heat until no longer pink; drain. Add the water, tomato juice, tomato paste and seasonings. Bring to a boil. Add uncooked spaghetti. Cover and simmer for 30 minutes or until the spaghetti is tender, stirring frequently. Sprinkle with Parmesan cheese if desired. **Yield:** 4-6 servings.

BACON VEGGIE ROLL-UPS

Sharon Wingo, El Paso, Texas

My husband and I are missionaries in the Sierra Madre Mountains of Mexico. This is a variation of a dish the locals make when zucchini is in season.

1/2 pound sliced bacon, diced
  3 medium zucchini, diced
  1 small onion, chopped
  1 jalapeno pepper, seeded and chopped*
  1 small tomato, chopped
  1 teaspoon chicken bouillon granules
1-1/2 cups (6 ounces) shredded cheddar
    cheese
  8 flour tortillas (10 inches)

In a skillet, cook bacon over medium heat until crisp. Remove to paper towels. Drain, reserving 1 teaspoon drippings. In the drippings, cook zuc-

chini, onion, jalapeno, tomato and bouillon for 5-10 minutes or until zucchini is almost tender, stirring occasionally. Sprinkle with cheese and bacon. Spoon down the center of tortillas and roll up. **Yield:** 8 servings.

  *Editor's Note:** When cutting or seeding hot peppers, use rubber or plastic gloves to protect your hands. Avoid touching your face.

HORSERADISH HONEY HAM
(Pictured below)

Beverly Loomis, Ithaca, Michigan

Horseradish definitely is the key to this delicious ham's tangy taste. I serve it for Easter and Christmas.

  1 boneless fully cooked ham (5 to 7
    pounds)
1/4 cup honey, warmed
1/8 teaspoon ground cloves
  1 cup packed brown sugar
1/2 cup prepared horseradish
1/4 cup lemon juice

Cut ham into 1/4-in. slices and tie with kitchen string. Place ham on a rack in a shallow roasting pan. Combine honey and cloves; drizzle over ham. Bake, uncovered, at 325° for 1-1/2 to 2 hours or until a meat thermometer reads 140° and ham is heated through, basting often with drippings.

Meanwhile, combine the brown sugar, horseradish and lemon juice. Increase oven temperature to 400°. Baste ham with brown sugar sauce so sauce penetrates between slices. Bake, uncovered, for 15-20 minutes. **Yield:** 15-18 servings.

■■■■■■■■■■■■■

CHICKEN SAUSAGE SKILLET

(Pictured below)

Connie Dowell, Orlando, Florida

My sister Mary, who is an excellent cook, shared this wonderful recipe with me. I've always loved its tantalizing blend of ingredients, and so do other folks I've served it to over the years. In fact, I'm often asked for the recipe myself.

- 1 medium onion, thinly sliced
- 1 medium green pepper, thinly sliced
- 1 cup sliced fresh mushrooms
- 1 cup sliced zucchini
- 2 tablespoons olive *or* vegetable oil
- 1/2 to 3/4 pound boneless skinless chicken breasts, thinly sliced
- 1/2 to 3/4 pound Italian sausage links, cut into 1/2-inch pieces
- 2 cans (14-1/2 ounces *each*) diced tomatoes, undrained
- 1 garlic clove, minced
- 3/4 teaspoon dried basil
- 3/4 teaspoon dried oregano

Hot cooked rice

In a large skillet, saute the onion, green pepper, mushrooms and zucchini in oil until tender. Remove vegetables with a slotted spoon; set aside. Add chicken and sausage to skillet; cook until

no longer pink. Drain. Stir in tomatoes, garlic, basil and oregano. Return vegetables to pan. Bring to a boil. Reduce heat; cover and simmer for 10 minutes or until heated through. Serve over rice. **Yield:** 6-8 servings.

■■■■■■■■■■■■■

BARBECUE SANDWICHES

Tina Wunker, Winston-Salem, North Carolina

This recipe makes the best barbecued meat sandwiches ever. The combination of beef, pork and spices just can't be beat. The recipe makes a lot...but these sandwiches don't last long. The first time I served them, I was sure I'd have leftovers—was I ever wrong!

- 1 boneless beef chuck roast (2-1/2 pounds), trimmed
- 1 boneless pork shoulder roast (2-1/2 pounds), trimmed
- 8 cups water
- 2 celery ribs, cut into 3-inch pieces
- 1 large onion, cut into 8 pieces
- 2 medium carrots, cut into 2-inch pieces
- 2 bay leaves
- 8 whole cloves
- 1 teaspoon salt
- 1/4 teaspoon pepper

BARBECUE SAUCE:

- 1 cup chopped onion
- 2 tablespoons butter *or* margarine
- 1 cup ketchup
- 1/2 cup cider vinegar
- 1/3 cup sugar
- 4 teaspoons Worcestershire sauce
- 1 tablespoon brown sugar
- 1 tablespoon celery salt
- 2 teaspoons paprika
- 1/2 teaspoon salt
- 1/2 teaspoon pepper
- 1/2 teaspoon chili powder
- 1/2 teaspoon ground cumin
- 16 to 20 hamburger buns, split

Place the first 10 ingredients in a large roasting pan; cover and bake at 325° for 3-4 hours or until pork is tender. Remove pork roast; set aside. Bake chuck roast, covered, 40 minutes longer or until beef is tender. Cut pork and beef into bite-size pieces. Strain pan drippings and set aside 1/2 cup for sauce.

In a large Dutch oven, saute onion in butter until tender. Add ketchup, vinegar, sugar, Worcestershire sauce, brown sugar and seasonings. Stir in reserved pan drippings. Add meat; bring to a boil. Reduce heat; cover and simmer for 15 minutes, stirring occasionally. Serve on buns. **Yield:** 16-20 servings.

Skillet Secrets

• I buy ground beef in bulk when it's on sale, then brown it with chopped onion and garlic...and freeze it in serving-size containers. I thaw portions as needed to get a jump start on supper.
—*Barbara Dailey*
Easton, Pennsylvania

• To prevent rice from boiling over, rub butter or margarine around the edge of the saucepan before cooking.
—*Mary Zacharias*
LaCrete, Alberta

• Slicing meat or chicken breasts into thin strips is easier if the meat is partially frozen. —*Darla Hardesty*
Northome, Minnesota

• For even cooking when stir-frying, cut all vegetables and meats into uniformly sized pieces. —*Vicky Monk*
Citrus Heights, California

• If you've run out of taco seasoning mix, make your own by combining 1 tablespoon dried minced onion, 4-1/2 teaspoons chili powder, 1 tablespoon garlic powder, 2 teaspoons paprika and 1 teaspoon ground cumin.
—*Cindy Grantz*
Stockton, Kansas

• To add a grilled flavor to foods without actually grilling them, put a small amount of liquid smoke in your favorite homemade barbecue sauce or marinade. —*Liz Blocker*
Crystal River, Florida

• Leftover stir-fry makes a great filling for pita bread sandwiches.
—*Shannon Witt, Clarksville, Indiana*

• To save time when preparing skillet dishes, casseroles and stir-fries, use frozen vegetables and measure them the same as you would fresh. It may take a bit longer for them to cook, but the time you'll save cleaning and cutting them makes up for it.
—*Sally Davis*
Gore, Oklahoma

• Whenever you want to add some spice to a recipe calling for regular canned tomatoes, try substituting either hot or mild salsa or picante sauce for all or part of the tomatoes.
—*Beth Becker, Leesburg, Indiana*

• Like a flavorful change of pace? Sprinkle a small amount of ground cinnamon in your favorite sloppy joe or barbecued beef recipe.
—*Brenda Gervais*
Paradise Hill, Saskatchewan

• To make a lighter stir-fry for yourself or a family member on a restricted diet, simply substitute reduced-sodium soy sauce and reduced-sodium broth, bouillon granules or cubes.
—*Susan Monaghan*
Central City, Nebraska

• For additional color and a nutritional boost, substitute shredded carrots for some of the potatoes called for in au gratin potato recipes.
—*Virginia Roberts, Oxnard, California*

• For a delightful caramelized flavor, add a teaspoon of sugar to vegetables when you stir-fry them.
—*Jeanette Pitts*
Laurel, Mississippi

THICK 'N' ZESTY RIBS

(Pictured below)

Helen Tucker, Wooster, Ohio

I got this recipe over 30 years ago from a co-worker and have made it many times. Everyone in our family loves it.

- 4 pounds pork baby back ribs, cut into serving-size pieces
- 1 teaspoon garlic salt
- 1 cup ketchup
- 1/2 cup vinegar
- 1/4 cup sugar
- 1-1/2 teaspoons chili powder
- 1 teaspoon salt
- 1 teaspoon paprika
- 1 teaspoon ground mustard
- 1 teaspoon celery seed
- 1/2 teaspoon pepper

Place ribs in a greased 13-in. x 9-in. x 2-in. baking dish. Rub with garlic salt. Bake, uncovered, at 350° for 45 minutes; drain. Combine the remaining ingredients; mix well. Pour over ribs. Bake, uncovered, for 40-50 minutes or until ribs are tender, basting several times. **Yield:** 4 servings.

TURKEY LATTICE PIE

Lorraine Naig, Emmetsburg, Iowa

With its pretty lattice crust, this cheesy baked dish is as eye-catching as it is delicious. It's easy to make, too, since it uses convenient crescent roll dough. It's a fun and different way to dress up leftover turkey.

- 3 tubes (8 ounces *each*) refrigerated crescent rolls
- 4 cups cubed cooked turkey
- 1-1/2 cups (6 ounces) shredded cheddar *or* Swiss cheese
- 1 package (10 ounces) frozen chopped broccoli, thawed and drained
- 1 can (10-3/4 ounces) condensed cream of chicken soup, undiluted
- 1-1/3 cups milk
- 2 tablespoons Dijon mustard
- 1 tablespoon dried minced onion
- 1/2 teaspoon salt
- Dash pepper
- 1 egg, lightly beaten

Unroll two tubes of crescent roll dough; separate into rectangles. Place rectangles in an ungreased 15-in. x 10-in. x 1-in. baking pan. Press onto the bottom and 1/4 in. up the sides of pan to form a crust, sealing seams and perforations. Bake at 375° for 5-7 minutes or until light golden brown.

In a bowl, combine the turkey, cheese, broccoli, soup, milk, mustard, onion, salt and pepper; mix well. Spoon over crust. Unroll remaining dough; divide into rectangles. Seal perforations. Cut each rectangle into four 1-in. strips. Using strips, make a lattice design on top of turkey mixture. Brush with egg. Bake 17-22 minutes longer or until top crust is golden brown and filling is hot. **Yield:** 12-16 servings.

APPLE HAM STEAK

Mildred Sherrer, Bay City, Texas

Whenever I take this ham steak to a get-together, I take along copies of the recipe. It's always a hit!

- 1-1/2 cups instant rice
- 1 medium onion, chopped
- 2 celery ribs, chopped
- 6 tablespoons butter *or* margarine, *divided*
- 2-1/2 cups apple juice, *divided*
- 1 teaspoon salt
- 1 pound fully cooked ham steak, cut into fourths
- 2 medium tart apples, peeled and sliced
- 2 tablespoons brown sugar
- 1/4 teaspoon ground cinnamon
- 2 tablespoons raisins
- 1 tablespoon cornstarch

In a saucepan, saute rice, onion and celery in 2 tablespoons butter until tender. Add 1-1/2 cups apple juice and salt. Bring to a boil. Cover and remove from the heat; let stand for 5 minutes. Meanwhile, in a skillet, cook ham in remaining butter until lightly browned. Remove and keep warm. In the same skillet, cook and stir apples, brown sugar and cinnamon over medium heat until apples are almost tender, about 5 minutes. Stir in raisins.

In a bowl, combine cornstarch and remaining apple juice until smooth; add to the skillet. Bring to a boil; cook and stir for 2 minutes or until thickened. Return the ham to skillet and heat through. Serve over the rice. **Yield:** 4 servings.

CREAMY SEAFOOD ENCHILADAS

Evelyn Gebhardt, Kasilof, Alaska

Two types of seafood and a flavorful sauce make these enchiladas outstanding. I prepare them for an annual fund-raiser, where they're always in demand. Spice up the recipe to your taste by adding more green chilies and salsa.

- 1/4 cup butter *or* margarine
- 1/4 cup all-purpose flour
- 1 cup chicken broth
- 1 can (10-3/4 ounces) condensed cream of chicken soup, undiluted
- 1 cup (8 ounces) sour cream
- 1/2 cup salsa
- 1/8 teaspoon salt
- 1 cup (8 ounces) small-curd cottage cheese
- 1 pound small shrimp, cooked, peeled and deveined
- 1 cup cooked *or* canned crabmeat, drained, flaked and cartilage removed
- 1-1/2 cups (6 ounces) shredded Monterey Jack cheese
- 1 can (4 ounces) chopped green chilies
- 1 tablespoon dried cilantro *or* parsley flakes
- 12 flour tortillas (7 inches)

Additional salsa

In a saucepan over low heat, melt butter; stir in flour until smooth. Gradually stir in broth and soup until blended. Bring to a boil; cook and stir for 2 minutes. Remove from the heat. Stir in sour cream, salsa and salt; set aside. Place cottage cheese in a blender; cover and process until smooth. Transfer to a bowl; add the shrimp, crab, Monterey Jack cheese, chilies and cilantro.

Spread 3/4 cup sauce in a greased 13-in. x 9-in. x 2-in. baking dish. Place about 1/3 cup seafood mixture down the center of each tortilla. Roll up and place, seam side down, over sauce. Top with the remaining sauce. Bake, uncovered, at 350° for 30-35 minutes or until heated through. Serve with additional salsa. **Yield:** 6 servings.

CHEDDAR CHICKEN SPAGHETTI
(Pictured above)

Ann Robinson, Dauphin Island, Alabama

I actually created this recipe out of desperation. My son Charlie was a picky eater when he was young, so I put together some of the things he likes. To this day, he says it's his favorite dish!

- 1 package (7 ounces) spaghetti, broken
- 2 cups cubed cooked chicken
- 2 cups (8 ounces) shredded cheddar cheese, *divided*
- 1 can (10-3/4 ounces) condensed cream of chicken soup, undiluted
- 1 cup milk
- 1 tablespoon diced pimientos, optional
- 1/4 teaspoon salt
- 1/4 teaspoon pepper

Cook spaghetti according to package directions. Meanwhile, in a bowl, combine the chicken, 1 cup cheese, soup, milk, pimientos if desired, salt and pepper. Drain spaghetti; add to the chicken mixture and toss to coat. Transfer to a greased 13-in. x 9-in. x 2-in. baking dish. Sprinkle with the remaining cheese. Bake, uncovered, at 350° for 20-25 minutes or until heated through. **Yield:** 6-8 servings.

SIMPLE SUBSTITUTION

If you don't have leftover chicken on hand, you can buy cubed cooked chicken in the frozen foods section of the supermarket.

Angela Harker, Superior, Wisconsin

I've shared this recipe many times over the years. Even folks who say they don't normally care for ground turkey love the taste of these patties.

✓ **Uses less fat, sugar or salt. Includes Nutritional Analysis and Diabetic Exchanges.**

  1 tablespoon sugar
  1 tablespoon cornstarch
1/8 teaspoon ground ginger
  1 cup chicken *or* turkey broth
  3 tablespoons reduced-sodium soy sauce
  2 teaspoons vinegar
  1 egg
1/3 cup dry bread crumbs
1/4 teaspoon salt
1/4 teaspoon garlic powder
1-1/4 pounds lean ground turkey
  1 large green pepper, cut into 1-inch pieces
  1 cup sliced celery
  2 medium tomatoes, cut into wedges
Hot cooked rice

In a small bowl, combine sugar, cornstarch and ginger; mix well. Whisk in the broth, soy sauce and vinegar until smooth; set aside. In another bowl, lightly beat egg. Add bread crumbs, salt and garlic powder; mix well. Crumble turkey over mixture and mix well. Shape into five patties.

In a nonstick skillet coated with cooking spray, cook patties over medium-high heat for 3-5 minutes on each side or until browned and juices run clear. Add green pepper and celery. Stir reserved broth mixture; add to pan and bring to a boil. Reduce heat; cover and simmer for 5 minutes or until vegetables are crisp-tender. Add tomatoes; simmer 6 minutes longer. Serve over rice. **Yield:** 5 servings.

Nutritional Analysis: One serving (calculated without rice) equals 260 calories, 1,064 mg sodium, 134 mg cholesterol, 15 gm carbohydrate, 23 gm protein, 12 gm fat, 2 gm fiber. **Diabetic Exchanges:** 3-1/2 lean meat, 1 starch.

██████████████████

HERB-CRUSTED CHUCK ROAST
(Pictured above)

Rita Drewes, Craig, Missouri

This recipe turns an inexpensive cut of beef into a delicious main dish. I got the recipe from a family member several years ago and have made it often.

1/4 cup dry bread crumbs
  2 tablespoons olive *or* vegetable oil
  1 garlic clove, minced
  1 teaspoon ground mustard
  1 teaspoon dried savory
  1 teaspoon pepper
1/2 teaspoon dried rosemary, crushed
  1 boneless chuck eye *or* top blade roast
    (about 3 pounds)
SAUCE:
  1 cup (8 ounces) sour cream
  3 tablespoons prepared horseradish
  1 teaspoon lemon juice
1/4 teaspoon salt

In a bowl, combine the first seven ingredients. Rub over entire roast. Place on a rack in a shallow roasting pan. Bake, uncovered, at 325° for 1-1/2 to 2 hours or until meat is tender and reaches desired doneness (for medium-rare, a meat thermometer should read 145°; medium, 160°; well-done, 170°). Let stand 10 minutes before carving. Meanwhile, in a bowl, combine the sauce ingredients. Serve with the roast. **Yield:** 8 servings.

██████████████████

BAKED CHICKEN AND ACORN SQUASH

Connie Svoboda, Elko, Minnesota

This eye-pleasing main dish is ideal for harvesttime, with its colorful acorn squash and sweet peaches. The fragrance of rosemary-seasoned chicken baking is heavenly. My family says it's every bit as delicious as its aroma.

2 small acorn squash (1-1/4 pounds *each*)
2 to 4 garlic cloves, minced
2 tablespoons vegetable oil, *divided*
4 chicken drumsticks
4 chicken thighs
1/4 cup packed brown sugar
1 teaspoon salt
1 tablespoon minced fresh rosemary *or* 1 teaspoon dried rosemary, crushed
1 can (15-1/4 ounces) sliced peaches, undrained

Cut squash in half lengthwise; discard seeds. Cut each half widthwise into 1/2-in. slices; discard ends. Place slices in an ungreased 13-in. x 9-in. x 2-in. baking dish. Sprinkle with garlic and drizzle with 1 tablespoon oil. In a large skillet, brown chicken in remaining oil. Arrange chicken over squash. Combine the brown sugar, salt and rosemary; sprinkle over chicken.

Bake, uncovered, at 350° for 45 minutes, basting with pan juices twice. Pour peaches over chicken and squash. Bake, uncovered, 15 minutes longer or until chicken juices run clear and peaches are heated through. **Yield:** 4 servings.

OLD-FASHIONED SWISS STEAK

Elaine DeWitt, Lake City, Minnesota

Our ladies' group held monthly dinners at our church to raise money, and this is one of the dishes we served. It was always a real crowd-pleaser. We never had to advertise these dinners—word about the good food got around quickly.

2 pounds round steak
1/2 cup all-purpose flour
1/2 teaspoon salt
1/2 teaspoon pepper, *divided*
2 tablespoons vegetable oil
1 cup chopped onion
1/2 cup chopped green pepper
1/4 cup soy sauce
1/2 teaspoon garlic salt
Hot cooked noodles, optional

Cut steak into serving-size pieces. Combine flour, salt and 1/4 teaspoon pepper; sprinkle over steak and pound into both sides. In a skillet over medium heat, brown steak on both sides in oil. Transfer to a greased 13-in. x 9-in. x 2-in. baking dish; top with onion and green pepper. Drizzle with soy sauce; sprinkle with garlic salt and remaining pepper. Cover and bake at 325° for 1-1/2 hours or until meat is tender. Serve over noodles if desired. **Yield:** 6-8 servings.

ORANGE-GLAZED TURKEY

(Pictured below)

Annette D'Onofrio, Malden, Massachusetts

I've used this recipe for our Thanksgiving meal for years. Everyone loves the flavor the orange marmalade gives the turkey.

2 teaspoons salt
2 teaspoons pepper
2 teaspoons dried savory
2 teaspoons rubbed sage
1 turkey (18 to 20 pounds)
2 medium pears, cored and thinly sliced
1 large onion, quartered
1 celery rib, quartered
1/2 cup butter *or* margarine, melted
3/4 cup orange marmalade
3/4 cup orange juice
1 tablespoon honey

In a small bowl, combine the salt, pepper, savory and sage. Rub 1 tablespoon of seasoning mixture in turkey cavity. Place the pears, onion and celery in turkey cavity; tie drumsticks together. Place, breast side up, on a rack in a roasting pan. Combine butter and remaining seasoning mixture; brush over turkey. Bake, uncovered, at 325° for 3-1/4 to 3-1/2 hours.

Meanwhile, combine marmalade, orange juice and honey in a saucepan. Bring to a boil. Reduce heat; simmer, uncovered, for 15 minutes or until thickened, stirring occasionally. Set aside and keep warm. When turkey begins to brown, cover lightly with a tent of foil. Bake 1 hour longer or until meat thermometer reads 180°, brushing occasionally with orange glaze. Cover and let stand 15 minutes before carving. Thicken pan juices for gravy if desired. **Yield:** 18-20 servings.

Speedy Skillet Suppers

LOOKING for a last-minute stovetop solution to satisfy your hungry bunch? These hearty suppers showcasing chicken, beef, pork and more can be stirred up in a half hour or less.

〰〰〰〰〰〰〰〰〰〰

CHICKEN VEGGIE SAUTE

(Pictured below)

Joyce Hiebert, Steinbach, Manitoba

Why serve plain chicken breasts when you can stir together this satisfying veggie and chicken saute in a matter of minutes?

  4 boneless skinless chicken breast halves
  1 tablespoon vegetable oil
1/2 cup sliced carrots
  1 cup broccoli florets
  1 cup sliced fresh mushrooms
  1 can (10-3/4 ounces) condensed cream
     of chicken soup, undiluted
1/3 cup milk
  1 tablespoon Dijon mustard
1/8 teaspoon pepper
Hot cooked noodles

In a large skillet, cook chicken in oil for 10 minutes or until juices run clear. Remove and keep warm. In the drippings, saute carrots for 2 minutes. Add broccoli; saute for 2 minutes. Add mushrooms; saute for 1 minute or until vegetables are crisp-tender. Stir in soup, milk, mustard and pepper. Bring just to a boil. Return chicken to pan. Reduce heat; cover and simmer for 10 minutes or until heated through. Serve over noodles. **Yield:** 4 servings.

〰〰〰〰〰〰〰〰〰〰

SAUSAGE STROGANOFF

Teresa Niesen, Rapid City, South Dakota

The addition of smoked sausage gives a unique and tasty twist to regular stroganoff. It's speedy, too.

  1 package (12 ounces) medium egg
     noodles
  1 pound fully cooked smoked sausage,
     cut into 1/2-inch pieces
  1 can (10-3/4 ounces) condensed cream
     of chicken soup, undiluted
  1 cup (8 ounces) sour cream

2 tablespoons grated Parmesan cheese
1/4 teaspoon seasoned salt
1/8 teaspoon pepper
2 tablespoons butter *or* margarine

Cook noodles according to package directions. Meanwhile, in a large skillet, cook sausage until heated through; drain. Remove with a slotted spoon and keep warm. Combine soup, sour cream, Parmesan cheese, seasoned salt and pepper; set aside. Melt butter in the skillet. Drain noodles and add to skillet. Add soup mixture and sausage; toss to coat. Heat through. **Yield:** 6 servings.

EASY BEEF AND NOODLES

Mildred Pavek, Eagle River, Wisconsin

I discovered this recipe in a magazine years ago and adapted it to fit my family's tastes. It's a very fast and flavorful meal.

1/2 pound sirloin steak, cut into 1/4-inch strips
1 medium onion, sliced
1 can (8 ounces) mushroom stems and pieces, drained
2 tablespoons vegetable oil
2 packages (3 ounces *each*) beef-flavored ramen noodles
4-1/4 cups water, *divided*

In a skillet, saute steak, onion and mushrooms in oil for 6-7 minutes or until meat is no longer pink. Set noodle seasoning packets aside. In a saucepan, bring 4 cups water to a boil. Add noodles; cook until tender. Drain. Add noodles, contents of seasoning packets and remaining water to skillet; heat through. **Yield:** 4 servings.

SAUSAGE AND WILD RICE

Gaye Whittington, Leesville, South Carolina

Since it has just four convenient ingredients, I can put this savory dish on the table for my hungry family in no time at all.

1 package (6.2 ounces) long grain and wild rice mix
1 can (15 ounces) black beans, rinsed and drained
1 can (11 ounces) Mexicorn, drained
1/2 pound fully cooked smoked sausage, cut into 1/2-inch slices

In a large skillet, prepare rice according to package directions. Add beans, corn and sausage. Cover and simmer for 10 minutes or until heated through. **Yield:** 4 servings.

SPEEDY SLOPPY JOES

Nancy Lambert, Punta Gorda, Florida

These quick-to-fix sloppy joe sandwiches get a nice zip from sweet pickle relish and barbecue sauce. Kids especially love them!

1 pound ground beef
1 can (10-3/4 ounces) condensed tomato soup, undiluted
2 tablespoons sweet pickle relish
2 tablespoons ketchup
2 tablespoons barbecue sauce
6 to 8 onion rolls *or* hamburger buns, split

In a large skillet over medium heat, cook beef until no longer pink; drain. Add soup, sweet pickle relish, ketchup and barbecue sauce; cover and simmer for 10 minutes. Serve on buns. **Yield:** 6-8 servings.

PORK 'N' PEPPER STIR-FRY

Opal Hoferer, Topeka, Kansas

I like the taste of chop suey, so I came up with my own recipe. This speedy stir-fry is the satisfying result.

1-1/2 cups julienned celery
1 medium green *or* sweet red pepper, julienned
1 medium onion, cut into wedges
1 garlic clove, minced
3 tablespoons vegetable oil
2 tablespoons cornstarch
1-1/4 cups cold water
1 cup cubed cooked pork, beef *or* chicken
2 tablespoons soy sauce
1/4 teaspoon salt
Hot cooked rice

In a skillet, stir-fry celery, green pepper, onion and garlic in oil until crisp-tender. Combine cornstarch and water until smooth; stir into vegetables. Add pork, soy sauce and salt. Bring to a boil; cook and stir for 2 minutes or until thickened. Serve over rice. **Yield:** 4 servings.

CHICKEN FAJITAS
(Pictured below)

Pamela Schroeder, Santee, California

Fajitas are my favorite dish when I'm at a Mexican restaurant, so I decided to try making them at home. They turned out so well that I served them the next time my husband's parents came to visit. Everyone said they were delicious!

    5 tablespoons vegetable oil, *divided*
    2 tablespoons Worcestershire sauce
    1 tablespoon soy sauce
    1 tablespoon lemon juice
    1 teaspoon cider *or* white wine vinegar
    1/4 teaspoon salt
    1/8 teaspoon pepper
1-1/4 pounds boneless skinless chicken breasts, cut into thin strips
   10 flour tortillas (7 inches), warmed
Shredded cheddar cheese
Guacamole

In a large resealable plastic bag, combine 4 tablespoons oil, Worcestershire sauce, soy sauce, lemon juice, vinegar, salt and pepper. Add chicken; seal bag and turn to coat. Refrigerate for at least 30 minutes. Drain and discard marinade. In a skillet, saute chicken in remaining oil for 8 minutes or until juices run clear. Serve in tortillas with cheese and guacamole. **Yield:** 5 servings.

TURKEY IN THE STRAWGANOFF

Phyllis Coning, North Manchester, Indiana

This attractive dish is a great way to use up leftover turkey. It's fast to fix and very filling.

    1 cup chopped onion
    1/2 cup butter *or* margarine
    2 garlic cloves, minced
    1/4 cup all-purpose flour
1 to 2 teaspoons salt
    1/2 teaspoon pepper
    2 cans (10-3/4 ounces *each*) condensed cream of chicken soup, undiluted
    4 cups cubed cooked turkey
    1 can (8 ounces) mushroom stems and pieces, drained
    2 cups (16 ounces) sour cream
    1/4 cup plus 2 tablespoons minced fresh parsley, *divided*
    1 pound fine noodles, cooked
    1 tablespoon diced pimientos, drained

In a large skillet, saute onion in butter. Add garlic; saute 2 minutes longer. Stir in flour, salt and pepper until blended. Add soup, turkey and mushrooms. Bring to a boil. Reduce heat; simmer, uncovered, for 10 minutes. Stir in sour cream and 1/4 cup parsley; heat for 6 minutes, stirring frequently. Serve over noodles. Garnish with pimientos and remaining parsley. **Yield:** 6-8 servings.

HAM WITH ORANGE SAUCE

Gloria Warczak, Cedarburg, Wisconsin

The light and citrusy glaze and sauce is what makes this ham so special. It's as good as it is good for you.

✓ **Uses less fat, sugar or salt. Includes Nutritional Analysis and Diabetic Exchanges.**

    1 reduced-sodium semi-boneless fully cooked ham half (6 pounds)
    1 cup orange juice
    1 cup reduced-sodium chicken broth
    1/4 teaspoon ground cloves
GLAZE:
    1 cup reduced-sugar orange marmalade
    1 tablespoon lemon juice
    1 tablespoon Worcestershire sauce
    1 teaspoon horseradish mustard*
    1/8 teaspoon garlic powder
SAUCE:
    1/4 cup orange juice
    1/4 cup packed brown sugar
    1/2 teaspoon ground ginger
    1 can (11 ounces) mandarin oranges, drained
    1/2 cup golden raisins

Remove skin from ham. Place on a rack in a shallow roasting pan. Combine orange juice and broth; pour over ham. Sprinkle with cloves.

Cover and bake at 325° for 1 to 1-1/2 hours. Combine glaze ingredients; spoon over ham. Bake, uncovered, 20-30 minutes longer or until a meat thermometer reads 140° and ham is heated through. Remove ham to a serving platter and keep warm. Strain pan drippings; skim fat.

In a saucepan, combine orange juice, brown sugar and ginger. Stir in pan drippings, oranges and raisins. Bring to a boil. Reduce heat; simmer, uncovered, for 15-20 minutes. Thicken if desired. Serve with the ham. **Yield:** 20 servings (about 3 cups of sauce).

Nutritional Analysis: One serving (with 2 tablespoons of sauce) equals 211 calories, 907 mg sodium, 43 mg cholesterol, 22 gm carbohydrate, 20 gm protein, 5 gm fat. **Diabetic Exchanges:** 2 lean meat, 1-1/2 fruit.

*Editor's Note: As a substitute for horseradish mustard, combine 1/2 teaspoon spicy brown mustard and 1/2 teaspoon prepared horseradish.

MEATY STUFFED ONIONS

Lorraine Grasso, Allentown, Pennsylvania

I won a prize for this recipe in a contest sponsored by our local newspaper. I got it from my mother-in-law, who's originally from Italy.

     4 large sweet onions
     1 pound ground beef
 1/2 pound bulk pork sausage
     1 package (10 ounces) frozen chopped
       spinach, thawed and drained
     5 slices day-old bread, crumbled
 1/2 to 2/3 cup beef broth
 1/2 cup grated Parmesan cheese
     1 egg, beaten
     1 tablespoon minced fresh parsley
 1/2 teaspoon salt
 1/4 teaspoon pepper
 1/8 teaspoon ground nutmeg

Peel onions and cut 1/2 in. off tops and bottoms. Place onions in a large saucepan. Cover with boiling water. Cook until tender, about 20 minutes; drain. Cool slightly. Carefully remove inside layers of onion, separating into eight individual shells (refrigerate remaining onion for another use). Drain on paper towels.

In a skillet, cook beef and sausage over medium heat until no longer pink; drain. Add spinach; cook and stir for 2 minutes. Remove from the heat; stir in the remaining ingredients. Spoon into the onion shells. Place in a greased 13-in. x 9-in. x 2-in. baking pan. Bake, uncovered, at 350° for 15-20 minutes or until heated through and lightly browned. **Yield:** 8 servings.

GRILLED PORK AND POBLANO PEPPERS

(Pictured above)

Donna Gay Harris, Springdale, Arkansas

My husband and I entertain a lot in summer, and this has quickly become the most-requested dish. I usually serve it with Mexican rice and a tossed salad.

     4 large poblano peppers*
     2 cups (8 ounces) shredded Monterey
       Jack cheese
 4-1/2 teaspoons chili powder
 1-1/2 teaspoons onion powder
 1-1/2 teaspoons ground cumin
 1/2 teaspoon garlic powder
 1/4 teaspoon salt
 1/8 teaspoon aniseed, ground
 1/8 teaspoon cayenne pepper
     2 pork tenderloins (about 1 pound *each*)

Cut the top off each pepper and set tops aside. Remove seeds. Stuff peppers with cheese. Replace tops and secure with toothpicks; set aside. Combine the seasonings; rub over pork. Grill, covered, over medium-hot heat for 18 minutes or until a meat thermometer reads 160°-170° and juices run clear. Place peppers on sides of grill (not directly over coals); heat for 10 minutes or until browned. **Yield:** 6-8 servings.

*Editor's Note: When cutting or seeding hot peppers, use rubber or plastic gloves to protect your hands. Avoid touching your face.

mometer reads 180° for the turkey and 165° for the stuffing. Baste occasionally with pan drippings. Cover loosely with foil if turkey browns too quickly. Cover and let stand for 20 minutes before removing the stuffing and carving the turkey. If desired, thicken pan drippings for gravy. **Yield:** 10-12 servings (6 cups stuffing).

Editor's Note: The stuffing may be prepared as directed and baked separately in a greased 2-qt. baking dish. Cover and bake at 325° for 50-60 minutes. Uncover and bake 10 minutes longer or until lightly browned.

BARBECUED TURKEY SANDWICHES

Pamela Siegrist, Fort Recovery, Ohio

I have an excellent source for turkey recipes, since many of our neighbors are poultry farmers! These satisfying sandwiches, with their mildly tangy sauce, are a great way to use up leftover turkey from the holidays.

 2 celery ribs, chopped
1/2 cup chopped onion
1/4 cup chopped green pepper
1/3 cup butter *or* margarine
1/2 cup ketchup
1/4 cup packed brown sugar
 3 tablespoons Worcestershire sauce
1-1/2 teaspoons chili powder
 1 teaspoon salt
1/8 teaspoon pepper
1/8 teaspoon hot pepper sauce
 4 cups shredded cooked turkey
 8 hamburger buns, split, toasted and buttered

In a saucepan, saute the celery, onion and green pepper in butter until tender. Add the next seven ingredients. Bring to a boil. Reduce heat; cover and simmer for 5 minutes. Add turkey; heat through. Serve on buns. **Yield:** 8 servings.

TURKEY WITH CHERRY STUFFING

(Pictured above)

Virginia Sacchetta, Leesburg, Florida

This moist stuffing, with its fruity blend of raisins and tart cherries, is a sweet twist on a traditional version. It's a tasty complement to tender poultry slices. Be prepared to dish up second helpings when you serve this bird.

3/4 cup chopped celery
1/3 cup chopped onion
 2 tablespoons butter *or* margarine
3/4 teaspoon dried thyme
1/4 teaspoon poultry seasoning
 5 cups seasoned stuffing cubes
3/4 cup golden raisins
3/4 cup chicken broth
 1 can (14-1/2 ounces) pitted tart cherries, drained
 1 turkey (10 to 12 pounds)
 2 tablespoons vegetable oil

In a saucepan, saute celery and onion in butter until tender. Stir in thyme and poultry seasoning. In a large bowl, combine stuffing, raisins and celery mixture. Add broth and cherries; toss to mix. Loosely stuff turkey just before baking. Skewer openings; tie drumsticks together.

 Place the turkey, breast side up, on a rack in a roasting pan. Brush with oil. Bake, uncovered, at 325° for 4 to 4-1/2 hours or until a meat ther-

APRICOT-FILLED PORK TENDERLOIN

Jo Ann Hettel, Bushnell, Florida

This flavorful main course is a great company offering. The tenderloin tastes wonderful and looks so pretty when it's sliced to reveal a golden apricot center. In the 15 plus years I've been using this recipe, it has never failed me.

 2 pork tenderloins (1 pound *each*)
 1 package (6 ounces) dried apricots

MARINADE:

- 1/3 cup sweet-and-sour salad dressing
- 1/4 cup packed brown sugar
- 3 tablespoons teriyaki sauce
- 2 tablespoons ketchup
- 1 teaspoon Dijon mustard
- 1 onion slice, separated into rings
- 1 garlic clove, minced
- 1/2 teaspoon ground ginger *or* 2 teaspoons minced fresh gingerroot
- 1/4 teaspoon pepper
- 1/8 teaspoon pumpkin pie spice

Make a lengthwise cut three-quarters of the way through each tenderloin; pound with a meat mallet to flatten evenly. Set aside three apricots for marinade. Stuff remaining apricots into tenderloins to within 1/2 in. of ends; secure with toothpicks or kitchen string. Place in a greased 11-in. x 7-in. x 2-in. baking dish.

In a blender, combine the marinade ingredients and reserved apricots. Cover and process until smooth; set aside 1/3 cup. Pour remaining marinade over tenderloins. Cover and refrigerate for at least 2 hours, turning meat often. Drain and discard marinade. Drizzle reserved marinade over meat. Bake, uncovered, at 400° for 30-35 minutes or until a meat thermometer reads 160°-170°. **Yield:** 6 servings.

PARMESAN HAM PASTA

Nancy Ringer, Dwight, Illinois

I always keep the ingredients for this pasta dish on hand, so I can whip it up pronto. People who try it always ask for the recipe.

- 1 package (16 ounces) bow tie pasta
- 2 cups cubed fully cooked ham
- 1 can (4 ounces) mushroom stems and pieces, drained
- 1/2 cup butter *or* margarine
- 1/2 cup all-purpose flour
- 1/2 teaspoon salt
- 2 cups milk
- 1 package (10 ounces) frozen chopped spinach, partially thawed
- 1 cup (4 ounces) shredded Parmesan cheese

Cook pasta according to package directions. Meanwhile, in a large skillet, saute ham and mushrooms in butter. Stir in flour and salt until blended. Gradually add milk. Bring to a boil; cook and stir for 2 minutes or until thickened. Reduce heat. Stir in spinach and cheese. Cook and stir until cheese is melted. Drain pasta; stir into the ham mixture. **Yield:** 6 servings.

STIR-FRIED STEAK AND VEGGIES

(Pictured below)

Inez Glover, Wainwright, Alberta

There's just enough ginger, chili powder and garlic powder in the sauce to spark the taste of this enjoyable steak specialty. For variety, you can substitute chicken or pork for the sirloin. If I'm in a hurry or don't have fresh vegetables on hand, I'll reach for two bags of frozen stir-fry vegetables instead.

- 1 tablespoon cornstarch
- 1 tablespoon brown sugar
- 3/4 teaspoon ground ginger
- 1/2 teaspoon chili powder
- 1/4 teaspoon garlic powder
- 1/4 teaspoon pepper
- 1/2 cup cold water
- 1/4 cup soy sauce
- 1 pound boneless sirloin steak, cut into thin strips
- 2 tablespoons vegetable oil
- 2 cups broccoli florets
- 2 cups cauliflowerets
- 1 large onion, chopped
- 1 cup sliced carrots

Hot cooked rice

In a small bowl, whisk together the first eight ingredients until smooth; set aside. In a skillet or wok, stir-fry steak in oil for 3-5 minutes. Add broccoli, cauliflower, onion, carrots and soy sauce mixture; cover and cook for 8 minutes or until vegetables are crisp-tender, stirring occasionally. Serve over rice. **Yield:** 4 servings.

TURKEY POTPIE

(Pictured below)

Marie Basinger, Connellsville, Pennsylvania

My family raves over this comforting dish, with its flaky homemade crust and saucy meat and veggie filling. Sometimes, I cook a bird specifically with this potpie in mind—when we just can't wait for leftovers to make it!

1 medium onion, chopped
1/3 cup butter *or* margarine
1/2 cup all-purpose flour
1 teaspoon salt
1/4 teaspoon pepper
1-3/4 cups chicken *or* turkey broth
2/3 cup milk
2 cups cubed cooked turkey
1 cup (4 ounces) shredded cheddar cheese
1 package (10 ounces) frozen peas and carrots, thawed

PASTRY:

2 cups all-purpose flour
2 teaspoons celery seed
1 teaspoon salt
2/3 cup plus 2 tablespoons shortening
4 to 5 tablespoons cold water

Milk, optional

In a saucepan, saute onion in butter. Stir in the flour, salt and pepper until blended. Gradually add broth and milk. Bring to a boil; cook and stir for 2 minutes or until thickened. Add the turkey, cheese and vegetables; cook until the cheese is melted. Set aside and keep warm.

For the crust, combine flour, celery seed and salt in a bowl. Cut in shortening until mixture resembles coarse crumbs. Add enough water until dough forms a ball. Divide dough in half. Line a 9-in. pie plate with bottom pastry; trim even with edge of plate. Pour hot turkey filling into crust.

Roll out remaining pastry to fit top of pie; place over the filling. Trim, seal and flute edges. Cut slits in pastry. Brush top with milk if desired. Bake at 375° for 40-45 minutes or until crust is golden brown. **Yield:** 6 servings.

APRICOT-STUFFED TURKEY BREAST

Bonnie De Meyer, New Carlisle, Indiana

For a new take on turkey, give this recipe a try. It cooks on the grill, and it's stuffed with a sensational apricot mixture.

✓ Uses less fat, sugar or salt. Includes Nutritional Analysis and Diabetic Exchanges.

1 bone-in turkey breast half (2-1/2 pounds), skin removed
1-1/2 cups soft bread crumbs
1/2 cup diced dried apricots
1/4 cup chopped pecans, toasted
3 tablespoons water *or* unsweetened apple juice, *divided*
1 tablespoon vegetable oil
1/4 teaspoon dried rosemary, crushed
1/4 teaspoon garlic salt
1 tablespoon Dijon mustard

Remove bone from turkey. Cut a horizontal slit into thickest part of turkey to form a 5-in. x 4-in. pocket. In a bowl, combine the bread crumbs, apricots, pecans, 2 tablespoons water or juice, oil, rosemary and garlic salt; toss gently. Stuff into pocket of turkey. Secure opening with metal or soaked bamboo skewers.

Grill, covered, over indirect heat for 30 minutes. Combine mustard and remaining water; brush over turkey. Grill 10 minutes longer or until golden brown and a meat thermometer inserted into stuffing reads 160°. Let stand 10 minutes before slicing. **Yield:** 8 servings.

Nutritional Analysis: One serving (calculated with water instead of apple juice) equals 268 calories, 313 mg sodium, 81 mg cholesterol, 20 gm carbohydrate, 33 gm protein, 6 gm fat, 2 gm fiber. **Diabetic Exchanges:** 4 very lean meat, 1 starch, 1/2 fruit, 1/2 fat.

MOTHER'S HAM CASSEROLE

Linda Childers, Murfreesboro, Tennessee

One of my mother's favorite dishes, this recipe always brings back fond memories of her when I prepare it. It's a terrific use of leftover ham from a holiday dinner.

2 cups cubed peeled potatoes
1 large carrot, sliced
2 celery ribs, chopped
3 cups water
2 cups cubed fully cooked ham
2 tablespoons chopped green pepper
2 teaspoons finely chopped onion
7 tablespoons butter *or* margarine, *divided*
3 tablespoons all-purpose flour
1-1/2 cups milk
3/4 teaspoon salt
1/8 teaspoon pepper
1 cup (4 ounces) shredded cheddar cheese
1/2 cup soft bread crumbs

In a saucepan, cook potatoes, carrot and celery in water until tender; drain. In a skillet, saute ham, green pepper and onion in 3 tablespoons butter until tender. Add to potato mixture. Transfer to a greased 1-1/2-qt. baking dish.

In a saucepan, melt remaining butter; stir in flour until smooth. Gradually add milk, salt and pepper. Bring to a boil; cook and stir for 2 minutes or until thickened. Stir in the cheese until melted; pour over the ham mixture. Sprinkle with bread crumbs. Bake, uncovered, at 375° for 25-30 minutes or until heated through. **Yield:** 4-6 servings.

ing dish. Drain skillet, reserving 2 tablespoons drippings. In the drippings, saute onion, green pepper and celery until tender. In a bowl, combine the ketchup, water, brown sugar, Worcestershire sauce, salt and pepper; add to vegetables. Bring to a boil. Pour over the chicken. Cover and bake at 350° for 30 minutes. Sprinkle with corn. Bake 18-20 minutes longer or until chicken juices run clear and corn is tender. **Yield:** 4-6 servings.

BARBECUE CHICKEN CASSEROLE

Gail Rector, Belle, Missouri

I am a minister's wife and have cooked for countless fellowships, funeral dinners and other church activities. This is a recipe I've used often for those occasions.

1 cup all-purpose flour
1 broiler/fryer chicken (3 to 4 pounds), cut up
2 tablespoons vegetable oil
1 cup chopped onion
1 cup chopped green pepper
1 cup thinly sliced celery
1 cup ketchup
1/2 cup water
3 tablespoons brown sugar
3 tablespoons Worcestershire sauce
1/2 teaspoon salt
1/4 teaspoon pepper
1 package (16 ounces) frozen corn, thawed

Place flour in a large resealable plastic bag. Add chicken, a few pieces at a time, and shake to coat. In a large skillet, brown the chicken in oil; transfer to an ungreased 13-in. x 9-in. x 2-in. bak-

SHRIMP STIR-FRY

(Pictured above)

Alberta Crowe, Staten Island, New York

When I need to fix a quick meal, I frequently turn to this well-loved dish that takes only a few minutes to cook. I've also used chicken instead of shrimp with delicious results.

1-1/2 cups broccoli florets
1 small sweet red pepper, julienned
1 small green pepper, julienned
1 to 2 tablespoons vegetable oil
1 pound uncooked shrimp, peeled and deveined
1 tablespoon cornstarch
2 teaspoons brown sugar
1 teaspoon ground ginger
1 cup orange juice
1/4 cup soy sauce
Hot cooked rice

In a skillet, stir-fry broccoli and peppers in oil until tender. Add shrimp; stir-fry for 3-5 minutes or until shrimp turn pink. Combine the cornstarch, brown sugar, ginger, orange juice and soy sauce until smooth; add to skillet. Bring to a boil; cook and stir for 2 minutes or until thickened. Serve over rice. **Yield:** 3-4 servings.

CURRIED HAM AND FRUIT
(Pictured below)

Brenda DenHollander
Chilliwack, British Columbia

This dish tastes as good as it looks! The curry and fruit go well with the ham.

- 4 slices fully cooked ham (1/2 inch thick and 4 to 6 ounces *each*)
- 1 can (5-1/2 ounces) peach-orange nectar
- 1 can (20 ounces) pineapple tidbits, drained
- 1 can (15-1/4 ounces) sliced peaches, drained and halved
- 1 can (15-1/4 ounces) sliced pears, drained and halved
- 10 maraschino cherries
- 1/4 cup butter *or* margarine, melted
- 3/4 cup packed brown sugar
- 4 teaspoons curry powder

Place ham in a single layer in an ungreased 13-in. x 9-in. x 2-in. baking dish. Top with nectar. Bake, uncovered, at 350° for 20 minutes, basting once. Combine fruits; spoon over ham. In a small bowl, combine butter, brown sugar and curry powder. Drop by spoonfuls over fruit. Bake 15-20 minutes longer, basting once. **Yield:** 4 servings.

BAVARIAN BRATWURST SUPPER

Jill Cook, Perry, Iowa

My family enjoys the flavors of hot German potato salad and bratwurst, especially during the cooler months. This original recipe is truly a one-dish meal, combining meat, potatoes, apple and sauerkraut.

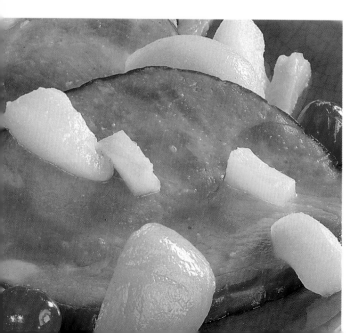

- 4 bacon strips, diced
- 4 fresh bratwurst, cut into 2-inch pieces
- 1 medium tart apple, chopped
- 1 medium onion, chopped
- 1/2 cup cider vinegar
- 3 tablespoons brown sugar
- 1 tablespoon spicy brown mustard
- 1/2 teaspoon salt
- 1/8 teaspoon pepper
- 4 cups frozen cubed hash brown potatoes, thawed
- 1 can (14 ounces) Bavarian-style sauerkraut, drained

In a skillet over medium heat, cook bacon until crisp. Remove with a slotted spoon to paper towels. In the drippings, cook and stir bratwurst for 10-12 minutes. Remove with a slotted spoon. Drain, reserving 2 tablespoons of drippings. Saute apple and onion in drippings until lightly browned. Add vinegar, brown sugar, mustard, salt, pepper and bratwurst.

Cover and cook for 12 minutes or until bratwurst are no longer pink and a meat thermometer reads 160°, stirring frequently. Add potatoes and sauerkraut; cook and stir 12 minutes longer or until heated through. Sprinkle with bacon. **Yield:** 4 servings.

HAM AND SWISS STRATA

Dorothy Smith, El Dorado, Arkansas

Layers of breakfast favorites will have folks digging into this all-in-one dish. The hearty combination of eggs, ham and cheese is just right to build a holiday brunch around—or to serve all by itself.

- 8 slices bread, crusts removed and cubed
- 1/4 cup minced fresh parsley
- 1 green onion, sliced
- 1 cup cubed fully cooked ham
- 1 cup (4 ounces) shredded Swiss cheese
- 3 eggs
- 2 cups milk
- 2 teaspoons Dijon mustard
- 1/8 teaspoon salt
- 1/8 teaspoon pepper
- 1/8 teaspoon hot pepper sauce

Place half of the bread cubes in a greased 11-in. x 7-in. x 2-in. baking dish. Sprinkle with half of the parsley, onion, ham and cheese. Repeat layers. In a bowl, beat eggs, milk, mustard, salt, pepper and hot pepper sauce. Pour over cheese. Bake, uncovered, at 350° for 35-40 minutes or until a knife inserted near the center comes out clean. **Yield:** 6 servings.

Helpful Ham Hints

• I find cooking my smoked ham in fruit juice instead of water gives it wonderful flavor. I use apple, orange or pineapple juice. —*Wendy Scott Herschel, Saskatchewan*

• Add cooked crumbled bacon to scalloped potatoes with ham to give them more flavor. Sprinkling them with cheese during the last half hour of baking adds color and taste, too. —*M. Louise Scanlan Ebensburg, Pennsylvania*

• For variety, use apple rings or slices to decorate a whole glazed ham. —*Mary Wilson, Booker, Texas*

• Before baking a ham with areas of fat on the outside, slice them off and freeze them. For extra flavor, drop a slice in with your green beans when you cook them. —*Phyllis Clinehens Maplewood, Ohio*

• When a ham casserole recipe calls for cheddar cheese, try using Monterey Jack or process cheese with peppers as a spicy alternative. —*Stacy Good Bakersfield, California*

• For a lovely glaze, drizzle melted jams or jellies over your baked ham 5 to 10 minutes before taking it out of the oven. —*Elizabeth Fagans North Springfield, Vermont*

• Sometimes it can be a cost savings to purchase a very thick slice of fully cooked ham from the deli rather than to buy vacuum-packed ham slices. —*Sarah Carpenter Trumansburg, New York*

• Don't have a kettle large enough to hold a ham bone for pea soup? Try putting the bone, soaked split peas and remaining soup ingredients in a roasting pan; cover and bake at 350° for 1-1/2 to 2 hours. —*Mary Ann Wiersma Whitinsville, Massachusetts*

• Ham rind is easier to remove if you make a lengthwise slit in the rind and cook the ham slit side down in the pan. As it bakes, the rind pulls away from the meat and can be removed easily right after baking. —*Audrey Waldo Mountain, Wisconsin*

• If you're making a soup with a ham bone and the broth is too salty, add a small peeled potato to soak up the salt. Discard the potato. —*Connie Stone Manchester, Tennessee*

• For a different basting sauce, spoon the syrup from pickled peaches over your baked ham. For another tasty glaze, rub the ham with apricot jam mixed with a little ground mustard. —*Mrs. Travis Baker, Litchfield, Illinois*

• I purchase ham slices that are 1/2 inch thick, freeze them on a cookie sheet and place them in plastic bags. When I need ham for soups, salads or casseroles, I take out the amount needed and return the rest to the freezer for later use. —*Barb Schoenefeld Herrick, South Dakota*

• For heartier fare, add strips or cubes of cooked ham to potato, chicken, macaroni or vegetable salads. —*Jill Kinder, Richlands, Virginia*

POACHED SALMON

(Pictured below)

Rose Mower, Chugiak, Alaska

My husband, our kids and grandkids enjoy fishing on the Kenai River in summer, so we never have a shortage of salmon. I like this tasty recipe because it's so easy to prepare.

- 1/4 cup finely chopped onion
- 1 garlic clove, minced
- 2 tablespoons butter *or* margarine
- 1-1/2 cups water
- 3/4 cup chicken broth
- 1/2 teaspoon dill weed
- 1/2 teaspoon lemon-pepper seasoning
- 1/2 teaspoon dried parsley flakes
- 1/2 teaspoon dried tarragon
- 4 salmon steaks (1 inch thick)

SAUCE:
- 1/2 cup finely chopped zucchini
- 1/4 cup mayonnaise
- 1/4 cup plain yogurt
- 2 tablespoons chopped green onions

In a large skillet, saute onion and garlic in butter. Add the water, broth and seasonings. Add salmon; bring to a boil. Reduce heat; cover and simmer for 20-25 minutes or until fish flakes easily with a fork. Meanwhile, in a small bowl, combine sauce ingredients. Serve with the salmon. **Yield: 4** servings.

TURKEY CROQUETTES WITH CRANBERRY SALSA

Jacque Capurro, Anchorage, Alaska

This recipe is a great way to use up leftover turkey after the holidays.

- 1/3 cup chopped onion
- 2 tablespoons butter *or* margarine
- 1/4 cup all-purpose flour
- 1/4 cup milk
- 1/4 cup chicken broth
- 2 cups finely chopped cooked turkey
- 1/2 cup mashed sweet potato
- 1/2 teaspoon salt
- 1/4 teaspoon pepper
- 1/8 teaspoon cayenne pepper

SALSA:
- 3/4 cup chopped tart green apple
- 1 tablespoon lemon juice
- 1/2 cup chopped cranberries
- 2 green onions, chopped
- 2 jalapeno peppers, seeded and chopped
- 3 tablespoons golden raisins, chopped
- 1 tablespoon honey

CROQUETTES:
- 2 eggs
- 1 tablespoon water
- 1/2 cup all-purpose flour
- 1/2 cup dry bread crumbs

Oil for deep-fat frying

In a saucepan, saute onion in butter until tender. Stir in flour until blended. Gradually add milk and broth. Bring to a boil; cook and stir for 2 minutes or until thickened. Remove from the heat; stir in turkey, sweet potato, salt, pepper and cayenne. Cover and refrigerate for 2 hours or until firm. Meanwhile, toss apple with lemon juice in a bowl. Stir in remaining salsa ingredients. Cover and chill for at least 1 hour.

For croquettes, beat eggs and water in a shallow bowl. Place flour and bread crumbs in separate shallow bowls. Shape turkey mixture into 1-1/2-in. balls. Roll in flour; shake off excess. Roll in egg mixture, then in crumbs. In an electric skillet or deep-fat fryer, heat 1-1/2 in. of oil to 375°. Fry croquettes, a few at a time, for 2 minutes or until golden brown. Drain on paper towels. Serve with cranberry salsa. **Yield: 16 croquettes (2 cups salsa).**

HASH BROWN HAM QUICHE

Sara Bowen, Upland, California

My family loves this cheesy ham quiche on Sunday morning after church. It's delicious for brunch and not hard to prepare. Shredded hash brown potatoes make a fuss-free crust.

> 3 cups frozen shredded hash brown potatoes, thawed
> 1/4 cup butter *or* margarine, melted, *divided*
> 1 cup (4 ounces) shredded pepper-Jack cheese
> 1 cup (4 ounces) shredded Swiss cheese
> 1 cup diced fully cooked ham
> 2 eggs
> 1/2 cup whipping cream
> 1/4 teaspoon seasoned salt

Press hash browns between paper towels to remove excess moisture. Grease a 9-in. pie plate with 2 teaspoons butter. Press hash browns onto the bottom and up the sides of plate. Drizzle with remaining butter. Bake, uncovered, at 425° for 20-25 minutes or until edges are browned.

Combine cheeses and ham; spoon into the crust. In a bowl, beat the eggs, cream and seasoned salt; pour over ham. Reduce heat to 350°. Bake, uncovered, for 20-25 minutes or until a knife inserted near the center comes out clean. Let stand 10 minutes before cutting. **Yield:** 6 servings.

in. baking dish. Combine topping ingredients; sprinkle over turkey mixture. Bake, uncovered, at 350° for 35-40 minutes or until bubbly and golden brown. **Yield:** 8-10 servings.

*Editor's Note: Reduced-fat or fat-free mayonnaise may not be substituted for regular mayonnaise.

ALMOND TURKEY CASSEROLE

Jill Black, Troy, Ontario

A special cousin shared the recipe for this comforting casserole. The almonds and water chestnuts give it a fun crunch.

> 2 cans (10-3/4 ounces *each*) condensed cream of mushroom soup, undiluted
> 1/2 cup mayonnaise*
> 1/2 cup sour cream
> 2 tablespoons chopped onion
> 2 tablespoons lemon juice
> 1 teaspoon salt
> 1/2 teaspoon white pepper
> 5 cups cubed cooked turkey
> 3 cups cooked rice
> 4 celery ribs, chopped
> 1 can (8 ounces) sliced water chestnuts, drained
> 1 cup sliced almonds

TOPPING:
> 1-1/2 cups crushed butter-flavored crackers (about 38 crackers)
> 1/3 cup butter *or* margarine, melted
> 1/4 cup sliced almonds

In a large bowl, combine the soup, mayonnaise, sour cream, onion, lemon juice, salt and pepper. Stir in the turkey, rice, celery, water chestnuts and almonds. Transfer to a greased 13-in. x 9-in. x 2-

HAM 'N' EGG PIZZA
(Pictured above)

Margaret Smith, Superior, Wisconsin

I like to fix this fun dish when we invite our children and grandchildren for brunch. There's never a slice left! The recipe is quick and easy to prepare, using refrigerated crescent rolls to form the crust. The ham makes it hearty.

> 1 tube (8 ounces) refrigerated crescent rolls
> 3 eggs
> 2 tablespoons milk
> 1/8 teaspoon pepper
> 2 cups finely chopped fully cooked ham
> 1 cup frozen shredded hash brown potatoes
> 1 cup (4 ounces) shredded cheddar cheese
> 1/2 cup shredded Parmesan cheese

Unroll crescent roll dough and place on an ungreased 12-in. pizza pan. Press onto the bottom and 1/4 in. up the sides, sealing seams and perforations. Bake at 375° for 5 minutes. Meanwhile, in a bowl, beat eggs, milk and pepper. Sprinkle ham, hash browns and cheddar cheese over crust. Carefully pour egg mixture over cheese. Sprinkle with Parmesan. Bake for 25-30 minutes or until eggs are completely set. **Yield:** 6 servings.

HERB-ROASTED TURKEY

Becky Goldsmith
Eden Prairie, Minnesota

Our guests always comment on how moist and flavorful this elegant entree is. Rubbed with garden-fresh herbs, this turkey has such a wonderful aroma when it's roasting that it lures everyone into the kitchen!

        1 turkey (14 pounds)
        1 tablespoon salt
        1 teaspoon pepper
       18 sprigs fresh thyme, *divided*
        4 medium onions, sliced
        4 celery ribs, sliced
        2 medium carrots, sliced
        3 bay leaves
        1 tablespoon peppercorns
      1/2 cup butter *or* margarine, melted
        1 teaspoon minced fresh sage *or* 1/2
           teaspoon rubbed sage
        1 teaspoon minced fresh thyme *or* 1/2
           teaspoon dried thyme
        1 teaspoon minced chives

Rub surface of turkey and sprinkle cavity with salt and pepper. Place 12 sprigs of thyme in cavity. In a large heavy roasting pan, place onions, celery, carrots, bay leaves, peppercorns and remaining thyme sprigs. Place the turkey, breast side up, over vegetables. Drizzle butter over turkey and sprinkle with minced herbs. Cover loosely with foil.

Bake at 325° for 2-1/2 hours. Remove foil; bake 1-1/2 to 2 hours longer or until a meat thermometer reads 180°, basting every 20 minutes. Cover and let stand for 20 minutes before carving. Discard bay leaves and peppercorns; thicken pan drippings for gravy if desired. **Yield:** 12-14 servings.

CAJUN PEPPER STEAK

(Pictured above)

Martha Sue Kinnaird, Ruston, Louisiana

Cajun recipes have become popular across the country, but they've always been loved here. See if this recipe doesn't become a family favorite at your house.

    1-1/2 pounds boneless round steak, cut into
           cubes
        2 tablespoons vegetable oil
        1 can (14-1/2 ounces) beef broth
        1 can (14-1/2 ounces) diced tomatoes,
           undrained
        1 cup chopped green pepper
      1/2 cup chopped onion
        3 garlic cloves, minced
        2 teaspoons Worcestershire sauce
        1 bay leaf
      1/2 teaspoon dried basil
      1/4 to 1/2 teaspoon Cajun seasoning
      1/8 teaspoon salt
      1/8 teaspoon pepper
        2 tablespoons cornstarch
        2 tablespoons cold water
Hot cooked rice *or* noodles

In a large skillet, cook beef in oil over medium heat until browned; drain. Stir in the broth, tomatoes, green pepper, onion, garlic, Worcestershire sauce and seasonings. Bring to a boil and reduce heat. Cover and simmer for 1 hour or until meat is tender. Discard bay leaf. Combine cornstarch and water until smooth and stir into meat mixture. Bring to a boil; cook and stir for 2 minutes or until thickened. Serve over rice or noodles. **Yield:** 4-6 servings.

HAM A LA KING

Jean Grubb, Austin, Texas

My mom and I used to have our own catering business, and this recipe was a popular choice from our menu. It looks elegant on the plate and always gets rave reviews.

        1 package (10 ounces) frozen puff pastry
           shells
      1/4 cup butter *or* margarine
      1/4 cup all-purpose flour
        1 teaspoon chicken bouillon granules
      1/2 cup hot water
    1-1/2 cups milk
        3 slices process American cheese

1 teaspoon Worcestershire sauce
1 teaspoon prepared mustard
2 cups cubed fully cooked ham
1/2 cup frozen peas, thawed, optional
1 can (2-1/4 ounces) sliced ripe olives, drained
2 tablespoons diced pimientos
2 tablespoons minced fresh parsley

Bake the pastry shells according to package directions. Meanwhile, in a saucepan, melt butter; stir in flour until smooth. Dissolve bouillon in water. Gradually add milk and bouillon to the saucepan. Bring to a boil; cook and stir for 2 minutes or until thickened. Stir in cheese, Worcestershire and mustard until the cheese is melted. Add the ham, peas if desired, olives, pimientos and parsley; heat through. Serve in pastry shells. **Yield:** 6 servings.

FREEZING HAM

Leftover cooked ham may be stored in the freezer for 2 months. If frozen for longer, the flavor and texture of the meat loses quality. Leftover ham can also be stored in the refrigerator for 4 to 5 days.

▲▼▲▼▲▼▲▼▲▼▲
TURKEY SCHNITZEL

Susan Nicholls, Palm Desert, California

If you like traditional schnitzel, you're going to love this deliciously different version using turkey breast slices. The bread crumb coating is tasty.

1/4 cup seasoned bread crumbs
1/4 cup grated Parmesan cheese
1/2 teaspoon garlic powder
1/4 teaspoon salt
1/4 teaspoon pepper
1 egg
1 tablespoon water
4 uncooked turkey breast slices (1/4 inch thick)
1/4 cup lemon juice
1/4 cup vegetable oil

In a shallow bowl, combine the bread crumbs, Parmesan, garlic powder, salt and pepper. In another shallow bowl, beat egg and water. Dip turkey slices in lemon juice and the egg mixture, then coat with bread crumbs. In a skillet, cook turkey in oil until browned on both sides and juices run clear. **Yield:** 4 servings.

▲▼▲▼▲▼▲▼▲▼▲
BEEF 'N' GREEN BEAN PIE
(Pictured below)

Jane Hotaling, Longmeadow, Massachusetts

This recipe is a family favorite and makes a wonderful Sunday night supper served with a salad.

1 pound ground beef
1/2 cup chopped onion
1/4 cup chopped green pepper, optional
1 can (8 ounces) tomato sauce
1 can (14-1/2 ounces) cut green beans, drained
1/2 teaspoon salt
1/4 teaspoon garlic salt
1 tube (8 ounces) refrigerated crescent rolls
1 egg
2 cups (8 ounces) shredded cheddar cheese, *divided*
Paprika

In a skillet over medium heat, cook beef, onion and green pepper if desired until meat is no longer pink; drain. Stir in the tomato sauce, beans, salt and garlic salt. Simmer for 8 minutes or until heated through. Meanwhile, separate crescent dough into eight triangles; place in an ungreased 9-in. pie plate with points toward the center. Press onto the bottom and up the sides to form a crust; seal perforations.

In a bowl, beat egg and 1 cup cheese; spread over crust. Stir 1/2 cup cheese into meat mixture; spoon into crust. Sprinkle with paprika and remaining cheese. Bake, uncovered, at 375° for 20-25 minutes or until golden brown. Let stand for 5 minutes before cutting. **Yield:** 4-6 servings.

UPSIDE-DOWN PIZZA

(Pictured below)

Debra Derstine, Mapleton, Pennsylvania

If you like pizza, I think you'll enjoy this recipe. I like making this better than regular pizza because I don't have to make a crust.

          1 pound bulk Italian sausage
          1 medium onion, chopped
      1/4 cup chopped green pepper
          2 tablespoons plus 1 cup all-purpose
               flour, *divided*
      1/2 teaspoon dried basil
      1/2 teaspoon fennel seed, crushed
          1 can (15 ounces) tomato sauce
          2 cups (8 ounces) shredded mozzarella
               cheese
          2 eggs
          1 cup milk
          1 tablespoon vegetable oil
      1/2 teaspoon salt
          2 tablespoons grated Parmesan
               cheese, optional

In a saucepan, cook sausage, onion and green pepper over medium heat until meat is no longer pink; drain. Stir in 2 tablespoons flour, basil and fennel; mix well. Add tomato sauce. Bring to a boil; cook and stir for 2 minutes. Transfer to an ungreased 13-in. x 9-in. x 2-in. baking dish. Sprinkle with mozzarella cheese.

Place the remaining flour in a mixing bowl. Beat in the eggs, milk, oil and salt until smooth; stir in Parmesan cheese if desired. Pour over casserole. Bake, uncovered, at 425° for 25-30 minutes or until browned. **Yield:** 8 servings.

APRICOT TURKEY AND RICE

Joan Gatling, Rio Rancho, New Mexico

Apricots, cinnamon and nutmeg add a touch of sweetness to this turkey and rice dish. It makes a very light and easy meal.

> ✓ **Uses less fat, sugar or salt. Includes Nutritional Analysis and Diabetic Exchanges.**

1-1/4 pounds uncooked boneless skinless
               turkey breast, cut into 1/2-inch strips
          1 large onion, chopped
          2 tablespoons reduced-fat margarine
1-1/2 cups reduced-sodium chicken broth
1-1/2 cups uncooked instant rice
      1/2 cup chopped dried apricots
      1/2 teaspoon dried thyme
      1/4 teaspoon ground cinnamon
      1/8 teaspoon ground nutmeg

In a skillet, saute turkey and onion in margarine until meat is lightly browned. Add broth; bring to a boil. Stir in the rice, apricots, thyme, cinnamon and nutmeg. Cover and remove from the heat; let stand for 5-7 minutes or until rice is tender. **Yield:** 6 servings.

Nutritional Analysis: One serving equals 269 calories, 117 mg sodium, 69 mg cholesterol, 30 gm carbohydrate, 28 gm protein, 4 gm fat. **Diabetic Exchanges:** 3-1/2 lean meat, 1 starch, 1 fruit.

DELUXE HAM BALLS

Joan Settle, Oceanside, California

Whenever I serve these saucy baked ham balls to guests, they ask me for the recipe. It's one I've had for many years and is a great use for leftover ham. I love to entertain, and know I can count on these ham balls to be a hit.

          2 eggs
      1/2 cup milk
      3/4 cup dry bread crumbs
      1/4 cup finely chopped onion
          1 pound ground fully cooked ham
      1/2 pound ground pork
          1 can (8 ounces) crushed pineapple
      1/2 cup packed brown sugar
      1/3 cup vinegar
      1/3 cup ketchup
          2 tablespoons soy sauce
          1 teaspoon ground ginger
Hot cooked rice

In a bowl, combine the eggs, milk, bread crumbs and onion. Crumble ham and pork over mixture;

mix well. Shape into 1-1/4-in. balls. Place in a greased 13-in. x 9-in. x 2-in. baking dish. In a saucepan, combine the pineapple, brown sugar, vinegar, ketchup, soy sauce and ginger. Cook and stir until sugar is dissolved. Pour over ham balls. Bake, uncovered, at 350° for 40-45 minutes or until a meat thermometer reads 160°. Serve over rice. **Yield:** 6 servings.

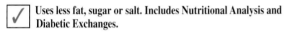

HEARTY SQUASH SKILLET

Vicki Berry, Galveston, Indiana

This skillet supper was a favorite of my family when we were watching our budget, since it calls for a lot of fresh vegetables we grew in our own backyard garden. The recipe feeds a crowd, but it can easily be cut in half, too.

✓ Uses less fat, sugar or salt. Includes Nutritional Analysis and Diabetic Exchanges.

- 2 pounds lean ground beef
- 3 medium onions, chopped
- 2 medium green peppers, chopped
- 2 garlic cloves, minced
- 2 small butternut squash, peeled, seeded and thinly sliced
- 1 small acorn squash, peeled, seeded and cubed
- 3 small potatoes, diced
- 2 cans (8 ounces *each*) tomato sauce
- 1 tablespoon Worcestershire sauce
- 6 large tomatoes, peeled, seeded and diced
- 1 small yellow squash, thinly sliced
- 1 medium zucchini, thinly sliced
- 1/2 teaspoon salt
- 1/4 teaspoon pepper
- 1 cup (4 ounces) shredded reduced-fat Swiss cheese
- 1 cup (4 ounces) shredded part-skim mozzarella cheese

In a large skillet, cook beef, onions, green peppers and garlic until meat is no longer pink; drain. Add butternut and acorn squash, potatoes, tomato sauce and Worcestershire sauce. Bring to a boil. Reduce heat; cover and cook until potatoes and squash are tender. Add the tomatoes, yellow squash, zucchini, salt and pepper; heat through. Sprinkle with cheeses; cover and cook until cheese is melted. **Yield:** 16 servings.

Nutritional Analysis: One serving (1 cup) equals 236 calories, 471 mg sodium, 28 mg cholesterol, 27 gm carbohydrate, 19 gm protein, 7 gm fat, 6 gm fiber. **Diabetic Exchanges:** 2 lean meat, 1 starch, 1 vegetable, 1/2 fat.

 ## GRILLED CHICKEN WITH PEACH SAUCE

(Pictured above)

Beverly Minton, Milan, Michigan

I've been cooking since I was a young girl growing up on a farm in Indiana. This recipe was adapted from a pie filling. I've served it many times to family and friends with great success.

- 1 cup sugar
- 2 tablespoons cornstarch
- 1 cup water
- 2 tablespoons peach gelatin powder
- 1 medium fresh peach, peeled and finely chopped
- 4 boneless skinless chicken breast halves

In a saucepan, combine sugar, cornstarch and water until smooth. Bring to a boil over medium heat; cook and stir for 2 minutes. Remove from heat. Stir in gelatin and peach; mix well. Set aside 1 cup for serving. Grill chicken, uncovered, over medium heat for 3 minutes on each side. Baste with some of the remaining peach sauce. Continue grilling for 6-8 minutes or until meat juices run clear, basting and turning several times. Serve with the reserved peach sauce. **Yield:** 4 servings.

COOKING CHICKEN

For the most tender results, cook boneless chicken to an internal temperature of 170°, bone-in chicken to 180°.

to simmering stew. Cover and simmer 15-20 minutes or until a toothpick inserted in a dumpling comes out clean (do not lift cover while simmering). Serve immediately. **Yield:** 10-12 servings

CHEESE-STUFFED BURGERS

Janet Wood, Windham, New Hampshire

Here's a sandwich that does regular burgers one better—with a surprise pocket of cheddar! Whenever I serve them, folks enjoy finding the melted cheese.

> 1/4 cup ketchup
> 1/4 cup finely chopped onion
> 4 teaspoons prepared mustard
> 2 teaspoons salt
> 1 teaspoon pepper
> 4 pounds ground beef
> 1-1/2 cups (6 ounces) shredded cheddar cheese
> 12 hamburger buns, split

In a bowl, combine the first five ingredients. Add beef and mix well. Shape into 24 thin patties. Sprinkle cheese in the center of 12 patties; top with remaining patties and press edges firmly to seal. Broil or grill until meat is no longer pink. Serve on buns. **Yield:** 12 servings.

SWEET-AND-SOUR PORK

Gloria Kubiak, Loveland, Colorado

This pork dinner has the perfect blend of sweet and sour flavors. Not only is it good—it's good for you!

> ✓ Uses less fat, sugar or salt. Includes Nutritional Analysis and Diabetic Exchanges.

> 1/4 cup cornstarch
> Egg substitute equivalent to 1 egg
> 1-1/2 pounds boneless pork, cut into 1/2-inch cubes
> 3 tablespoons vegetable oil, *divided*
> 1 medium onion, chopped
> 2 medium carrots, sliced
> 1 garlic clove, minced
> 1 medium green pepper, cut into 1-inch pieces
> 2 tablespoons water
> 1 can (8 ounces) unsweetened pineapple chunks
> SAUCE:
> 1 tablespoon cornstarch
> 1/3 cup packed brown sugar
> 1/4 teaspoon ground ginger *or* 1/2 teaspoon minced fresh gingerroot

BEEF STEW WITH HERB DUMPLINGS
(Pictured above)

Anna Broschart, Elkins, West Virginia

Nothing could be more comforting on a chilly day than a bowlful of this nicely seasoned stew.

> 1/2 cup all-purpose flour
> 2 teaspoons salt
> 1/4 teaspoon pepper
> 2 pounds beef stew meat
> 2 tablespoons vegetable oil
> 4 cups water
> 5 medium potatoes, peeled and cubed
> 2 medium onions, chopped
> 1-1/2 cups sliced carrots (1/2-inch pieces)
> 1 cup chopped celery
> 2 tablespoons minced fresh parsley
> 1/2 teaspoon dried thyme
> 1 bay leaf
> Browning sauce, optional
> DUMPLINGS:
> 1-1/2 cups all-purpose flour
> 2 teaspoons baking powder
> 3/4 teaspoon salt
> 1/2 teaspoon dried thyme
> 1/4 teaspoon rubbed sage
> 3 tablespoons shortening
> 3/4 cup milk

In a resealable plastic bag, combine flour, salt and pepper. Add beef, a few pieces at a time, and shake to coat. In a Dutch oven, brown meat in oil. Add water; bring to a boil. Reduce heat; cover and simmer 1-1/2 hours. Add vegetables, parsley, thyme and bay leaf. Cover and simmer until meat and vegetables are tender, about 30 minutes. Discard bay leaf. Add browning sauce if desired.

For dumplings, combine flour, baking powder, salt, thyme and sage. Cut in shortening until the mixture resembles coarse crumbs. Stir in milk until moistened. Drop by heaping tablespoonfuls on-

1 tablespoon reduced-sodium soy sauce
1/4 cup cider *or* white wine vinegar
1/4 cup reduced-sodium chicken broth
Hot cooked rice

In a bowl, combine cornstarch and egg substitute until smooth. Add pork; toss to coat. In a skillet or wok, stir-fry half of the pork in 1 tablespoon oil until no longer pink; remove. Repeat with remaining pork and 1 tablespoon oil; set pork aside and keep warm.

Stir-fry onion, carrots and garlic in the remaining oil for 3 minutes. Add green pepper and water; stir for 2 minutes. Drain pineapple, reserving 1/4 cup juice. Add pineapple and pork to skillet. For sauce, combine the cornstarch, brown sugar, ginger, soy sauce, vinegar, broth and reserved pineapple juice; add to skillet. Bring to a boil; cook and stir for 2 minutes. Serve over rice. **Yield:** 6 servings.

Nutritional Analysis: One serving (calculated without rice) equals 351 calories, 245 mg sodium, 67 mg cholesterol, 28 gm carbohydrate, 26 gm protein, 15 gm fat. **Diabetic Exchanges:** 3 meat, 1 starch, 1 fruit.

Meaty Mexican Meal

PILING ON loads of hearty flavor at mealtime is a snap for Bernice Janowski of Stevens Point, Wisconsin. She simply rolls out her skillet specialty, Chuck Wagon Tortilla Stack!

This busy grandmother of two first cooks up a concoction of ground beef, veggies and spices. "Then I layer the meat mixture with tortillas in a deep skillet and let it simmer a little longer," details Bernice.

"It's easy to cut and spoon out of the pan. What's most satisfying, though, is everyone's reaction. The first time I served it, my husband, daughter, son-in-law and even the grandkids asked for seconds. Now, I know I need to make two skillets' worth!"

CHUCK WAGON TORTILLA STACK

1 pound ground beef
2 to 3 garlic cloves, minced
1 can (16 ounces) baked beans
1 can (14-1/2 ounces) stewed tomatoes, undrained
1 can (11 ounces) whole kernel corn, drained
1 can (4 ounces) chopped green chilies
1/4 cup barbecue sauce
4-1/2 teaspoons chili powder
1-1/2 teaspoons ground cumin
4 flour tortillas (10 inches)
1-1/2 cups shredded pepper Jack, cheddar *or* Monterey Jack cheese
Shredded lettuce, chopped red onion, sour cream *and/or* chopped tomatoes, optional

In a skillet, cook beef and garlic until meat is no longer pink; drain. Add beans, tomatoes, corn, chilies, barbecue sauce, chili powder and cumin. Bring to a boil. Reduce heat; simmer, uncovered, for 10-12 minutes or until liquid is reduced. Coat a large deep skillet with nonstick cooking spray. Place one tortilla in skillet; spread with 1-1/2 cups meat mixture. Sprinkle with 1/3 cup cheese. Repeat layers three times. Cover and cook on low for 15 minutes or until cheese is melted and tortillas are heated through. Cut into wedges. Serve with toppings of your choice. **Yield:** 4-6 servings.

BAKED COD

Ginny Morgan
Marblehead, Massachusetts

Fish is a New England staple. This easy and delicious recipe featuring that fresh catch has become a family favorite over the years.

1/4 cup butter *or* margarine, melted
1/4 cup lemon juice
1/4 cup chopped green onions
2 tablespoons water
1/2 teaspoon dill weed
1/2 teaspoon garlic salt
1 pound cod *or* haddock fillets, cut into serving-size pieces
Lemon-pepper seasoning
Lemon slices and dill sprigs, optional

In an ungreased 11-in. x 7-in. x 2-in. baking dish, combine the butter, lemon juice, onions, water, dill weed and garlic salt. Add fish fillets; turn to coat. Cover and refrigerate for 1 hour. Loosely cover and bake at 350° for 25-30 minutes or until fish flakes easily with a fork. Sprinkle with lemon-pepper. Garnish with lemon slices and dill if desired. **Yield:** 3-4 servings.

TERIYAKI GLAZED CHICKEN
(Pictured above)

Kelly Brenneman, Kapolei, Hawaii

I love to experiment with food. For this recipe, I took advantage of the sweet onions grown on Maui. My whole family just loves this main dish.

4 boneless skinless chicken breast halves, cut into strips
3 tablespoons vegetable oil, *divided*
4 medium carrots, julienned
1 medium sweet onion, julienned
1/2 cup soy sauce
1/4 cup packed brown sugar
Hot cooked rice
Sesame seeds, toasted, optional
Sliced green onions, optional

In a large skillet or wok, stir-fry chicken in 2 tablespoons oil for 6-8 minutes or until juices run clear. Remove chicken and set aside. In the same skillet, stir-fry carrots in remaining oil for 2 minutes. Add onion; stir-fry about 2-4 minutes longer or until vegetables are tender.

Combine soy sauce and brown sugar; add to skillet. Bring to a boil. Return chicken to skillet. Boil for 5 minutes or until sauce is slightly thickened. Serve over rice. Sprinkle with sesame seeds and green onions if desired. **Yield:** 4 servings.

ITALIAN RIBS AND RICE

Ruth Seitz, Columbus Junction, Iowa

With meat, vegetables and rice, here's a dish that can be a whole meal by itself. It'll satisfy the hunger of anyone at your table.

3 pounds country-style pork ribs
1 tablespoon vegetable oil
1 can (14-1/2 ounces) diced tomatoes, undrained
1 cup water
1 cup uncooked long grain rice
1 small green pepper, thinly sliced
1 garlic clove, minced
1 tablespoon sugar
2 teaspoons salt, *divided*
1/2 teaspoon Italian seasoning

In a Dutch oven, brown pork ribs in oil over medium-high heat. Cover and cook over low heat for 1-1/4 hours, turning occasionally. Remove ribs and set aside; drain. In same pan, bring tomatoes and water to a boil. Stir in rice, green pepper, garlic, sugar, 1 teaspoon salt and Italian seasoning. Place the ribs over the rice; sprinkle with remaining salt. Cover and cook on low for 30 minutes or until the rice is tender and meat juices run clear. **Yield:** 6 servings.

HOT TURKEY SALAD PITAS

Rachael Vandendool, Barrys Bay, Ontario

Fresh fruit and cooked turkey tastily combine in these yummy pita bread sandwiches.

- 1 medium navel orange, peeled and quartered
- 1 cup fresh *or* frozen cranberries
- 1/2 cup green grapes
- 1/2 cup sugar
- 1/8 teaspoon ground ginger *or* 3/4 teaspoon minced fresh gingerroot
- 2 cups cubed cooked turkey
- 1 celery rib, chopped
- 1/2 cup mayonnaise
- 1/2 teaspoon salt
- 1/8 teaspoon pepper
- 2 pita breads (6 inches), halved

Place the orange, cranberries, grapes, sugar and ginger in a blender or food processor. Cover and process until finely chopped. Set aside 1/2 cup. Cover and refrigerate remaining relish. In a bowl, combine the turkey, celery, mayonnaise, salt, pepper and reserved relish. Spoon into pita halves. Place on an ungreased baking sheet. Bake, uncovered, at 375° for 8-10 minutes or until heated though. Serve with relish. **Yield:** 2-4 servings.

SPINACH ENCHILADAS

(Pictured at right)

William Parman, Oxnard, California

We moved to Southern California many years ago from Minnesota. We especially like the Mexican food that's served here, like this flavorful dish.

- 1 can (14-1/2 ounces) chicken broth
- 1 can (6 ounces) tomato paste
- 3 to 4 teaspoons chili powder
- 1 package (10 ounces) frozen chopped spinach, thawed and well drained
- 3 green onions, chopped
- 1/3 cup sour cream
- 1/4 cup small-curd cottage cheese, drained
- 1-1/2 cups (6 ounces) shredded Colby/ Monterey Jack cheese, *divided*
- 6 to 8 corn tortillas (7 inches)

For the sauce, whisk the broth, tomato paste and chili powder in a saucepan. Simmer, uncovered, for 5 minutes. Meanwhile, combine spinach, onions, sour cream and cottage cheese in a bowl; stir in 1 cup Colby/Monterey Jack cheese. Spoon 1/2 cup of the sauce into a greased 11-in. x 7-in. x 2-in. baking dish.

Dip tortillas into the remaining sauce; spoon about 1/4 cup spinach mixture down the center of each tortilla. Roll up and place, seam side down, in the baking dish. Top with the remaining sauce and cheese. Bake, uncovered, at 350° for 20 minutes or until bubbly. **Yield:** 6-8 servings.

SPINACH SWISS PIE

Phoebe Martin, Hampstead, Maryland

This egg dish has a wonderful flavor from the nutmeg, which combines well with the Swiss cheese. Every time I've served it, it's been well received.

- 1 package (10 ounces) frozen chopped spinach
- 1 cup (4 ounces) shredded Swiss cheese
- 2 tablespoons chopped onion
- 1-1/2 cups milk
- 3 eggs
- 3/4 cup biscuit/baking mix
- 1 teaspoon salt
- 1/4 teaspoon pepper
- 1/4 teaspoon ground nutmeg

Cook spinach according to package directions; drain well. In a bowl, combine cheese, onion and spinach. Transfer to a greased 9-in. pie plate. In a blender, combine milk, eggs, biscuit mix, salt, pepper and nutmeg; cover and process until smooth. Pour over spinach mixture. Bake at 350° for 45-50 minutes or until a knife inserted near the center comes out clean. **Yield:** 6-8 servings.

SIRLOIN WITH BERNAISE SAUCE

(Pictured below)

Willa Govoro, Nevada, Missouri

When I want a meal to be extra special, I feature this beef roast as the centerpiece. The pale yellow sauce with flecks of green looks lovely draped over the slices. I'm almost 90 years old and have been cooking almost my whole life.

    1/2 teaspoon garlic salt
    1/2 teaspoon pepper
      1 boneless sirloin roast (5 to 6 pounds)
BERNAISE SAUCE:
    1/4 cup cider *or* white wine vinegar
    1/2 cup chopped green onions
      1 tablespoon minced fresh tarragon *or* 1
        teaspoon dried tarragon
    1/4 teaspoon pepper
      4 egg yolks, lightly beaten
      1 tablespoon cold water
    1/4 teaspoon salt
    1/8 teaspoon cayenne pepper
    3/4 cup cold butter (no substitutes)
      1 tablespoon minced fresh parsley

Combine garlic salt and pepper; rub over roast. Place on a rack in a shallow roasting pan. Bake, uncovered, at 350° for 2-1/2 to 3 hours or until meat reaches desired doneness (for rare, a meat thermometer should read 140°; medium, 160°;

well-done, 170°). Let stand for 10-15 minutes before slicing. Meanwhile, in a saucepan, combine the vinegar, onions, tarragon and pepper; bring to a boil. Strain, reserving liquid; discard onions and tarragon.

Place egg yolks in a heavy saucepan. Gradually whisk in water, vinegar mixture, salt and cayenne. Cook until the mixture begins to thicken, stirring constantly. Add butter, 1 tablespoon at a time, until the mixture has thickened and reaches 160°, stirring constantly. Remove from the heat; stir in parsley. Serve warm with sliced beef. **Yield:** 12 servings.

EGG SALAD PITAS

Ricquel Stinson, Mt. Orab, Ohio

I came up with this recipe purely by accident. I was making egg salad and just kept adding different seasonings. When my friend tried it, she raved about it.

    2/3 cup mayonnaise
      2 tablespoons sweet pickle relish
      1 teaspoon prepared mustard
    1/4 teaspoon pepper
    1/4 teaspoon celery salt
    1/4 teaspoon paprika
    1/4 teaspoon dried basil
    1/4 teaspoon salt
      6 hard-cooked eggs, coarsely chopped
    1/2 cup shredded cheddar cheese
      1 small onion, finely chopped
      1 large carrot, grated
      2 bacon strips, cooked and crumbled
      3 pita breads (6 inches), halved
Lettuce leaves and sliced tomatoes, optional

In a bowl, combine the first eight ingredients. Stir in the eggs, cheese, onion, carrot and bacon. Spoon about 1/2 cup into each pita half. Add lettuce and tomatoes if desired. **Yield:** 3-6 servings.

ROASTED PEPPER AND ONION SANDWICHES

James McNaughton, Tallahassee, Florida

Due to diet restrictions, I tried making sandwiches without meat. This sandwich turned out to be one of my favorites.

      8 onion slices (1/4 inch thick)
    1/4 cup olive *or* vegetable oil
    1/4 cup cider *or* red wine vinegar

4 teaspoons chopped fresh oregano *or* 1
   teaspoon dried oregano
2 garlic cloves, minced
4 jars (7 ounces *each*) roasted red
   peppers, drained
1 loaf (1 pound) French bread
1 cup (4 ounces) shredded mozzarella
   cheese

Place onion slices in a 13-in. x 9-in. x 2-in. baking pan. Combine the oil, vinegar, oregano and
garlic; brush half over the onions. Set remaining
dressing aside. Bake onions, uncovered, at 375° for
10 minutes or until tender. Add red peppers;
bake 10 minutes longer or until heated through.

   Meanwhile, slice bread in half lengthwise, then
cut into fourths. Carefully hollow out bottom of
loaf, leaving 1/2-in. shells (discard removed bread
or save for another use). Place bread, cut side up,
on a baking sheet. Broil 4 in. from the heat for 1
minute or until toasted. Layer onions, red peppers
and mozzarella cheese on bottom halves of bread.
Drizzle with remaining dressing. Broil 4 in. from
the heat for 4 minutes or until cheese is melted.
Top with remaining bread. **Yield:** 4 servings.

■■■■■■■■■■■■■

TURKEY STIR-FRY

(Pictured above)

Sally Moulton, Greene, Maine

*My family loves this fast-to-fix stir-fry featuring turkey
instead of the usual chicken. It's very colorful and*

*has a nice crunch from the snowpeas and chunks of
sweet red pepper.*

2 tablespoons sugar
1 tablespoon cornstarch
3 tablespoons water
3 tablespoons soy sauce
1 cup fresh *or* frozen snow peas
1 medium sweet red pepper, cut into
   chunks
10 large fresh mushrooms, quartered
2 tablespoons vegetable oil
2 cups cubed cooked turkey
Hot cooked rice

In a bowl, combine the sugar and cornstarch. Stir
in water and soy sauce until smooth; set aside. In
a skillet, saute the peas, red pepper and mushrooms in oil until tender. Add the turkey and soy
sauce mixture. Bring to a boil; cook and stir for 2
minutes or until thickened. Serve over rice. **Yield:**
6 servings.

STIR-FRYING SECRETS

Choose stir-fry vegetables that are harmo-
nious both in color, texture and flavor. The
cooking time will depend on how the veggies
are cut—matchstick pieces will take less time
to cook than chunks of food. Always start with
the vegetable that will take the longest to cook.

Soups & Salads

AVOCADO MALIBU SALAD

(Pictured at left)

Brenda Brinkley, Watsonville, California

One of the first things I learned when I moved to California from Oregon was to make light yet filling salads like this tasty blend. They're practical, easy and delicious.

- 1/4 cup sour cream
- 1/4 teaspoon curry powder
- 1/8 teaspoon salt
- 1 cup diced cooked chicken
- 1 can (8 ounces) pineapple chunks, drained
- 1/4 cup chopped green pepper
- 1/4 cup frozen or canned crabmeat, drained, flaked and cartilage removed
- 1 tablespoon diced pimientos
- 2 large avocados, peeled and sliced
- 2 tablespoons lemon juice

Lettuce leaves
Red grapes, optional

In a large bowl, combine sour cream, curry powder and salt. Add the chicken, pineapple, green pepper, crab and pimientos. Cover and refrigerate for 1-2 hours. Just before serving, toss avocados with lemon juice. Place avocados and crab mixture on lettuce. Garnish with grapes if desired. **Yield:** 4 servings.

ALMOND MANDARIN SALAD

(Pictured at left)

Jacquelyn Smith, Soperton, Georgia

After my daughters-in-law and I enjoyed a delightful salad at a restaurant one day, I decided to come up with my own similar version. It has quickly become a family favorite.

- 1/2 cup sliced almonds
- 1 tablespoon sugar

DRESSING:
- 1/4 cup vegetable oil
- 2 tablespoons orange juice
- 1 tablespoon lemon juice
- 1 tablespoon cider or red wine vinegar
- 1 teaspoon sugar
- 1/4 teaspoon salt
- 1/4 teaspoon grated orange peel

SALAD:
- 8 cups torn mixed salad greens
- 1 can (11 ounces) mandarin oranges, drained
- 2 celery ribs, chopped
- 1/4 cup chopped green onions

In a small skillet, heat the almonds and sugar over low heat. Cook and stir until almonds are coated with sugar glaze; remove and cool. In a jar with a tight-fitting lid, combine the dressing ingredients; shake well. In a large bowl, combine the mixed salad greens, oranges, celery and onions. Add dressing and almonds; toss to coat. **Yield:** 10-12 servings.

PICNIC RICE SALAD

Carol Galow, Bay City, Texas

My husband has grown rice, soybeans, cotton and maize on our farm, located on the Gulf Coast of Texas. I've tried to fix rice in many different ways to promote the rice industry. This rice salad is one of our favorite dishes.

- 3 cups cooked rice, cooled
- 2 hard-cooked eggs, chopped
- 1/2 cup chopped celery
- 1/3 cup chopped green pepper
- 1/4 cup chopped onion
- 1 jar (2 ounces) diced pimientos, drained
- 1/4 cup dill pickle relish
- 1/3 cup mayonnaise
- 1/3 cup sweet pickle relish
- 1/4 cup French salad dressing
- 1 teaspoon salt
- 1/4 teaspoon pepper

Leaf lettuce

In a large bowl, combine the first seven ingredients. In a small bowl, combine the mayonnaise, sweet pickle relish, salad dressing, salt and pepper. Fold into the rice mixture. Serve in a lettuce-lined bowl. Refrigerate leftovers. **Yield:** 4-6 servings.

HOPPIN' GOOD SALAD
(Pictured above)

Gail Kuntz, Dillon, Montana

I have to admit, anything containing cream cheese is automatically a winner with me. With that ingredient plus tangy oranges, gelatin and fluffy marshmallows, this salad is always a hit with others, too. Especially when I serve it as part of my Easter supper.

  1 package (8 ounces) cream cheese, softened
  1 package (3 ounces) orange gelatin
1-1/2 cups boiling water
  2 cans (15 ounces *each*) mandarin oranges, drained
  1 cup whipping cream, whipped
1-1/2 cups miniature pastel marshmallows, *divided*
Maraschino cherry, optional

In a bowl, beat cream cheese and gelatin powder. Stir in water until gelatin is dissolved. Refrigerate for 1 hour or until thickened, stirring frequently. Set aside 10-12 oranges for garnish. Fold whipped cream, 3/4 cup marshmallows and remaining oranges into gelatin mixture. Transfer to a 2-1/2-qt. serving bowl. Sprinkle with the remaining marshmallows. Chill until firm. Garnish with reserved oranges and a maraschino cherry if desired. **Yield:** 8-10 servings.

CITRUS PINEAPPLE COLESLAW

Carol Ross, Anchorage, Alaska

A blue-ribbon recipe, this slaw was a winner in our state fair competition. Alaska is famous for its giant cabbages, but any garden-variety head will taste great dressed in pineapple and marshmallow bits.

1/3 cup sugar
1/4 cup cornstarch
1/4 teaspoon salt
  1 cup unsweetened pineapple juice
1/4 cup orange juice
  3 tablespoons lemon juice
  2 eggs, lightly beaten
  2 packages (3 ounces *each*) cream cheese, cubed
  1 medium head cabbage, shredded
  2 large carrots, shredded
  1 can (8 ounces) crushed pineapple, drained
  1 cup miniature marshmallows
Carrot curls, optional

In a saucepan, combine the first six ingredients until smooth. Bring to a boil over medium heat; cook and stir for 2 minutes or until thickened. Stir a small amount into the eggs. Return all to saucepan, stirring constantly. Cook and stir until mixture reaches 160°. Cool for 5 minutes. Stir in cream cheese until melted. Refrigerate.

In a large salad bowl, combine the cabbage, carrots, pineapple and marshmallows. Add dressing; toss to coat. Garnish with carrot curls if desired. **Yield:** 8-12 servings.

CHILI NON CARNE

Janis Winfrey, Beulah, North Dakota

You won't miss the meat in this zesty chili, which gets its fantastic flavor from veggies, beans and a nice blend of seasonings.

✓ **Uses less fat, sugar or salt. Includes Nutritional Analysis and Diabetic Exchanges.**

  1 large onion, chopped
  2 garlic cloves, minced
  3 tablespoons olive *or* vegetable oil
  4 cups diced zucchini
  1 cup coarsely chopped carrots
  2 tablespoons chili powder
1/4 teaspoon dried oregano
1/4 teaspoon dried basil
1/4 teaspoon ground cumin
  2 cans (one 28 ounces, one 14-1/2 ounces) stewed tomatoes
  3 cans (16 ounces *each*) kidney beans, rinsed and drained

In a large saucepan, saute onion and garlic in oil. Add the zucchini, carrots, chili powder, oregano, basil and cumin; mix well. Add tomatoes and beans; bring to a boil. Reduce heat; cover and simmer for 30-45 minutes or until tender. **Yield:** 10 servings.

Nutritional Analysis: One serving equals 266 calories, 269 mg sodium, 0 cholesterol, 44 gm carbohydrate, 12 gm protein, 5 gm fat, 15 gm fiber. **Diabetic Exchanges:** 2-1/2 vegetable, 2 starch, 1 fat.

APPLE DELIGHT SALAD

Joyce Dancey, Clearwater, Florida

This refreshing fruit salad gets a triple crunch from apples, celery and walnuts. The simple yogurt dressing really enhances the flavor.

✓ Uses less fat, sugar or salt. Includes Nutritional Analysis and Diabetic Exchanges.

3-1/2 cups chopped unpeeled apples
1/3 cup chopped celery
1/4 cup raisins
1/4 cup chopped walnuts
1/2 cup plain reduced-fat yogurt
Sugar substitute equivalent to 6 teaspoons
  sugar
1/8 teaspoon ground cinnamon

In a bowl, combine the apples, celery, raisins and walnuts. In another bowl, combine the yogurt, sugar substitute and cinnamon until blended. Pour over apple mixture; toss to coat. Refrigerate until serving. **Yield:** 6 servings.

Nutritional Analysis: One serving equals 88 calories, 22 mg sodium, 1 mg cholesterol, 13 gm carbohydrate, 2 gm protein, 4 gm fat, 2 gm fiber. **Diabetic Exchanges:** 1 fruit, 1/2 fat.

 ## NAVY BEAN SQUASH SOUP

Linda Eggers, Albany, California

On a chilly day, what could be more comforting than a pot of this homemade soup? The mix of ham, beans and squash is a hearty combination.

1 pound dry navy beans, sorted and
  rinsed
2 cans (14-1/2 ounces *each*) chicken
  broth
2 cups water
1 meaty ham bone
2 to 2-1/2 pounds butternut squash,
  peeled, seeded and cubed (about 5 cups)
1 large onion, chopped
1/2 teaspoon salt
1/2 teaspoon pepper

Place beans in a large saucepan or Dutch oven; add water to cover by 2 in. Bring to a boil; boil for 2 minutes. Remove from the heat; cover and let stand for 1 hour. Drain and discard liquid; return beans to pan. Add the broth, water, ham bone, squash, onion, salt and pepper. Bring to a boil. Reduce heat; cover and simmer for 1-1/2 to 1-3/4 hours or until beans are tender.

Remove ham bone. Mash the soup mixture, leaving some chunks if desired. Remove ham from bone; cut into chunks. Discard bone and fat. Return meat to the soup; heat through. **Yield:** 12-14 servings (about 3 quarts).

CAULIFLOWER TOMATO SOUP

(Pictured below)

Katherine Stallwood, Kennewick, Washington

We usually have tomato soup at least once a week, so I've tried to find ways to dress it up. This recipe is one of my favorites.

1/4 cup sliced leek (white portion only)
1/4 cup chopped celery
1 tablespoon butter *or* margarine
1 can (10-3/4 ounces) condensed tomato
  soup, undiluted
1-1/4 cups water
1 cup fresh cauliflowerets
1/2 cup frozen peas
1/4 to 1/2 teaspoon dill weed
1/4 teaspoon salt

In a saucepan, saute leek and celery in butter until tender. Stir in the remaining ingredients. Bring to a boil; reduce heat. Cover and simmer for 12-16 minutes or until the vegetables are tender. **Yield:** 2-4 servings.

Ham Salad Puff

(Pictured below)

Cheryl McGarva, Taber, Alberta

Rarely do I come home with leftovers when I take this appetizing salad to family gatherings and potlucks at work. It's hearty yet refreshing, and the edible "bowl" makes it fun to serve.

       1 cup water
    1/2 cup butter (no substitutes)
       1 cup all-purpose flour
    1/4 teaspoon salt
       4 eggs
 1-1/2 cups cubed fully cooked ham
       2 celery ribs, chopped
    1/2 cup cooked small shrimp
    1/2 cup chopped green pepper
    1/2 cup sliced green onions
    1/2 cup mayonnaise
       1 teaspoon dill weed
Salt and pepper to taste
Lettuce leaves
Additional dill weed, optional

In a large saucepan, bring water and butter to a boil. Add flour and salt all at once, stirring until a smooth ball forms. Remove from the heat; let stand for 5 minutes. Add eggs, one at a time, beating well after each addition. Continue beating until mixture is smooth and shiny.

Spread dough onto the bottom and up the sides of a greased 9-in. pie plate. Bake at 400° for 30-35 minutes or until puffed and golden brown. Prick the puff with a fork. Cool on a wire rack. In a bowl, combine the ham, celery, shrimp, green pepper, onions, mayonnaise, dill, salt and pepper. Line puff with lettuce; fill with ham mixture. Garnish with dill if desired. Refrigerate leftovers. **Yield:** 4 servings.

Hearty Bean Soup

Nelda Cameron, Cleveland, Texas

This hearty soup is a real crowd-pleaser served with fresh corn bread. No one can believe how quick and easy it is to make.

       1 large onion, chopped
    1/2 cup chopped green pepper
       2 tablespoons butter *or* margarine
       2 garlic cloves, minced
       2 cans (15-1/2 ounces *each*) great
         northern beans, rinsed and drained
       2 cans (15 ounces *each*) pinto beans,
         rinsed and drained
       2 cans (11-1/2 ounces *each*) condensed
         bean with bacon soup, undiluted
       2 cups diced fully cooked ham
       2 cups water
       2 tablespoons canned diced jalapeno
         peppers

In a skillet, saute onion and green pepper in butter for 3 minutes. Add garlic; cook 1 minute longer. Transfer to a Dutch oven or soup kettle. Add remaining ingredients. Cover and cook over medium-low heat for 20 minutes or until heated through, stirring occasionally. **Yield:** 10 servings.

Ham Pasta Salad

Ruth Bolduc, Conway, New Hampshire

A bowl of this pasta salad is popular at potlucks. It's always one of the first dishes to go.

✓ **Uses less fat, sugar or salt. Includes Nutritional Analysis and Diabetic Exchanges.**

       1 package (7 ounces) small shell pasta
    3/4 cup fat-free mayonnaise
    3/4 cup salsa
 1-1/2 teaspoons prepared mustard
    1/4 teaspoon celery seed
 1-1/2 cups reduced-sodium cubed fully
         cooked ham
 1-1/2 cups sliced celery
       1 medium green pepper, chopped
    1/4 cup chopped fresh tomato
       2 tablespoons finely chopped onion
       2 tablespoons minced fresh parsley

Cook pasta according to package directions. Rinse in cold water and drain. Place in a large bowl; stir in the mayonnaise, salsa, mustard and celery seed. Cover and refrigerate. Just before serving, stir in remaining ingredients. **Yield:** 9 servings.

MOM'S VEGETABLE SOUP

Betty Van Kuiken, Oak Lawn, Illinois

I make this vegetable-packed soup whenever we have a family get-together. It's been a favorite with us for a number of years.

  1 beef chuck roast (3 to 4 pounds)
  2 tablespoons vegetable oil
2-1/2 quarts water
  3 cans (28 ounces *each*) diced tomatoes, undrained
 10 celery ribs, chopped
  6 large carrots, thinly sliced
  3 large onions, chopped
3/4 cup medium pearl barley
2/3 cup cut fresh green beans (1/2-inch pieces)
  1 can (15-1/4 ounces) whole kernel corn, drained
Salt and pepper to taste

In a large soup kettle, brown the roast in oil. Add water; cover and simmer for 2-1/2 to 3 hours or until meat is tender. Drain; set roast aside. In the same kettle, combine the tomatoes, celery, carrots, onions, barley and beans. Cover and simmer for 50 minutes or until the barley is tender. Cut beef into 1/2-in. cubes; add to soup. Stir in corn, salt and pepper; heat through. **Yield:** 26 servings (6-1/2 quarts).

FRUITY CHICKEN SALAD

Roberta Freedman, Mesilla Park, New Mexico

I've been using this recipe whenever we go to a potluck dinner. It always gets rave reviews. It's a great way to use up leftover chicken.

  8 ounces uncooked spiral pasta
  1 can (20 ounces) pineapple chunks
  3 to 4 cups cubed cooked chicken
  1 can (15-1/2 ounces) sliced peaches, drained and diced
  2 tablespoons raisins
1/3 cup vegetable oil
1/4 cup soy sauce
  1 teaspoon curry powder
1/2 cup chopped pecans

Cook pasta according to package directions; rinse with cold water and drain. Drain pineapple, reserving 1/2 cup juice. Dice the pineapple and place in a large bowl. Add cooked pasta, chicken, peaches and raisins. In a small bowl, whisk together the oil, soy sauce, curry powder and reserved pineapple juice. Pour over pasta mixture; toss to coat. Cover and refrigerate for 2 hours. Stir in pecans just before serving. **Yield:** 6-8 servings.

SWEET 'N' SOUR TOSSED SALAD

(Pictured above and on front cover)

Dolores Kastello, Waukesha, Wisconsin

This recipe has been with our family so long that no one knows who originated it. The dressing is also great on any lettuce salad or even over a fruit salad.

1-1/2 cups *each* torn fresh spinach, romaine and iceberg lettuce
  1 can (11 ounces) mandarin oranges, drained
1/3 cup thinly sliced red onion
  1 cup vegetable oil
1/2 cup cider vinegar
1/2 cup sugar
  1 tablespoon finely chopped onion
  1 teaspoon salt
  1 to 2 teaspoons ground mustard

In a large bowl, combine lettuces, oranges and onion. In a blender or food processor, combine remaining ingredients. Cover and process until slightly thickened. Pour 1/3 cup over the salad and toss to coat; serve immediately. Refrigerate remaining dressing. **Yield:** 4 servings.

vegetables and bay leaf. Return broth to kettle; add onion, celery, carrots and beans. Bring to a boil. Reduce heat; cover and simmer for 10 minutes or until vegetables are tender. Add corn, peas and reserved turkey. Bring to a boil; reduce heat.

Combine biscuit mix and milk. Drop by teaspoonfuls onto simmering broth. Cover and simmer for 10 minutes or until a toothpick inserted in a dumpling comes out clean (do not lift the cover while simmering). **Yield:** 16 servings (4 quarts).

▪▪▪▪▪▪▪▪▪▪▪▪▪

CHICKEN CAESAR SALAD
(Pictured on page 65)

Kim Blanda, Neptune, New Jersey

After tasting this salad at a friend's going-away party, I made sure to request the recipe. Now I fix it for my husband just about every week. It's great with a potato or pasta side dish and chunks of crusty bread.

      6 cups torn romaine
      1 pound boneless skinless chicken breasts, cooked and cut into strips
      2 cups seasoned salad croutons
  3/4 cup shredded Parmesan cheese
  1/2 teaspoon salt
      6 tablespoons olive *or* vegetable oil
  1/3 cup lemon juice
      3 to 4 garlic cloves, minced
  1/4 teaspoon coarsely ground pepper

In a salad bowl, combine the first five ingredients. In a jar with a tight-fitting lid, combine the oil, lemon juice, garlic and pepper; shake well. Drizzle over salad; toss to coat. Serve immediately. **Yield:** 4-6 servings.

▪▪▪▪▪▪▪▪▪▪▪▪▪

FRENCH DRESSING OVER ICEBERG WEDGES
(Pictured on page 65)

Carol Underhill, Bathurst, New Brunswick

This dressing has long been a favorite in our family. I got the recipe from a friend years ago, who apparently picked it up from a local restaurant.

  3/4 cup ketchup
  1/2 cup vegetable oil
  1/2 cup cider vinegar
  1/2 cup packed brown sugar
  1/4 cup chopped onion
      1 garlic clove
  1/2 teaspoon Worcestershire sauce

▪▪▪▪▪▪▪▪▪▪▪▪▪

TURKEY DUMPLING SOUP
(Pictured above)

Debbie Wolf, Mission Viejo, California

Simmering up a big pot of this soup is one of my favorite holiday traditions. This is a variation on a recipe my mom made while I was growing up. We can't get enough of the tender dumplings.

      1 meaty leftover turkey carcass (from an 11-pound turkey)
      6 cups chicken broth
      6 cups water
      2 celery ribs, cut into 1-inch slices
      1 medium carrot, cut into 1-inch slices
      1 tablespoon poultry seasoning
      1 bay leaf
  1/2 teaspoon salt
  1/2 teaspoon pepper
SOUP INGREDIENTS:
      1 medium onion, chopped
      2 celery ribs, chopped
      2 medium carrots, sliced
      1 cup fresh *or* frozen cut green beans
      1 package (10 ounces) frozen corn
      1 package (10 ounces) frozen peas
      2 cups biscuit/baking mix
  2/3 cup milk

In a large soup kettle or Dutch oven, combine the first nine ingredients. Bring to a boil. Reduce heat; cover and simmer for 3 hours. Remove carcass and allow to cool. Remove meat and set aside 4 cups for soup (refrigerate any remaining meat for another use); discard bones. Strain broth, discarding

Soups & Salads

1/4 teaspoon salt
1/4 teaspoon paprika
Dash hot pepper sauce
Iceberg lettuce, cut into wedges

Combine the first 10 ingredients in a blender; cover and process until smooth. Store in a jar with a tight-fitting lid; refrigerate. Shake; serve over lettuce wedges. **Yield:** 2-1/4 cups.

ARTICHOKE STEAK SALAD
(Pictured on page 64)

Pat Briggs, Sarasota, Florida

I came up with my hearty main-course salad to take to picnics. It's perfect for potlucks, too. Feel free to substitute other meats for the steak, such as leftover roast beef, grilled pork or chicken.

    3/4 cup vegetable oil
    1/4 cup cider *or* red wine vinegar
    1/4 cup soy sauce
    1/2 teaspoon dried thyme
    1/2 teaspoon ground mustard
    1/2 teaspoon pepper
    1/4 teaspoon dried oregano
  1-1/2 pounds boneless sirloin steak
    1/2 pound fresh mushrooms, quartered
      1 can (14 ounces) artichoke hearts,
        drained and quartered
     12 cherry tomatoes, halved
      5 green onions, chopped
      2 heads Bibb lettuce, separated
        into leaves
      2 hard-cooked eggs, cut into wedges

In a jar with a tight-fitting lid, combine the first seven ingredients; set aside. Grill or broil steak until a meat thermometer reaches at least 145° (medium-rare). Slice meat across the grain into thin strips.

In a bowl, combine the steak, mushrooms, artichokes, tomatoes and onions. Shake dressing; pour over steak mixture and toss to coat. Cover and refrigerate for at least 4 hours, stirring occasionally. Line a serving platter with lettuce; top with steak mixture and dressing. Garnish with eggs. **Yield:** 6-8 servings.

LETTUCE HEADS-UP

Lettuce should be torn, not cut with a knife, to prevent the edges from turning brown.

STRAWBERRY-BANANA GELATIN SALAD
(Pictured below)

Betty Claycomb, Alverton, Pennsylvania

Our family gatherings wouldn't be the same without this classic gelatin salad with its festive fruity layers. Since it stays nice and firm, it travels well and is ideal for taking to covered-dish suppers and church potlucks.

      1 package (6 ounces) strawberry gelatin
      1 cup boiling water
      2 packages (10 ounces *each*) frozen
        sweetened sliced strawberries, partially
        thawed
      1 can (20 ounces) crushed pineapple,
        undrained
      1 cup mashed firm bananas (about 3
        medium)
    1/2 to 3/4 cup chopped walnuts
      2 cups (16 ounces) sour cream
      2 teaspoons sugar
    1/2 teaspoon vanilla extract

In a bowl, dissolve gelatin in water. Stir in strawberries, pineapple, bananas and nuts. Pour half of the mixture into a 13-in. x 9-in. x 2-in. dish. Refrigerate for 1 hour or until set. Set the remaining gelatin mixture aside. Combine the sour cream, sugar and vanilla; mix well. Spread over the chilled gelatin. Spoon remaining gelatin mixture over top. Chill overnight. **Yield:** 12-15 servings.

PLAIN SALADS *will be a thing of the past when you toss together these fresh creations that are anything but garden variety!*

GREAT GREENS. Clockwise from top right: Chicken Caesar Salad (p. 62), Creamy Dressing Over Asparagus (p. 66), French Dressing Over Iceberg Wedges (p. 62), Artichoke Steak Salad (p. 63) and Lettuce with Blue Cheese Dressing (p. 66).

nonstick cooking spray. Bake, uncovered, at 425° for 25-30 minutes or until tender. In a Dutch oven coated with nonstick cooking spray, saute garlic for 2 minutes. Add broth, beans, peas, vinegar, seasonings and roasted vegetables. Bring to a boil. Reduce heat; cover and simmer for 10-12 minutes or until heated through. **Yield:** 16 servings (about 4 quarts).

▪▪▪▪▪▪▪▪▪▪▪▪
LETTUCE WITH BLUE CHEESE DRESSING
(Pictured on page 64)

Gayle Lewis, Yucaipa, California

A yummy combination of cream, spices and blue cheese, this old-fashioned favorite will cover greens with pizzazz! The texture is extra rich, thanks to the cream cheese.

>   1 package (3 ounces) cream cheese, softened
>   1/2 cup half-and-half cream
>   1/2 cup mayonnaise
>   4 ounces crumbled blue cheese
>   1/2 teaspoon garlic powder
>   1/4 teaspoon salt
>   1/8 teaspoon pepper
> Dash cayenne pepper
> Leaf lettuce *or* mixed salad greens

In a small mixing bowl, beat cream cheese until smooth. Beat in the cream, mayonnaise, blue cheese, garlic powder, salt, pepper and cayenne; mix well. Refrigerate overnight. Serve over salad greens. **Yield:** about 1 cup.

▪▪▪▪▪▪▪▪▪▪▪▪
ROASTED VEGETABLE SOUP
(Pictured above)

Brought to you by the folks at the Bean Education and Awareness Network, this veggie- and bean-packed soup will appease the heartiest of appetites.

>   1 medium eggplant, cut into 3/4-inch pieces
>   2 medium zucchini, cut into 3/4-inch pieces
>   2 large sweet red peppers, cut into 3/4-inch pieces
>   1/2 pound fresh mushrooms, quartered
>   1 large sweet potato, peeled and cut into 3/4-inch pieces
>   1 large potato, peeled and cut into 3/4-inch pieces
>   1 medium leek (white part only), sliced
>   6 garlic cloves, minced
>   4 cans (14-1/2 ounces *each*) vegetable *or* chicken broth
>   1 can (16 ounces) kidney beans, rinsed and drained
>   1 can (15 ounces) garbanzo beans, rinsed and drained
>   1 can (15-1/2 ounces) black-eyed peas, rinsed and drained
>   2 to 3 teaspoons cider *or* red wine vinegar
>   1 teaspoon dried rosemary, crushed
>   1 teaspoon dried marjoram
>   1/2 teaspoon rubbed sage
>   1/2 teaspoon dried thyme
> Salt and pepper to taste

Line two 15-in. x 10-in. x 1-in. baking pans with foil; coat the foil with nonstick cooking spray. Place eggplant, zucchini, peppers, mushrooms, potatoes and leek on pans; generously coat with

▪▪▪▪▪▪▪▪▪▪▪▪
CREAMY DRESSING OVER ASPARAGUS
(Pictured on page 65)

Marie Hattrup, The Dalles, Oregon

There's a sweet story behind this versatile dressing, which can be used on all kinds of salads. After baking an angel food cake, my mother would whip up the dressing using leftover egg yolks.

>   3 egg yolks, lightly beaten
>   1/3 cup cider vinegar
>   3 tablespoons sugar
>   1/4 teaspoon salt
> Pinch ground mustard
>   3/4 cup whipping cream
> Cooked fresh asparagus spears

Sliced tomato
Escarole *or* endive

In a heavy saucepan, combine the first five ingredients. Cook and stir over low heat until mixture reaches 160° and is thickened. Remove from the heat; whisk for 1 minute. Cover and refrigerate. Just before serving, whisk in the cream until blended. Arrange asparagus and tomato on lettuce-lined plates; spoon dressing over top. **Yield:** about 1 cup.

SHRIMP RICE SALAD

Joyce Pappert, Mars, Pennsylvania

I enjoy this salad because it's so easy to prepare and makes a refreshing meal on a hot day. My husband is not a big fan of seafood, so I often make it with chicken, which is just as tasty.

- 1 pound cooked medium shrimp, peeled and deveined
- 1 package (10 ounces) frozen peas, thawed
- 3 cups cooked rice
- 1-1/2 cups chopped celery
- 1/4 cup chopped onion
- 1/2 cup vegetable oil
- 3 tablespoons cider vinegar
- 2 tablespoons brown sugar
- 1 tablespoon soy sauce
- 2 teaspoons curry powder
- 1/2 teaspoon celery seed
- 1/2 teaspoon salt

Leaf lettuce
Cherry tomatoes

In a bowl, combine the first five ingredients; toss gently. In a jar with a tight-fitting lid, combine the next seven ingredients; shake well. Add to shrimp mixture; toss. Cover and refrigerate for several hours or overnight. Serve on lettuce; garnish with tomatoes. **Yield:** 8 servings.

TWO-BEAN TURKEY SALAD
(Pictured below)

Turkey, beans and more combine in this salad from the Bean Education and Awareness Network.

- 12 cups torn fresh spinach
- 2 cups cubed cooked turkey *or* chicken
- 2 cups broccoli florets
- 1 can (15-1/2 ounces) black-eyed peas *or* navy beans, rinsed and drained
- 1 can (15 ounces) garbanzo beans, rinsed and drained
- 1 large unpeeled red apple, cubed
- 1/2 cup coarsely chopped walnuts
- 1/3 cup dried cranberries *or* raisins
- 3/4 cup ranch salad dressing
- 1/2 cup apricot preserves *or* jam
- 1 teaspoon Dijon mustard
- 3/4 teaspoon ground ginger

In a large salad bowl, toss the first eight ingredients. In a small bowl, combine salad dressing, preserves, mustard and ginger until blended. Pour over salad and toss to coat. **Yield:** 8-10 servings.

SPECIAL TURKEY SALAD

Connie Laux, Englewood, Ohio

I used to buy turkey salad from a local deli until I experimented and came up with this recipe myself. It's even better than the store-bought kind.

- 1/4 cup mayonnaise
- 1/4 cup plain yogurt
- 1 tablespoon honey Dijon mustard
- 3 cups cubed cooked turkey
- 1 cup halved green grapes
- 2 celery ribs, chopped
- 1/2 cup chopped cashews
- 5 green onions, thinly sliced
- Lettuce leaves

In a bowl, combine first three ingredients. Add turkey, grapes, celery, cashews and onions; stir to coat. Serve on lettuce. **Yield:** 4 servings.

HOT HAM SALAD

(Pictured below)

Frances Kellner, Sheboygan Falls, Wisconsin

I make this quite often for my husband. A quick, hot meal that's perfect served with dinner rolls, it's a real hit at our house.

- 3 cups cubed fully cooked ham
- 1 can (8 ounces) pineapple tidbits, drained
- 1/4 cup chopped green pepper
- 1/4 cup chopped sweet red pepper
- 1 cup mayonnaise*
- 1/4 cup shredded mozzarella cheese
- 1 can (11 ounces) mandarin oranges, drained
- 1/2 cup slivered almonds

In a bowl, combine the first six ingredients. Gently fold in the oranges. Transfer to a greased 1-1/2-

qt. baking dish. Sprinkle with almonds. Bake, uncovered, at 350° for 30 minutes or until heated through. **Yield:** 4 servings.

*Editor's Note: Reduced-fat or fat-free mayonnaise may not be substituted for regular mayonnaise.

ARTICHOKE TOSSED SALAD

Karin Graw, Hudson, Wisconsin

It's a cinch to mix this zesty salad together for a potluck. It'll feed a crowd and then some. For a lighter version, I use less oil and a sugar substitute for the dressing and toss in turkey bacon.

- 2 bunches (1 pound *each*) romaine, torn
- 1 pound sliced bacon, diced, cooked and drained
- 1 jar (6-1/2 ounces) marinated artichoke hearts, drained and sliced
- 1 package (4 ounces) crumbled blue cheese
- 1 cup sliced celery
- 1 medium sweet red pepper, sliced
- 1 medium sweet yellow pepper, sliced
- 6 tablespoons cider vinegar
- 1/4 cup chopped onion
- 4 teaspoons brown sugar
- 4 teaspoons spicy brown mustard
- 1 teaspoon salt
- 1/2 teaspoon pepper
- 1/4 cup vegetable oil

In a large salad bowl, combine the first seven ingredients; cover and refrigerate. In a blender or food processor, combine the vinegar, onion, brown sugar, mustard, salt and pepper; cover and process until smooth. With blender running, add oil in a steady stream; blend until thickened. Drizzle over salad; toss gently. Serve immediately. **Yield:** 20-24 servings.

CAULIFLOWER HAM CHOWDER

Arline Hofland, Deer Lodge, Montana

I came up with this recipe myself when I had a ham hock and wanted to make something other than the usual split pea soup. The resulting chowder was satisfying and good-tasting. Mashed potatoes help give it a rich, creamy texture.

- 1 meaty ham bone
- 2 quarts water
- 1 large onion, chopped
- 1 medium green pepper, chopped

1/2 cup butter *or* margarine
3/4 cup all-purpose flour
1-1/2 teaspoons salt
1/4 teaspoon pepper
4 cups milk
4 cups cauliflowerets, cooked and drained
2 cups mashed potatoes (prepared with milk and butter)
Minced fresh parsley, optional

In a soup kettle, simmer ham bone in water for 1-1/2 hours. Remove ham bone; set cooking liquid aside. When cool enough to handle, remove meat from bone; discard bone. Return ham to cooking liquid; set aside.

In a saucepan, saute onion and green pepper in butter until tender. Stir in flour, salt and pepper until blended. Gradually add milk. Bring to a boil; cook and stir for 2 minutes or until thickened. Add to ham and liquid. Add cauliflower and potatoes. Cook until heated through. Sprinkle with parsley if desired. **Yield:** 14 servings.

SPINACH RICE SALAD

Eleanor Harris, Knoxville, Tennessee

Here's a salad that goes well with many menus. It has a hint of Oriental flavor, with spinach and green onions for color and bacon for a bit of crunch.

1/2 cup Italian salad dressing
1 tablespoon soy sauce
1/2 teaspoon sugar
2 cups cooked rice
1 celery rib, thinly sliced
4 green onions, thinly sliced
2 cups thinly sliced fresh spinach
5 bacon strips, cooked and crumbled

In a bowl, combine the salad dressing, soy sauce and sugar. Stir in rice, celery and onions. Cover and refrigerate for at least 1 hour. Just before serving, stir in spinach and bacon. **Yield:** 6-8 servings.

MARINATED TOMATOES

Isabella Lynch, South San Francisco, California

This has been a favorite of family and friends for years. The dressing gives it a wonderful flavor.

1 garlic clove, minced
3/4 teaspoon salt
1/2 teaspoon pepper
1 teaspoon dried oregano
1/4 teaspoon ground mustard
3 tablespoons cider *or* red wine vinegar

1/2 cup olive *or* vegetable oil
1/2 cup minced fresh parsley
4 large tomatoes, cut into 1/2-inch slices
1 medium sweet onion, sliced into 1/4-inch rings

In a small bowl, combine garlic, salt, pepper, oregano and mustard. Whisk in vinegar and oil until well mixed. Stir in parsley. In a shallow serving dish, layer half of the tomato and onion slices. Drizzle with half of the dressing. Repeat layers. Cover and refrigerate for at least 1 hour. Serve with a slotted spoon. **Yield:** 6-8 servings.

 ## SESAME CUCUMBER SALAD
(Pictured above)

Linda Hodge, Kannapolis, North Carolina

I learned to cook at an early age and have collected many recipes. Whenever I take this salad to a church supper, it's the first one to disappear!

8 cups thinly sliced cucumbers
1 tablespoon salt
2 green onions, sliced
1 garlic clove, minced
2 to 3 tablespoons soy sauce
2 tablespoons vinegar
1 tablespoon vegetable oil
1 tablespoon sesame seeds, toasted
1/8 teaspoon cayenne pepper

Place cucumbers in a colander. Set the colander on a plate; sprinkle cucumbers with salt and toss. Let stand for 30 minutes. Rinse and drain well. In a bowl, combine the onions, garlic, soy sauce, vinegar, oil, sesame seeds and cayenne. Add cucumbers and toss to coat. Cover and refrigerate until serving. **Yield:** 8-10 servings.

RED, WHITE AND BLUEBERRY SALAD

Linnea Tucker, Dolores, Colorado

Lovely and layered, this delightful gelatin salad rounds out any meal fruitfully. Originally my grandmother's recipe, this is a standby of mine for potlucks. My father would eat the entire dish himself if I let him!

> 2 packages (3 ounces *each*) raspberry gelatin
> 2 cups boiling water, *divided*
> 1-1/2 cups cold water, *divided*
> 1 envelope unflavored gelatin
> 1 cup half-and-half cream
> 3/4 to 1 cup sugar
> 1 package (8 ounces) cream cheese, cubed
> 1/2 cup chopped pecans
> 1 teaspoon vanilla extract
> 1 can (15 ounces) blueberries in syrup, undrained

In a bowl, dissolve one package of raspberry gelatin in 1 cup boiling water. Stir in 1 cup cold water. Pour into a 13-in. x 9-in. x 2-in. dish; chill until set. In a small bowl, soften unflavored gelatin in the remaining cold water; set aside.

In a saucepan, combine cream and sugar; whisk over medium heat until sugar is dissolved. Add cream cheese and softened unflavored gelatin; cook and stir until smooth. Cool. Stir in pecans and vanilla. Spoon over raspberry gelatin. Refrigerate until completely set. In a bowl, dissolve second package of raspberry gelatin in remaining boiling water. Stir in blueberries. Carefully spoon over cream cheese layer. Chill several hours or overnight. **Yield:** 12-16 servings.

Editor's Note: This salad takes time to prepare since each layer must be set before the next layer is added.

BLT MACARONI SALAD

(Pictured above)

Mrs. Hamilton Myers Jr., Charlottesville, Virginia

A friend served this salad, and I just had to get the recipe. My husband loves BLT sandwiches, so this has become a favorite of his. It's nice to serve on hot and humid days, which we frequently get during summer here in Virginia.

> 1/2 cup mayonnaise
> 3 tablespoons chili sauce
> 2 tablespoons lemon juice
> 1 teaspoon sugar
> 3 cups cooked elbow macaroni
> 1/2 cup chopped seeded tomato
> 2 tablespoons chopped green onions
> 3 cups shredded lettuce
> 4 bacon strips, cooked and crumbled

In a large bowl, combine the first four ingredients; mix well. Add the macaroni, tomato and onions; toss to coat. Cover and refrigerate. Just before serving, add lettuce and bacon; toss to coat. **Yield:** 6 servings.

PERFECT PASTA

When making pasta salad, always cook the pasta al dente—cooked just long enough to retain a somewhat firm texture. This will allow the pasta to absorb some of the dressing without becoming mushy.

MARINATED CITRUS SALAD

Katrina Heinrich, Underhill, Vermont

This citrusy salad evolved over the years by combining a little bit of what everyone in my family likes.

> ✓ **Uses less fat, sugar or salt. Includes Nutritional Analysis and Diabetic Exchanges.**

> 1-1/2 cups orange juice
> 1/2 cup cider *or* red wine vinegar
> 1/4 cup orange marmalade
> 1/4 cup sugar
> 1/2 teaspoon pepper
> 1/4 teaspoon salt
> 3 medium grapefruit, peeled and sectioned

3 medium navel oranges, peeled and
  sectioned
32 fresh asparagus tips
1 medium cucumber, thinly sliced
1 medium onion, sliced and separated into
  rings
1 medium ripe avocado, peeled and cubed
6 cups torn romaine
6 cups torn red leaf lettuce
1 teaspoon minced fresh mint, optional

In a bowl, combine the orange juice, vinegar, marmalade, sugar, pepper and salt; stir until sugar is dissolved. In another bowl, combine the grapefruit, oranges, asparagus, cucumber, onion and avocado. Add the marinade and toss to coat. Cover and refrigerate for 2 hours. Drain and reserve marinade. Arrange lettuce on plates; top with fruit mixture. Sprinkle with mint if desired. Serve with reserved marinade. **Yield:** 12 servings.

Nutritional Analysis: One serving (1 cup) equals 143 calories, 65 mg sodium, 0 cholesterol, 31 gm carbohydrate, 4 gm protein, 2 gm fat, 8 gm fiber. **Diabetic Exchanges:** 1-1/2 fruit, 1/2 starch.

FRUIT SLAW IN A CABBAGE BOWL
(Pictured at right)

Darlene Markel, Stayton, Oregon

I like to serve this fruity coleslaw inside a hollowed-out cabbage. Both the flavor and "bowl" never fail to draw compliments.

1 medium head cabbage
1 can (11 ounces) mandarin oranges,
  drained
1 can (8 ounces) pineapple chunks,
  drained
2 medium carrots, shredded
1 medium tart apple, chopped
1/2 cup halved green grapes
2 tablespoons vegetable oil
2 tablespoons lemon juice
2 tablespoons honey
1/8 teaspoon ground ginger

To prepare the cabbage serving bowl, gently peel back outer leaves of the cabbage. Hollow out cabbage, leaving a 1/4-in. shell and the core intact; set aside. Chop removed cabbage leaves. Place 2 cups chopped cabbage in a bowl (refrigerate remaining cabbage for another use). Add oranges, pineapple, carrots, apple and grapes.

In a jar with a tight-fitting lid, combine oil, lemon juice, honey and ginger; shake well. Pour over slaw and toss to coat. Spoon into cabbage bowl. Serve immediately. **Yield:** 6-8 servings.

TUTTI-FRUTTI CUPS
(Pictured below)

Holly Keithley, Lowell, Indiana

Scooping up spoonfuls of this tangy slush is a tongue-tingling treat! The convenient single-serving cups burst with wholesome chunks of strawberries, bananas and more. Mix in diet pop instead of the regular kind to make the fruit salad cups lower in calories.

2 cans (11 ounces *each*) mandarin
  oranges, undrained
1 can (20 ounces) crushed pineapple,
  undrained
5 medium firm bananas, thinly sliced
1-1/2 cups fresh *or* frozen sliced strawberries
1-1/2 cups fresh *or* frozen blueberries
1 can (12 ounces) lemon-lime soda
1 cup water
3/4 cup lemonade concentrate
1/2 cup sugar

In a large bowl, combine all ingredients. Fill 8-oz. plastic cups three-fourths full; cover and freeze for 4 hours or until solid. Remove from freezer 30 minutes before serving. **Yield:** 20 servings.

1 pound ground beef
1/2 teaspoon Italian seasoning
6 cups water, *divided*
2 large onions, chopped
3 celery ribs, chopped
1 cup uncooked wild rice
2 teaspoons beef bouillon granules
1/2 teaspoon pepper
1/4 teaspoon hot pepper sauce
3 cans (10-3/4 ounces *each*) condensed cream of mushroom soup, undiluted
1 can (4 ounces) mushroom stems and pieces, drained

In a Dutch oven or soup kettle, cook beef and Italian seasoning over medium heat until meat is no longer pink; drain. Add 2 cups water, onions, celery, rice, bouillon, pepper and hot pepper sauce; bring to a boil. Reduce heat; cover and simmer for 45 minutes. Stir in the soup, mushrooms and remaining water. Cover and simmer for 30 minutes or until heated through. **Yield:** 10-12 servings (3 quarts).

▰▰▰▰▰▰▰▰▰▰▰

RAINBOW PASTA SALAD
(Pictured above)

Debbie Albright, Salisbury, North Carolina

I sometimes add extra color by substituting sweet red pepper for half of the green one. But the secret ingredient in this salad is actually the sweetened condensed milk.

1 package (1 pound) tricolor spiral pasta
2 medium carrots, shredded
1 large red onion, chopped
1 medium green pepper, chopped
1/2 teaspoon celery seed *or* 2 celery ribs, chopped
1 can (14 ounces) sweetened condensed milk
1 cup vinegar
1 cup mayonnaise
3/4 cup sugar
1 teaspoon salt
1/2 to 1 teaspoon pepper

Cook pasta according to package directions. Rinse in cold water and drain; place in a large bowl. Add carrots, onion, green pepper and celery seed. In another bowl, combine remaining ingredients. Pour over pasta mixture; toss to coat. Cover; refrigerate 8 hours or overnight. **Yield:** 12-14 servings.

▰▰▰▰▰▰▰▰▰▰▰

BEEFY WILD RICE SOUP

Marilyn Chesbrough, Wautoma, Wisconsin

Living in central Wisconsin, we experience many days of snow and cold temperatures. I like to prepare soup often, especially this one, which warms you through and through. My whole family loves it.

▰▰▰▰▰▰▰▰▰▰▰

SWEET FLORET SALAD

Kathi Lavier, Hillsboro, Oregon

Everywhere I take this crunchy and fresh-tasting salad with its sweet creamy dressing, people invariably want a copy of the recipe. It's perfect for a potluck— best made the night before you serve it and very easy to transport.

1/2 cup mayonnaise*
1/3 cup sugar
1/4 cup vegetable oil
1/4 cup vinegar
1 medium head cauliflower, broken into florets
1-3/4 pounds fresh broccoli, broken into florets
1 medium red onion, sliced
1 medium sweet yellow pepper, cut into 1-inch pieces, optional
1/2 pound sliced bacon, cooked and crumbled

In a small saucepan, combine the mayonnaise, sugar, oil and vinegar. Bring to a boil, whisking constantly. Cool to room temperature. In a large bowl, combine the remaining ingredients. Add dressing and toss to coat. Cover and refrigerate for several hours or overnight, stirring occasionally. **Yield:** 10-12 servings.

*Editor's Note: Reduced-fat or fat-free mayonnaise may not be substituted for regular mayonnaise.

NECTARINE CHICKEN SALAD

Cathy Ross, Van Nuys, California

When guests are coming for lunch or dinner in the warm summer months, I like to serve this attractive colorful salad. The dressing is refreshingly tart. A neighbor shared the recipe years ago.

1/4 **cup lime juice**
  1 **tablespoon sugar**
  1 **tablespoon minced fresh thyme** *or* 1 **teaspoon dried thyme**
  1 **tablespoon olive** *or* **vegetable oil**
  1 **garlic clove, minced**
  6 **cups torn mixed salad greens**
  1 **pound boneless skinless chicken breasts, cooked and sliced**
  5 **medium ripe nectarines, thinly sliced**

In a jar with a tight-fitting lid, combine the lime juice, sugar, thyme, oil and garlic; shake well. On a serving platter, arrange the mixed salad greens, chicken breast slices and nectarines. Drizzle with the dressing. Serve immediately. **Yield:** 4 servings.

"Souper" Squash Bowls

FOLKS are sure to be bowled over when you serve them Pat Hoffman's yummy Maple Squash Soup in pretty squash shells!

It's simple to create the hollowed-out shell. Begin by cutting the neck off a butternut squash, leaving the round bulb intact. With a sharp knife, cut around the seeds and membranes, leaving about a 1/2-in. shell (see photo below left).

Next, with an ice cream scoop or large spoon, remove the seeds and membrane from the shell. Place shells in a foil-lined 13-in. x 9-in. x 2-in. baking pan; bake as directed in the recipe.

Be ready for compliments on the gourdgeous results (see photo below right)!

MAPLE SQUASH SOUP

(Pictured below and on page 56)

  4 **medium butternut squash (about 2-1/4 pounds** *each***)**
  4 **teaspoons plus 1/2 cup butter** *or* **margarine, divided**
1/2 **teaspoon salt**
1/4 **teaspoon pepper**
  3 **cups chopped onions**
  1 **medium leek, chopped**
  1 **celery rib, chopped**
  3 **cans (14-1/2 ounces** *each***) vegetable** *or* **chicken broth**
  1 **cup maple syrup**
Additional maple syrup
1/4 **teaspoon ground nutmeg**

Pierce neck end of squash in several places with a sharp knife. Microwave, uncovered, on high for 4-5 minutes. Cut squash between neck and bulb. Peel neck and cut into cubes; set aside. Remove and discard seeds and membrane from bulb, leaving about a 1/2-in. shell.

Place 1 teaspoon of butter in each shell; sprinkle with salt and pepper. Place in a foil-lined 13-in. x 9-in. x 2-in. baking pan. Bake at 350° for 15-20 minutes or until butter is melted and squash is heated through.

In a soup kettle, saute onions, leek and celery in remaining butter until tender. Add squash cubes, broth and syrup; bring to a boil. Reduce heat; cover and simmer for 20 minutes or until squash is tender.

In a blender, puree soup in small batches until smooth. Return to the pan. Drizzle additional syrup into squash bowls. Fill with soup; drizzle with syrup if desired. Sprinkle with nutmeg. Freeze remaining soup to serve at another time or serve in regular soup bowls. **Yield:** 3 quarts (4 squash bowls).

MARINATED ITALIAN PASTA

(Pictured above)

Gail Buss, Westminster, Maryland

When I have guests coming over or a busy day ahead, I like to make this convenient pasta salad because I prepare it the day before.

  1 package (16 ounces) medium shell pasta
1/4 pound hard salami, cubed
1/4 pound sliced pepperoni, halved
  1 block (4 ounces) provolone cheese, cubed
  4 medium tomatoes, seeded and chopped
  4 celery ribs, chopped
  1 medium green pepper, chopped
1/2 cup sliced stuffed olives
1/2 cup sliced ripe olives
  1 bottle (8 ounces) Italian salad dressing
  2 teaspoons dried oregano
1/2 teaspoon pepper

Cook pasta according to package directions; rinse in cold water and drain. Place in a large bowl; add salami, pepperoni, cheese, vegetables and olives. Add salad dressing, oregano and pepper; toss to coat. Cover and refrigerate overnight. **Yield:** 12-16 servings.

FESTIVE FRUIT SALAD

Faith Bowman, Selah, Washington

One year I was asked to bring a fruit salad to a family Christmas dinner. I devised this recipe and every-

one loved it. After that, I became the "official fruit salad person" for all family get-togethers.

✓ **Uses less fat, sugar or salt. Includes Nutritional Analysis and Diabetic Exchanges.**

  1 can (15 ounces) mandarin oranges, drained
1-1/2 cups halved red seedless grapes
1-1/2 cups halved green grapes
  1 jar (10 ounces) red maraschino cherries, halved, rinsed and drained
  1 jar (10 ounces) green maraschino cherries, halved, rinsed and drained
  1 can (8 ounces) unsweetened pineapple chunks, drained
  2 cups miniature marshmallows
  1 cup flaked coconut
  1 cup (8 ounces) fat-free sour cream

In a large bowl, combine the first eight ingredients. Just before serving, add sour cream and toss to coat. **Yield:** 12-16 servings.

Nutritional Analysis: One 1/2-cup serving equals 149 calories, 18 mg sodium, 1 mg cholesterol, 33 gm carbohydrate, 2 gm protein, 3 gm fat, 1 gm fiber. **Diabetic Exchanges:** 2 fruit, 1/2 fat.

CAJUN CORN AND SHRIMP

Carolyn Whetstone, Zachary, Louisiana

My dad's Cajun concoctions inspired me to experiment in the kitchen. Dishes like this flavorful soup are the rewarding result.

  1 large onion, chopped
  1 medium green pepper, chopped
  2 garlic cloves, minced
1/4 cup butter *or* margarine
  2 packages (16 ounces *each*) frozen corn
  1 can (10 ounces) diced tomatoes and green chilies, undrained
  1 tablespoon sugar
1/4 teaspoon salt
1/8 teaspoon pepper
Cayenne pepper to taste
  1 can (5 ounces) evaporated milk
1/3 cup chopped green onions
  2 pounds uncooked medium shrimp, peeled and deveined

In a skillet, saute onion, green pepper and garlic in butter until crisp-tender. Add corn, tomatoes, sugar, salt, pepper and cayenne. Cook 10 minutes or until heated through. Stir in milk and green onions; simmer 10 minutes. Add shrimp; cook 8 minutes or until shrimp turn pink. **Yield:** 8 servings.

CURRIED LEEK SOUP

Arnold Foss, Mercer, Maine

I like to come up with new recipes, and this is one I developed the first year I grew leeks in my garden.

- 3 medium leeks (white portion only), thinly sliced
- 1 garlic clove, minced
- 2 tablespoons butter *or* margarine
- 1 can (14-1/2 ounces) chicken broth
- 3/4 cup water
- 1-1/2 cups thinly sliced carrots
- 2 celery ribs, thinly sliced
- 2 teaspoons chicken bouillon granules
- 1/2 teaspoon curry powder
- 1/8 teaspoon pepper
- 1 can (12 ounces) evaporated skim milk

In a 3-qt. saucepan, saute leeks and garlic in butter over medium heat until tender. Add the broth, water, carrots, celery, bouillon, curry powder and pepper. Bring to a boil. Reduce heat; cover and simmer for 20-25 minutes or until vegetables are tender. Cool slightly. Place 1 cup soup in a blender or food processor; cover and process until smooth. Return to pan. Add milk; heat through (do not boil). **Yield:** 4 servings.

OLD-FASHIONED POTATO SALAD

Nancy Grove-Nichols, Dillsburg, Pennsylvania

We live at the edge of Pennsylvania Dutch Country, where there are lots of small farms. Country markets are plentiful here, so potatoes are a staple.

- 4 cups cubed peeled potatoes
- 3 hard-cooked eggs, chopped
- 2 celery ribs, thinly sliced
- 1/4 cup chopped green onions
- 1/2 cup sour cream
- 1/2 cup mayonnaise
- 2 tablespoons vinegar
- 2 tablespoons sugar
- 1 teaspoon prepared mustard
- 1/2 teaspoon salt
- 1/4 teaspoon pepper

Place potatoes in a saucepan and cover with water; bring to a boil. Reduce heat. Cook for 20-25 minutes or until tender; drain. Place in a large bowl; add eggs, celery and onions. In a small bowl, combine the remaining ingredients. Pour over potato mixture and toss to coat. Cover and refrigerate for at least 1 hour. **Yield:** 6-8 servings.

CHILLED ASPARAGUS SOUP

(Pictured below)

Kim Gilliland, Simi Valley, California

This is a delightful soup that's perfect for hot weather. The curry seasoning comes through just right.

- 1 pound fresh asparagus
- 5 cups chicken broth
- 1/2 cup water
- 1/4 cup butter *or* margarine
- 1/4 cup all-purpose flour
- 3 egg yolks, beaten
- 3/4 cup whipping cream
- 1 teaspoon curry powder
- 1/8 teaspoon pepper

Dash lemon juice

Cut asparagus into 1-in. pieces; set tips aside. Place the remaining asparagus in a saucepan; add broth. Bring to a boil; reduce heat. Cover and simmer for 40-45 minutes. Cool slightly. Process in batches in a blender or food processor until smooth; set aside. In a small saucepan, bring water to a boil. Add the asparagus tips; cook for 2-3 minutes or until tender. Drain and chill until serving.

In a saucepan, melt butter. Stir in flour until smooth. Gradually add pureed asparagus. Bring to a boil; cook and stir for 2 minutes or until thickened. Remove from the heat. Stir a small amount of hot soup into egg yolks; return all to the pan, stirring constantly. Cook over low heat for 5 minutes or until mixture is heated through and reaches 160°. Stir in the cream, curry powder, pepper and lemon juice. Remove from the heat; cool slightly. Cover and chill until serving. Garnish with asparagus tips, gently adding to each bowl. **Yield:** 8-10 servings.

TOMATO TURKEY SOUP

(Pictured below)

Judy Lloyd, Alta Vista, Kansas

During winter, we often have this hearty soup along with a salad at our senior citizen's center. It's always well received.

✓ Uses less fat, sugar or salt. Includes Nutritional Analysis and Diabetic Exchanges.

  6 cups chicken *or* turkey broth
  2 cans (14-1/2 ounces *each*) diced
     tomatoes, undrained
1/3 cup quick-cooking barley
  1 tablespoon dried parsley flakes
  1 teaspoon salt
1/2 teaspoon garlic powder
1/2 teaspoon dried oregano
1/2 teaspoon dried basil
1/4 teaspoon pepper
  2 cups cubed cooked turkey
1-1/2 cups sliced carrots
1-1/2 cups sliced celery
  1 medium onion, chopped
  1 cup chopped green pepper
  1 package (10 ounces) frozen chopped okra

In a large saucepan or Dutch oven, combine the first nine ingredients. Bring to a boil. Reduce heat; cover and simmer for 50 minutes. Add turkey and vegetables. Cover and simmer 50 minutes longer or until vegetables are tender. **Yield:** 14 servings.

Nutritional Analysis: One serving (1 cup) equals 85 calories, 714 mg sodium, 14 mg cholesterol, 11 gm carbohydrate, 5 gm protein, 2 gm fat, 3 gm fiber. **Diabetic Exchanges:** 1 vegetable, 1/2 starch, 1/2 meat.

RAISIN BROCCOLI TOSS

Bernice Morris, Marshfield, Missouri

Packed with fresh flavor, this raisin salad is a lively addition to a down-home meal. It's easy to prepare and good for you, too. The walnuts and broccoli add lots of crunch.

  4 cups broccoli florets
3/4 cup coarsely chopped walnuts
1/2 cup raisins
1/2 cup golden raisins
  1 cup mayonnaise *or* salad dressing
1/4 cup sugar
  2 tablespoons lemon juice
  2 tablespoons half-and-half cream
  1 tablespoon vinegar

In a large salad bowl, toss broccoli, walnuts and raisins. In a small bowl, combine the remaining ingredients. Pour over salad; toss to coat. Cover and refrigerate for 1 hour. **Yield:** 8 servings.

HAM AND CORN CHOWDER

Sherry Akers, Forest, Virginia

This comforting ham chowder has become a staple at my house throughout the year. This calls for sweet potatoes instead of white potatoes for a nutritional twist.

✓ Uses less fat, sugar or salt. Includes Nutritional Analysis and Diabetic Exchanges.

  3 garlic cloves, minced
  1 teaspoon vegetable oil
  2 cans (14-1/2 ounces *each*) reduced-
     sodium chicken broth
1-1/2 cups frozen corn
1-1/2 cups cubed peeled sweet potatoes
1-1/2 cups chopped sweet red pepper
1-1/2 teaspoons dried thyme
1-1/4 cups reduced-sodium cubed fully
     cooked ham
  3 green onions, thinly sliced
  2 tablespoons cornstarch
  2 cups plain reduced-fat yogurt

In a large saucepan, saute garlic in oil for 1 minute. Add broth, corn, sweet potatoes, red pepper and thyme. Bring to a boil. Reduce heat; cover and simmer for 10 minutes or until vegetables are tender. Stir in ham and onions. Remove from the heat. In a bowl, combine cornstarch and yogurt until smooth. Gradually add to soup. Return to heat. Bring to a boil; cook and stir for 2 minutes or until thickened. **Yield:** 8 servings.

Nutritional Analysis: One serving equals 157 calories, 254 mg sodium, 13 mg cholesterol, 24 gm carbohydrate, 10 gm protein, 3 gm fat. **Diabetic Exchanges:** 1 starch, 1 vegetable, 1 lean meat.

CARROT BROCCOLI SALAD

Heather Hibbs, Middleburg, Pennsylvania

I created this salad one summer for a round of family reunions and picnics. My in-laws provided me with all the fresh vegetables from their garden.

> 6 medium carrots, shredded
> 1 small bunch broccoli (about 12 ounces), chopped
> 1 cup raisins
> 1 small onion, chopped
> 1 garlic clove, minced
> 2/3 to 1 cup mayonnaise
> 1/2 cup sugar
> 1 teaspoon gound mustard
> 1/2 pound sliced bacon, cooked and crumbled

In a large bowl, combine the first five ingredients. In another bowl, combine the mayonnaise, sugar and mustard; mix well. Add to vegetable mixture and toss to coat. Cover and refrigerate. Stir in bacon just before serving. **Yield:** 6 servings.

VEGETABLE BEAN SOUP

Beans add extra texture and flavor to this vegetable soup shared by the Bean Education and Awareness Network.

> 1-1/2 cups chopped onion
> 1 cup sliced celery
> 3 medium carrots, sliced
> 2 to 3 garlic cloves, minced
> 1 tablespoon vegetable oil
> 2 cans (14-1/2 ounces *each*) chicken broth
> 2 cans (15 ounces *each*) navy *or* great northern beans, rinsed and drained, *divided*
> 2 cups broccoli florets
> 1/2 teaspoon dried rosemary, crushed
> 1/4 teaspoon dried thyme
> 1/2 teaspoon salt
> 1/4 teaspoon pepper
> 1 cup fresh spinach

In a Dutch oven or soup kettle, saute onion, celery, carrots and garlic in oil until tender. Add broth, one can of beans, broccoli and seasonings; bring to a boil. Reduce heat; simmer, uncovered, for 5-7 minutes. Place remaining beans in a blender or food processor; cover and process un-

til smooth. Add to the soup with the spinach; simmer for 2 minutes or until heated through. **Yield:** 8 servings (2 quarts).

SALAD WITH HONEY-MUSTARD DRESSING

(Pictured above)

Chris Rufener, Rittman, Ohio

This salad is my most-requested recipe. The dressing, eggs and almonds can be prepared ahead of time, so it can be made at the last minute.

> 1 cup vegetable oil
> 1/2 cup plus 3 tablespoons sugar, *divided*
> 1/4 cup vinegar
> 1/4 cup honey
> 2 tablespoons lemon juice
> 1 teaspoon onion powder
> 1 teaspoon salt
> 1 teaspoon celery seed
> 1 teaspoon ground mustard
> 1 teaspoon paprika
> 1/2 cup slivered almonds
> 9 cups torn romaine
> 1 cup (4 ounces) shredded cheddar cheese
> 2 hard-cooked eggs, diced

In a saucepan, combine the oil, 1/2 cup sugar, vinegar, honey, lemon juice and seasonings; cook and stir until sugar is dissolved. Remove from the heat; set aside to cool. In a skillet over low heat, cook almonds and remaining sugar until nuts are glazed; cool. In a salad bowl, toss the romaine, cheese and almonds. Top with eggs. Drizzle with dressing. Serve immediately. Refrigerate any leftover dressing. **Yield:** 10-12 servings.

FOR SOMETHING sensational to serve alongside main entrees, turn to these complementary side dishes and condiments.

ON THE SIDE. From top: Cheesy Zucchini Saute (p. 79), Scalloped Potatoes and Carrots (p. 79) and Macaroni and Cheese Casserole (p. 79).

Side Dishes & Condiments

CHEESY ZUCCHINI SAUTE
(Pictured at left)
Doris Biggs, Felton, Delaware

Friends keep me supplied with zucchini. As a thank-you, I tell them how to make this saute.

- 1/2 cup chopped onion
- 1/4 cup butter *or* margarine
- 3 cups coarsely shredded zucchini
- 2 teaspoons minced fresh basil *or* 1/2 teaspoon dried basil
- 1/2 teaspoon salt
- 1/8 teaspoon garlic powder
- 1 cup (4 ounces) shredded cheddar cheese
- 1 cup diced fresh tomato
- 2 tablespoons sliced ripe olives

In a skillet, saute onion in butter until crisp-tender. Stir in zucchini, basil, salt and garlic powder. Cook and stir for 4-5 minutes or until zucchini is crisp-tender. Sprinkle with cheese, tomato and olives. Cover and cook for 4-5 minutes or until cheese is melted. **Yield:** 6 servings.

SCALLOPED POTATOES AND CARROTS
(Pictured at left)
Rosemary Wehinger, Monroe, Wisconsin

I feel this recipe deliciously represents our region because it contains dairy products.

- 2-1/2 pounds potatoes (about 9 medium), peeled and sliced
- 5 medium carrots, cut into 1/4-inch slices
- 1-1/2 cups sliced onions
- 2 cups boiling water
- 1 teaspoon salt

CHEESE SAUCE:
- 3 tablespoons butter *or* margarine
- 2 tablespoons all-purpose flour
- 1 teaspoon salt
- 1/8 teaspoon pepper
- 1-1/2 cups milk
- 1-1/2 cups (6 ounces) shredded cheddar cheese, *divided*

In a large Dutch oven, combine potatoes, carrots, onions, water and salt. Bring to a boil. Reduce heat; cover and cook for 10 minutes. Meanwhile, in a saucepan, melt butter. Remove from the heat; stir in flour, salt and pepper until smooth. Gradually stir in milk. Bring to a boil over medium heat, stirring constantly. Cook and stir for 2 minutes. Stir in 1 cup cheese. Reduce heat; stir until cheese is melted.

Drain the vegetables; layer half in a greased 3-qt. baking dish. Top with half of the cheese sauce. Repeat layers. Sprinkle with remaining cheese. Cover and bake at 375° for 20 minutes. Uncover and bake 10 minutes longer or until potatoes are tender. **Yield:** 6-8 servings.

MACARONI AND CHEESE CASSEROLE
(Pictured at left)
Eve-Lyn Woodard, Canandaigua, New York

Families with small children love this casserole. After all, what kid doesn't like macaroni and cheese?

- 1-1/2 cups milk
- 1-1/2 cups (6 ounces) shredded sharp cheddar cheese
- 3 tablespoons butter *or* margarine, melted
- 1 cup soft bread crumbs
- 1 cup elbow macaroni, cooked and drained
- 3 eggs, *separated*
- 1/4 cup diced pimientos
- 1 tablespoon minced fresh parsley
- 1 tablespoon finely chopped onion
- 1 teaspoon salt

In a saucepan, heat milk over medium heat until bubbles form around edge of pan. Remove from the heat; stir in the cheese and butter. Let stand for 1 minute. Stir until cheese is almost melted. Stir in bread crumbs.

In a bowl, combine the macaroni, egg yolks, pimientos, parsley, onion and salt. Stir in cheese mixture; mix well. Beat egg whites until stiff peaks form; fold into macaroni mixture. Transfer to a greased 2-qt. baking dish. Bake, uncovered, at 350° for 30-35 minutes or until puffed and lightly browned. **Yield:** 4-6 servings.

ZESTY ZUCCHINI SKILLET

JoseAnn Engle, Spanish Fork, Utah

For a fast and flavorful side dish that goes great with a variety of main dishes, give this recipe a try. It's a cinch to stir together using just one skillet. Ground cumin and picante sauce add a nice zip.

4 cups chopped zucchini
1 cup chopped onion
2 garlic cloves, minced
2 tablespoons vegetable oil
1/2 teaspoon ground cumin
1/4 teaspoon dried oregano
1/4 teaspoon salt
1/3 cup picante sauce
1 medium tomato, peeled, seeded and chopped
1/2 cup shredded Monterey Jack cheese

In a large skillet, saute the zucchini, onion and garlic in oil for 2 minutes. Add cumin, oregano and salt. Stir in picante sauce; cook and stir for 5-7 minutes or until vegetables are crisp-tender. Add tomato; cook for 1-2 minutes or until heated through. Remove from the heat; sprinkle with cheese. **Yield:** 4 servings.

GRANDPA'S PARTY POTATOES

(Pictured below)

Mary Kay Elert, St. Paul Park, Minnesota

This casserole will please even the pickiest eaters. My grandpa, who gave the recipe to me, liked the way the cream cheese and onion dip created a wonderful velvety texture. I often assemble it the night before, then pop it in the oven the next day.

8 to 9 cups diced peeled potatoes
2 tablespoons butter *or* margarine
2 tablespoons milk
3/4 teaspoon salt
1/4 teaspoon pepper
1 package (8 ounces) cream cheese, softened
1 carton (8 ounces) French onion dip
Paprika

In a large saucepan, cook potatoes in boiling salted water until tender; drain. Mash the potatoes with butter, milk, salt and pepper until smooth. Add cream cheese and onion dip; mix well. Spread in a greased 2-1/2-qt. baking dish. Sprinkle with paprika. Cover and refrigerate for 8 hours or overnight. Remove from the refrigerator 30 minutes before baking. Bake, uncovered, at 350° for 50-60 minutes or until heated through. **Yield:** 12-14 servings.

ASPARAGUS ONION CASSEROLE

Judy Fleetwood, Beulah, Michigan

This vegetable dish goes great with just about any meal. I've prepared it ahead of time, then put it in the oven so it's ready with the meal.

1 pound fresh asparagus, cut into 1-inch pieces *or* 2 packages (10 ounces *each*) asparagus cuts, thawed
2 medium onions, sliced
5 tablespoons butter *or* margarine, *divided*
2 tablespoons all-purpose flour
1 cup milk
1 package (3 ounces) cream cheese, cubed

1 teaspoon salt
1/8 teaspoon pepper
1/2 cup shredded cheddar cheese
1 cup soft bread crumbs

In a skillet, saute the asparagus and onions in 1 tablespoon of butter until crisp-tender, about 8 minutes. Transfer to an ungreased 1-1/2-qt. baking dish. In a saucepan, melt 2 tablespoons butter. Stir in flour until smooth; gradually add milk. Bring to a boil; cook and stir for 2 minutes or until thickened. Reduce heat.

Add cream cheese, salt and pepper; stir until cheese is melted. Pour over the vegetables. Sprinkle with cheddar cheese. Melt remaining butter; toss with bread crumbs. Sprinkle over casserole. Bake, uncovered, at 350° for 35-40 minutes or until heated through. **Yield:** 4-6 servings.

AUTUMN SQUASH BAKE

Patty Baumann, Savannah, Missouri

The sweetness of pears and tangy flavor of cranberries really complement the squash. This dish has become a favorite at family holiday meals.

✓ **Uses less fat, sugar or salt. Includes Nutritional Analysis and Diabetic Exchanges.**

9 cups diced peeled Hubbard squash
2 medium pears, cut into 1-inch pieces
1 cup fresh *or* frozen cranberries
1 tablespoon margarine
2 tablespoons water

Combine all ingredients in a 3-qt. baking dish coated with nonstick cooking spray. Cover and bake at 350° for 50-55 minutes or until squash is tender. **Yield:** 14 servings.

Nutritional Analysis: One serving (3/4 cup) equals 102 calories, 22 mg sodium, 0 cholesterol, 21 gm carbohydrate, 4 gm protein, 2 gm fat, 5 gm fiber. **Diabetic Exchanges:** 1 starch, 1/2 fruit.

PICKLED MUSHROOMS

Linda Keiper-Quinn, Hazleton, Pennsylvania

Pennsylvania is known for its mushrooms. In the region where I live, fresh mushrooms are used prominently in many recipes.

1/2 cup cider *or* red wine vinegar
1/2 cup water
2 bay leaves
2 tablespoons sugar
1-1/2 teaspoons salt

1 garlic clove, minced
1 pound fresh mushrooms, quartered

In a saucepan over medium heat, combine vinegar, water, bay leaves, sugar, salt and garlic. Add mushrooms. Bring to a boil; boil for 2 minutes. Transfer to a glass bowl; cover and refrigerate for 8 hours or overnight. Discard bay leaves before serving. **Yield:** about 2-1/2 cups.

CREAMY CORN CASSEROLE

(Pictured above)

Monica Digman, Dubuque, Iowa

The cheese and noodles give this dish a unique flavor. I got the recipe from a cousin, who brought this casserole to a family reunion.

1 can (15-1/4 ounces) whole kernel corn, drained
1 can (14-3/4 ounces) cream-style corn
1 cup cooked wide egg noodles
1 small onion, chopped
1 small carrot, shredded
1/4 cup cubed process American cheese
1/4 teaspoon salt
1/4 teaspoon pepper
1/3 cup crushed saltines (about 10 cracers)
1 tablespoon butter *or* margarine, melted

In a bowl, combine the first eight ingredients. Transfer to a greased 1-qt. baking dish. Toss cracker crumbs and butter; sprinkle over the top. Bake, uncovered, at 350° for 45-50 minutes or until heated through. **Yield:** 4-6 servings.

FIT-FOR-A-KING BAKED BEANS

These nicely seasoned, savory baked beans from the Bean Education and Awareness Network really live up to their name. They're extra special.

      3 bacon strips, diced
      2 small onions, chopped
      3 garlic cloves, minced
  2-1/4 teaspoons ground ginger *or* 3
        tablespoons minced fresh gingerroot
      4 cans (15 ounces *each*) great northern
        beans, rinsed and drained
    1/2 cup apple cider *or* juice
    1/2 cup salsa
    1/2 cup molasses
    1/2 cup packed brown sugar
    1/2 cup crushed gingersnaps, optional
      1 tablespoon Dijon mustard
    1/2 teaspoon dried thyme
    1/2 teaspoon ground allspice
      2 bay leaves

In a skillet, cook bacon until crisp. Remove with a slotted spoon to paper towels. Drain, reserving 1 teaspoon drippings. In the drippings, saute onions, garlic and ginger until tender. In a bowl, combine remaining ingredients. Stir in onion mixture and bacon. Transfer to a greased 2-qt. baking dish. Cover and bake at 300° for 2 hours. Uncover; bake 30-35 minutes longer or until beans reach desired thickness. Discard bay leaves. **Yield:** 12-14 servings.

FRUITY CRANBERRY RELISH

(Pictured below)

Holly Cosentino, Templeton, Massachusetts

This relish recipe has been in my family for years. It has a zippy taste that everyone seems to enjoy. I like serving it with pork, turkey and chicken.

  2-1/2 cups cranberries
      1 medium navel orange, peeled and
        sectioned
      2 cups chopped peeled tart apples
      1 can (8 ounces) crushed pineapple,
        drained
      1 cup sugar
    1/2 cup chopped green *or* red grapes
      4 teaspoons grated orange peel
    1/2 teaspoon salt
    1/3 cup chopped walnuts

In a food processor, combine cranberries and orange sections. Cover and process until chopped. Transfer to a bowl; add apples, pineapple, sugar, grapes, orange peel and salt. Cover and refrigerate overnight. Stir in the walnuts just before serving. **Yield:** 6-8 servings.

GRILLED DIJON SUMMER SQUASH

Ruth Lee, Troy, Ontario

A niece gave this mustard-seasoned squash recipe to me. My husband, Doug, and our three grandchildren love the zesty flavor and slightly crunchy texture. The kabobs are perfect partners to any grilled meat and reheat easily.

    1/2 cup olive *or* vegetable oil
    1/4 cup cider *or* red wine vinegar
      1 tablespoon minced fresh oregano *or* 1
        teaspoon dried oregano
      1 tablespoon Dijon mustard
      2 garlic cloves, minced
    1/2 teaspoon salt
    1/4 teaspoon pepper
      4 medium zucchini, cut into 1/2-inch
        slices
      4 medium yellow squash, cut into
        1/2-inch slices
      2 medium red onions, quartered
      1 large sweet red pepper, cut into 2-inch
        pieces
      1 large sweet yellow pepper, cut into
        2-inch pieces
     12 to 16 whole fresh mushrooms
     12 cherry tomatoes

In a jar with a tight-fitting lid, combine the oil, vinegar, oregano, mustard, garlic, salt and pepper. Place the zucchini, squash, onions, peppers, mushrooms and tomatoes in a shallow baking dish. Add marinade and toss to coat. Let stand for 15 minutes. Drain and discard marinade; arrange vegetables on a vegetable grill rack. Grill, covered, over indirect heat for 10-12 minutes or until tender. **Yield:** 16-18 servings.

Squash Suggestions

• When preparing my favorite Italian or Mexican recipes, I often substitute shredded zucchini for half of the ground beef or sausage. It reduces the fat and makes the recipe more economical, too. —*Trudy Overlin*
Rigby, Idaho

• Here's a quick and easy way to grill acorn squash. Generously sprinkle each half with brown sugar, cinnamon, nutmeg and pepper. Dot each with 2 tablespoons butter and wrap tightly in foil. Cook, covered, over medium heat for 25-35 minutes or until tender.
—*Theresa Hoffmann*
Hatley, Wisconsin

• My family loves fried squash blossoms! Pick fully opened blossoms that do not have a small squash growing behind the flower. Remove the stamen and wash gently. Dip in a mixture of egg and milk, dredge in flour, fry in butter and sprinkle with salt and pepper.
—*Carolyn Manz, Tiffin, Ohio*

• Here's an easy way to cook several winter squash. In a large roaster, place halved and seeded squash, cut side down; add 2 cups water. Cover and bake for 45-60 minutes or until tender. The peel will easily pull away and the squash will be ready to mash.
—*Mary Burkman, Gary, South Dakota*

• Try placing crumpled aluminum foil around the sides of filled squash shells to keep them from tipping during baking. Lining pans with foil before baking squash can also cut down on the cleanup time. —*Jan Roberts*
Grain Valley, Missouri

• When preparing an autumn oven meal, I fill up the extra oven space with a baking pan of squash. When the squash is cool enough to handle, I mash it and freeze in measured amounts for use throughout the year.
—*June Mueller, Sioux City, Iowa*

• I remove and set aside the seeds before I cook my winter squash. If it tastes especially good, I let the seeds dry thoroughly on paper towels, then place them in a jar and use for planting the next year. —*Mary Romig*
Lebanon, Pennsylvania

• It's easy to remove seeds from winter squash with an ice cream scoop.
—*Michele Decoteau*
Millbury, Massachusetts

• I make homemade baby food for my 6-month-old twins from acorn squash. I put pureed cooked squash in ice cube trays, then freeze. Once the squash cubes are frozen, I place them in freezer bags. Each cube can be quickly reheated and ready for my boys to enjoy. —*Muriel Villalta*
Godfrey, Ontario

• Try topping your favorite squash soup with a dollop of sour cream or plain yogurt. It is an attractive garnish and adds a nice tang.
—*Linda Orchard, Omaha, Nebraska*

CREAMED CAULIFLOWER
(Pictured below)

Peggie De Chick, Auburn, New York

This is a Hungarian recipe from my mother. It's easy to make and flavorful.

  1 medium head cauliflower, broken into
      florets (about 7 cups)
1-1/2 teaspoons salt, *divided*
  1/2 cup dry bread crumbs, *divided*
  1 cup half-and-half cream
  1 tablespoon butter *or* margarine
Minced fresh parsley

Place cauliflower in a saucepan; add 1 in. of water and 1 teaspoon salt. Bring to a boil. Reduce heat. Cover and simmer for 6-7 minutes or until crisp-tender; drain. Grease the bottom and sides of a 2-qt. baking dish; sprinkle with 2 tablespoons bread crumbs. Add cauliflower. Pour cream over top. Dot with butter; sprinkle with remaining salt and bread crumbs. Bake, uncovered, at 350° for 25-30 minutes or until cauliflower is tender. Garnish with parsley. **Yield:** 6-8 servings.

MICROWAVE ACORN SQUASH

Rita McPherson, Nashua, New Hampshire

Acorn squash is my favorite fall vegetable—and it goes to great use in this quick-and-easy side dish.

  2 medium acorn squash
  2/3 cup crushed butter-flavored crackers
  1/3 cup butter *or* margarine, melted
  3 tablespoons brown sugar
  1/8 teaspoon ground nutmeg

Pierce squash several times with a knife or fork; place on a microwave-safe plate. Microwave on high for 5 minutes. Cut in half; remove seeds and strings. Place, cut side down, in a microwave-safe dish; cover with waxed paper. Microwave for 7 minutes. Meanwhile, combine the crushed crackers, butter, brown sugar and nutmeg. Turn squash over; fill with cracker mixture. Microwave for 2-3 minutes or until squash is tender. **Yield:** 4 servings.

Editor's Note: This recipe was tested in an 850-watt microwave.

ALMOND-TOPPED CARROTS

Karen Regennitter, Ritzville, Washington

Here's a different way to cook plain carrots. It's a nice addition to a fancy meal and also jazzes up an everyday dinner. I treat family and friends to these tender carrots often.

  2 pounds carrots, julienned
  2 cups water
  1/2 cup golden raisins
  1/2 cup butter *or* margarine, melted
  6 tablespoons honey
  2 tablespoons lemon juice
  1/2 teaspoon ground ginger
Dash pepper
  1/2 cup slivered almonds, toasted

In a saucepan, bring carrots and water to a boil. Reduce heat. Cover and cook for 10 minutes or until crisp-tender; drain. Add the raisins, butter, honey, lemon juice, ginger and pepper. Place in a greased 2-qt. baking dish. Cover and bake at 350° for 35 minutes or until the carrots are tender. Sprinkle with almonds before serving. **Yield:** 12 servings.

PARTY POTATOES AU GRATIN

Debbie Carlson, San Diego, California

Hearty helpings of these cheesy spuds will please hungry folks in a hurry. The rich creamy sauce makes this recipe of my mother's the one folks request most. The potatoes are just as delicious the next day, reheated in the microwave with a little milk added.

  1/2 cup butter *or* margarine
  1/3 cup all-purpose flour
  2 teaspoons salt, *divided*
  2 teaspoons pepper, *divided*
  4 cups milk
  7 large potatoes, peeled and thinly sliced

2 medium onions, chopped
8 cups (32 ounces) shredded cheddar
   cheese

In a saucepan, melt butter. Stir in flour, 1 teaspoon salt and 1 teaspoon pepper until smooth. Gradually add milk; bring to a boil. Cook and stir for 2 minutes or until thickened and bubbly; set aside.

Combine the potatoes, onions, cheese, and remaining salt and pepper. Place a third of the mixture in a greased 5-qt. baking dish; top with a third of the sauce. Repeat layers twice. Cover and bake at 350° for 2-1/2 hours. Uncover; bake 30 minutes longer or until potatoes are tender. **Yield:** 14-18 servings.

POTATO SQUASH SKILLET

Robbie Harris, Philadelphia, Tennessee

I've tried different ways to fix zucchini and yellow squash and finally came up with this recipe. It's easy to make and tastes good with any meat entree.

   2 cups cooked cubed red potatoes
      (1/2-inch pieces)
   2 cups cubed zucchini (1/2-inch pieces)
   2 cups cubed yellow summer squash
      (1/2-inch pieces)
1-1/2 teaspoons lemon-pepper seasoning
   2/3 cup cornmeal
   1 teaspoon baking powder
   1/4 teaspoon salt
   3 tablespoons vegetable oil
   2 tablespoons butter *or* margarine

In a large bowl, toss the potatoes, zucchini and yellow squash with lemon-pepper. Let stand for 10 minutes. In a bowl, combine cornmeal, baking powder and salt. Add to potato mixture; toss to coat. In a large skillet, heat oil and butter over medium heat. Add vegetable mixture; cook and stir for 15 minutes or until golden brown. **Yield:** 4-6 servings.

SQUASH DESCRIPTION

Squash are divided into two categories. Summer squash have thin edible skins and soft seeds. These include crookneck, pattypan and zucchini. Winter squash have hard thick skins and seeds. The most popular varieties are acorn, buttercup, butternut, Hubbard, spaghetti and turban.

CABBAGE-TOMATO PASTA TOSS
(Pictured above)

Alcy Thorne, Los Molinos, California

Here's an unusual combination of ingredients that blend very well together. It's a nice side dish for any beef entree.

   2 medium tomatoes, peeled and diced
   2 tablespoons cider *or* red wine vinegar
   1 teaspoon dried basil
   1/2 cup minced fresh parsley
   8 ounces uncooked bow tie pasta
   2 cups shredded cabbage
1-1/2 cups soft bread crumbs
   1/2 cup slivered almonds
   2 to 3 garlic cloves, minced
   1/4 cup olive *or* vegetable oil
   1/4 cup butter *or* margarine

In a bowl, combine the tomatoes, vinegar, basil and parsley; set aside. Cook pasta according to package directions, adding the cabbage during the last 2 minutes. Meanwhile, in a skillet, saute bread crumbs, almonds and garlic in oil and butter for 6 minutes or until golden brown. Drain pasta and cabbage; place in a large bowl. Add tomato and crumb mixtures; toss and serve immediately. **Yield:** 6 servings.

1 package (16 ounces) frozen corn, thawed
1 large tomato, seeded and chopped
4 tablespoons butter *or* margarine, *divided*
3 tablespoons all-purpose flour
1/2 teaspoon salt
1/8 teaspoon pepper
Dash cayenne pepper
1 cup milk
1 cup (4 ounces) shredded sharp cheddar cheese
4 eggs, *separated*
1/4 teaspoon cream of tartar

In a skillet, saute corn and tomato in 1 tablespoon butter until tomato is heated through; set aside. In a large saucepan, melt the remaining butter; stir in flour, salt, pepper and cayenne until smooth. Gradually add milk. Bring to a boil; cook and stir for 2 minutes or until thickened. Remove from the heat. Add cheese and the reserved corn mixture.

In a small mixing bowl, beat egg yolks until thick and lemon-colored, about 3 minutes. Stir in 1/3 cup hot corn mixture; return all to the pan. Cool to room temperature. In another mixing bowl, beat egg whites until soft peaks form. Add cream of tartar; beat until stiff peaks form. Gently fold into corn mixture. Transfer to a greased 2-1/2-qt. baking dish. Bake, uncovered, at 350° for 40-45 minutes or until a thermometer reads 160° and top is golden brown. Let stand for 5 minutes before serving. **Yield:** 4-6 servings.

▰▰▰▰▰▰▰▰▰▰▰▰
CRUMB-TOPPED BROCCOLI BAKE

Hope Huggins, Santa Cruz, California

Broccoli is one of the main crops grown in this area. This recipe has pleased just about everyone who has tried it, including some who said they didn't normally care for broccoli.

1/4 cup chopped onion
2 tablespoons butter *or* margarine
2 tablespoons all-purpose flour
1/2 cup milk
1 jar (8 ounces) process cheese sauce
2 packages (10 ounces *each*) frozen broccoli cuts
3 eggs, beaten
1/2 cup crushed butter-flavored crackers (about 12 crackers), *divided*
Salt and pepper to taste

In a saucepan, saute onion in butter until tender. Stir in flour until blended. Gradually add milk. Bring to a boil; cook and stir for 2 minutes or until thickened. Reduce heat; stir in cheese sauce until smooth. Remove from the heat. Cook broc-

▰▰▰▰▰▰▰▰▰▰▰▰
CASHEW RICE PILAF
(Pictured above)

Tina Coburn, Tucson, Arizona

This hearty dish will add pizzazz to your plate, thanks to its beautiful blend of flavors and colors. I often serve it as a main course with salad and bread.

1-1/2 cups uncooked long grain rice
1 cup chopped onion
1 cup diced carrots
1 cup golden raisins
1/4 cup butter *or* margarine
3 cups chicken broth
1 teaspoon onion salt
2 cups frozen peas
1-1/2 cups cooked wild rice
1 cup cashews
1/4 cup thinly sliced green onions, optional

In a Dutch oven, saute the long grain rice, onion, carrots and raisins in butter until onion is tender. Add the broth and onion salt; bring to a boil. Reduce heat; cover and simmer for 20 minutes or until liquid is absorbed and rice is tender. Stir in peas, wild rice and cashews; heat through. Sprinkle with sliced green onions if desired. **Yield:** 12 servings.

▰▰▰▰▰▰▰▰▰▰▰▰
GOLDEN CORN PUFF

Barbara Merrick, Van Etten, New York

My mother-in-law shared this recipe with me. It's something different and very simple to make. My husband, Rich, and I especially like it because corn is our favorite vegetable.

Side Dishes & Condiments

coli according to package directions; drain and place in a bowl. Add cheese sauce mixture, eggs, 1/4 cup cracker crumbs, salt and pepper. Transfer to a greased 1-1/2-qt. baking dish; sprinkle with remaining cracker crumbs. Place dish in a larger baking pan. Fill pan with hot water to a depth of 1 in. Bake, uncovered, at 350° for 50 minutes or until golden brown. **Yield:** 6 servings.

TOMATO HAM PASTA

Colleen Harvel, Big Bear City, California

I got this recipe from a cooking show years ago and have been making it often ever since. I like to use tomatoes fresh from my garden.

> ✓ Uses less fat, sugar or salt. Includes Nutritional Analysis and Diabetic Exchanges.

- 3 cups uncooked penne pasta
- 2 garlic cloves, minced
- 2 tablespoons vegetable oil
- 4 medium tomatoes, peeled, seeded and chopped
- 1 cup diced fully cooked low-sodium ham
- 1/2 teaspoon salt-free seasoning blend
- 1/4 teaspoon pepper
- 1/8 teaspoon crushed red pepper flakes

Cook pasta according to package directions. Meanwhile, in a skillet, saute garlic in oil until tender. Add tomatoes; simmer for 5 minutes. Stir in ham and seasonings. Cook 8 minutes longer or until heated through. Drain pasta; add to ham mixture. **Yield:** 8 servings.

Nutritional Analysis: One serving equals 187 calories, 125 mg sodium, 6 mg cholesterol, 29 gm carbohydrate, 7 gm protein, 5 gm fat. **Diabetic Exchanges:** 2 starch, 1 lean meat.

BIG-BATCH BAKED BEANS

Kathy Herron, Jamestown, New York

All in the family is how I describe my tasty baked beans. My mom got the recipe from my aunt, then shared it with me when she saw how much my husband enjoyed the dish. It's great to take to potlucks and picnics.

- 1/2 pound ground beef
- 1/2 cup chopped onion
- 1 can (55 ounces) pork and beans
- 1 can (16 ounces) kidney beans, rinsed and drained
- 1 can (15-1/2 ounces) black-eyed peas, rinsed and drained

- 1/2 cup ketchup
- 5 bacon strips, cooked and crumbled
- 1/3 cup sugar
- 1/3 cup packed brown sugar
- 1/3 cup barbecue sauce
- 2 tablespoons molasses
- 2 tablespoons prepared mustard
- 1/2 teaspoon chili powder
- 1/2 teaspoon salt
- 1/4 teaspoon pepper

In a Dutch oven, cook beef and onion over medium heat until meat is no longer pink; drain. Stir in the remaining ingredients. Transfer to a greased 3-qt. baking dish. Cover and bake at 350° for 1 hour or until beans reach desired thickness. **Yield:** 14 servings.

CREAMY POTATO CASSEROLE
(Pictured below)

June DeWeese, Greencastle, Indiana

A friend gave this recipe to me and I've made it often. I've tried others, but always go back to this one. It's great when you need to feed a large gathering.

- 1 package (30 ounces) frozen shredded hash brown potatoes, thawed
- 2 cups (16 ounces) sour cream
- 2 cups (8 ounces) shredded sharp cheddar cheese
- 1 can (10-3/4 ounces) condensed cream of chicken soup, undiluted
- 1/2 cup chopped onion
- 1/4 cup butter *or* margarine, melted
- 2 tablespoons chopped fresh parsley
- 1/2 teaspoon pepper
- 1/4 teaspoon salt

In large bowl, combine all ingredients. Transfer to ungreased 2-qt. baking dish. Bake, uncovered, at 350° for 1 hour or until heated through. **Yield:** 8-10 servings.

■■■■■■■■■■■■■■

CORN BREAD CASSEROLE
(Pictured below)

Margaret Mayes, La Mesa, California

We live very close to the Mexican border, so recipes featuring corn and green chilies are popular here. This dish has always been a hit whenever I've taken it to a potluck dinner.

> 2 packages (8-1/2 ounces *each*) corn bread/muffin mix
> 1 can (15-1/4 ounces) whole kernel corn, drained
> 1 can (14-3/4 ounces) cream-style corn
> 1 can (4 ounces) chopped green chilies, drained
> 1 cup (4 ounces) shredded Monterey Jack cheese

Prepare corn bread mixes according to package directions. Pour half of the batter into a greased 11-in. x 7-in. x 2-in. baking pan. Combine corn and creamed corn; spread over batter. Top with chilies and cheese. Carefully spread with remaining corn bread batter. Bake, uncovered, at 375° for 25-30 minutes or until a toothpick comes out clean. Serve warm. **Yield:** 12 servings.

■■■■■■■■■■■■■■

SAVORY PLUM SAUCE

Nancy Mendoza, Yakima, Washington

This flavorful sauce tastes fantastic served with pork or poultry dishes. Plus, it's very quick and easy to stir together.

> 2 cans (30 ounces *each*) purple plums, drained and pitted
> 1/4 cup sugar
> 3 tablespoons orange juice concentrate
> 4-1/2 teaspoons lemon juice
> 1-1/2 teaspoons cider vinegar
> 1/2 to 3/4 teaspoon salt
> 1/2 teaspoon ground ginger
> 1/4 teaspoon cayenne pepper
> 1/4 teaspoon curry powder
> 1-1/2 teaspoons cornstarch
> 1 tablespoon cold water

Place plums in a blender or food processor; cover and process until smooth. Transfer to a saucepan; add sugar, orange juice concentrate, lemon juice, vinegar and seasonings. Bring to a boil. Combine cornstarch and water until smooth; gradually add to plum mixture. Bring to a boil; cook and stir for 2 minutes or until thickened. Serve as a condiment with pork or poultry. **Yield:** about 2-3/4 cups.

■■■■■■■■■■■■■■

ZUCCHINI SUPREME

Bette Cimino, Vancouver, Washington

Zucchini recipes are popular around here in late summer. I'm always on the lookout for new ones. This dish featuring that garden-fresh ingredient has a very pleasant flavor and nice combination of color and texture.

> 4 cups water
> 6 cups sliced zucchini
> 1 cup shredded carrot
> 1/4 cup chopped onion
> 1 teaspoon salt
> 1 can (10-3/4 ounces) condensed cream of mushroom soup, undiluted
> 1 cup (8 ounces) sour cream
> 1/2 teaspoon garlic powder
> 1/2 teaspoon pepper
> 4 cups seasoned stuffing croutons
> 1/2 cup butter *or* margarine, melted

In a Dutch oven or soup kettle, bring water to a boil. Add the zucchini, carrot, onion and salt. Cook for 8-10 minutes or until vegetables are tender; drain. In a large bowl, combine the soup, sour cream, garlic powder and pepper. Fold in vegetable mixture.

Combine croutons and butter; place half in a greased 13-in. x 9-in. x 2-in. baking dish. Top with vegetable mixture and remaining croutons. Cover and bake at 350° for 30 minutes. Uncover; bake 10 minutes longer or until golden brown. **Yield:** 8-10 servings.

COLORFUL VEGETABLE SAUTE

Regena Hofer, Meadows, Manitoba

This fresh-tasting mixture is so pretty and tasty—and a great way to enjoy your garden's bounty. A sprinkling of toasted sesame seeds adds a pleasant crunch to the savory saute.

2 medium sweet red peppers, julienned
2 medium green peppers, julienned
2 medium zucchini, julienned
4 medium carrots, julienned
1 tablespoon olive *or* vegetable oil
4 cups thinly sliced red cabbage
1/4 teaspoon salt
1/4 teaspoon pepper
4 teaspoons cider *or* white wine vinegar
1/4 cup water
1 tablespoon sesame seeds, toasted

In a large skillet, saute peppers, zucchini and carrots in oil for 5 minutes. Add cabbage, salt and pepper; saute 1 minute longer. Combine vinegar and water; pour over the vegetables. Saute 3 minutes more. Sprinkle with sesame seeds; cook and stir for 1 minute. **Yield:** 8-10 servings.

WILTED GREENS OVER POTATOES

Bonnie Black, Sligo, Pennsylvania

This recipe is representative of my Pennsylvania Dutch heritage. I remember not liking this dish as a child, but I've become fond of it over the years.

4 cups packed fresh spinach, dandelion, collard, mustard, beet *or* turnip greens
2 cups plus 2 tablespoons water, *divided*
5 thick-sliced bacon strips, diced
4 teaspoons all-purpose flour
1 tablespoon sugar
1 cup milk
1/2 teaspoon salt
1 egg yolk, beaten
1/3 cup cider vinegar
Hot mashed potatoes

In a saucepan, bring greens and 2 cups water to a boil. Reduce heat; cover and simmer for 4-8 minutes or until tender. Drain and set aside. In a skillet, cook bacon until crisp. Remove with a slotted spoon to paper towels to drain. Discard drippings.

Combine flour and sugar; stir in milk, salt and remaining water until smooth. Pour into skillet and bring to a boil. Cook and stir for 2 minutes or until thickened. Remove from the heat. Stir a small amount of the hot mixture the into egg yolk; return all to pan. Bring to a gentle boil; cook and stir for 2 minutes. Add vinegar, greens and bacon; heat through. Serve over mashed potatoes. **Yield:** 4 servings.

SIX-VEGGIE CASSEROLE

(Pictured above)

Eudora Nelson, Glenview, Illinois

I like this convenient casserole because it can be assembled ahead of time. I'm a country girl at heart. I guess I inherited that from my mom, who was raised on a farm.

1 package (16 ounces) frozen cut green beans, thawed
2 cups sliced celery
1-1/2 cups sliced carrots
1-1/2 cups sliced onions
3/4 cup sliced green pepper
1 can (14-1/2 ounces) diced tomatoes, undrained
1/4 cup butter *or* margarine, melted
3 tablespoons quick-cooking tapioca
1 tablespoon sugar
1 teaspoon salt
1/2 teaspoon pepper
1 can (2.8 ounces) french-fried onions

In large bowl, combine the beans, celery, carrots, onion, green pepper and tomatoes. Add butter, tapioca, sugar, salt and pepper; mix well. Transfer to an ungreased 2-1/2-qt. baking dish. Cover and bake at 350° for 50 minutes. Uncover; sprinkle with onions. Bake 20 minutes longer or until vegetables are tender. **Yield:** 12-14 servings.

MOUTHS WILL WATER *when you put any of these from-scratch yeast and quick breads, rolls, muffins and more into the oven.*

HEAVEN-SCENT. From top: Orange Swirl Coffee Cake (p. 91), Butternut Squash Dinner Rolls (p. 92) and Lemon-Cranberry Mini Loaves (p. 91).

Breads & Rolls

LEMON-CRANBERRY MINI LOAVES

(Pictured at left)

Betsy Weigle, Spokane, Washington

I concocted this colorful bread for a Christmas tea buffet. The lemony loaves received so many compliments that I now often give this bread, as well as the recipe and a tea mix, to my friends as Christmas gifts.

2/3 cup butter *or* margarine, softened
1-1/2 cups sugar
   3 tablespoons lemon juice
   2 tablespoons grated lemon peel
   4 eggs
   3 cups all-purpose flour
   2 teaspoons baking powder
   2 teaspoons salt
   1 cup milk
   2 cups dried cranberries
   1 cup chopped walnuts
GLAZE:
   1/4 cup sugar
   1/4 cup lemon juice

In a mixing bowl, cream the butter, sugar, lemon juice and peel. Add the eggs, one at a time, beating well after each addition. Combine the flour, baking powder and salt; add to the creamed mixture alternately with milk. Stir in cranberries and walnuts. Pour into four greased 5-3/4-in. x 3-in. x 2-in. loaf pans.

Bake at 350° for 40-45 minutes or until a toothpick inserted near the center comes out clean. Cool for 10 minutes before removing from pans to wire racks. With a toothpick or skewer, poke 12 holes in each loaf. For glaze, combine sugar and lemon juice until sugar is dissolved. Spoon over loaves. Cool completely before slicing. **Yield: 4 loaves.**

ORANGE SWIRL COFFEE CAKE

(Pictured at left)

Barbara Daniel, Ducor, California

My family and I look forward to warm slices of this citrus-flavored coffee cake every Christmas and Easter morning. It's a tasty tradition we've been doing for a number of years.

   1 package (1/4 ounce) active dry yeast
  1/4 cup warm water (110° to 115°)
   1 cup sugar, *divided*
   2 eggs
  1/2 cup sour cream
   8 tablespoons butter *or* margarine, *divided*
   1 teaspoon salt
3-1/4 to 3-1/2 cups all-purpose flour
  3/4 cup flaked coconut, toasted
   2 tablespoons grated orange peel
ORANGE GLAZE:
   6 tablespoons sugar
1-1/2 teaspoons cornstarch
  1/4 cup sour cream
   2 tablespoons butter *or* margarine
   1 tablespoon orange juice
  1/4 cup flaked coconut, toasted

In a mixing bowl, dissolve yeast in warm water. Add 1/4 cup sugar, eggs, sour cream, 6 tablespoons butter and salt; mix well. Stir in enough flour to form a soft dough. Turn onto a floured surface; knead until smooth and elastic, about 6-8 minutes. Place in a greased bowl, turning once to grease top. Cover and let rise in a warm place until doubled, about 1 hour.

Meanwhile, combine coconut, orange peel and remaining sugar; set aside. Punch dough down. Turn onto a floured surface; roll into an 18-in. x 10-in. rectangle. Melt remaining butter; brush over dough. Spread coconut mixture over dough. Roll up, jelly-roll style, starting with a long side; pinch seam to seal. Place seam side near the top and facing the center tube in a greased fluted 10-in. tube pan; pinch ends together. Cover and let rise in a warm place until doubled, about 1 hour.

Bake at 350° for 30 minutes or until golden brown. Cool for 10 minutes before removing from pan to a wire rack. For orange glaze, combine the sugar, cornstarch, sour cream, butter and orange juice in a saucepan. Bring to a boil; boil and stir for 2 minutes. Spoon or brush over warm coffee cake. Sprinkle with coconut. **Yield: 16-20 servings.**

CARDAMOM BRAIDS
(Pictured below)

Walter Dust, Rapid City, Michigan

This is an old recipe that I like to make for breakfast. The bread is great for dunking in a cup of coffee.

    1 package (1/4 ounce) active dry yeast
1-1/2 cups warm milk (110° to 115°), *divided*
    1 cup sugar, *divided*
    3 egg yolks, beaten
  1/2 cup butter *or* margarine, softened
    1 tablespoon ground cardamom
  1/2 teaspoon salt
    5 to 6 cups all-purpose flour
    2 tablespoons milk

In a large mixing bowl, dissolve yeast in 1/2 cup warm milk. Add 3/4 cup sugar, egg yolks, butter, cardamom, salt, 3 cups of flour and remaining warm milk; beat until smooth. Stir in enough remaining flour to form a soft dough. Turn onto a floured surface; knead until smooth and elastic, about 6-8 minutes. Place in a greased bowl, turning once to grease top. Cover and let rise in a warm place until doubled, about 1-1/4 hours.

Punch dough down; divide into six pieces. Shape each piece into a 16-in. rope. Place three ropes on a greased baking sheet; braid. Pinch ends firmly and tuck under. Repeat with remaining three ropes on another baking sheet. Cover and let rise until doubled, about 45 minutes. Brush braids with milk and sprinkle with remaining sugar. Bake at 350° for 25-30 minutes or until golden brown. Remove to wire racks to cool. **Yield:** 2 loaves.

BUTTERNUT SQUASH DINNER ROLLS
(Pictured on page 90)

Ula Kessler, Liberty Center, Ohio

These wholesome rolls are a pleasant addition to any entree. I get so many requests for them at holiday time, I make about 100 dozen in December.

     2 tablespoons plus 1 teaspoon active
       dry yeast
   3/4 teaspoon plus 1 cup sugar, *divided*
   1/2 cup warm water (110° to 115°)
     2 cups warm milk (110° to 115°)
   1/4 cup butter *or* margarine, softened
     2 cups mashed cooked butternut squash
     2 teaspoons salt
   1/4 cup wheat germ
    10 to 11-1/2 cups all-purpose flour
Additional butter *or* margarine, melted

In a large mixing bowl, dissolve yeast and 3/4 teaspoon sugar in warm water; let stand for 5 minutes. Add the milk, butter, squash, salt and remaining sugar; mix until smooth. Add wheat germ and 4 cups flour; beat until smooth. Stir in enough remaining flour to form a soft dough. Turn onto a floured surface; knead until smooth and elastic, about 6-8 minutes. Place in a greased bowl, turning once to grease top. Cover and let rise in a warm place until doubled, about 1 hour.

Punch dough down and divide into thirds; divide each portion into 20 pieces. Shape into balls. Place on greased baking sheets. Cover and let rise until doubled, about 30 minutes. Bake at 350° for 15-17 minutes or until golden brown. Brush with butter. Remove to wire racks. **Yield:** 5 dozen.

MASHED POTATO ROLLS

Glenda Suit, Boise, Idaho

Potatoes are synonymous with our state. Because it makes a large batch, this recipe is great for company.

     1 package (1/4 ounce) active dry yeast
   1/4 cup warm water (110° to 115°)
 1-3/4 cups warm milk (110° to 115°)
   1/4 cup butter *or* margarine, softened
   1/4 cup vegetable oil
     6 tablespoons sugar
     1 egg
   1/2 cup warm mashed potatoes (prepared
       with milk and butter)
 1-1/2 teaspoons salt
     1 teaspoon baking powder
   1/2 teaspoon baking soda

Hearty Ham Bread

"A TWO-FOR-ONE SPECIAL" —that's what Sue Stamper of Grayson, Kentucky serves up with her homemade Country Ham Bread. The ham is baked right into the bread!

"I often serve wedges of this hearty bread warm from the oven with my zesty herb butter and a simple tossed salad for dinner," she relates. "My husband and teenage son just love it!"

Sue shares her family-pleasing recipe here, so you can round up a satisfying snack or meal for your own brood, too. She's sure they'll love it as much as her own family does.

※※※※※※※※※※
COUNTRY HAM BREAD

    2 tablespoons plus 1 cup
      cornmeal, *divided*
    1 package (1/4 ounce)
      active dry yeast
  1/2 cup warm water (110°
      to 115°)
    2 cups warm buttermilk*
      (110° to 115°)
    1 egg
    3 tablespoons sugar
    3 tablespoons butter (no
      substitutes), melted
1 to 2 teaspoons coarsely
      ground pepper
    1 teaspoon salt
  1/2 teaspoon cayenne pepper
    5 to 5-1/2 cups all-purpose
      flour
2-1/2 cups ground fully cooked
      ham
HERB BUTTER:
    1 cup butter (no
      substitutes), softened
    1 cup chopped chives
  1/2 cup minced fresh parsley
    2 tablespoons lemon juice
Dash pepper

Grease two 9-in. round baking pans. Sprinkle each with 1 tablespoon cornmeal; set aside. In a large mixing bowl, dissolve yeast in water. Add buttermilk, egg, sugar, butter, pepper, salt, cayenne, 3 cups flour and remaining cornmeal; beat until smooth. Beat in ham. Add enough remaining flour to form a soft dough. Turn onto a floured surface; knead until smooth and elastic, about 6-8 minutes. Place in a greased bowl, turning once to grease top. Cover and let rise in a warm place until doubled, about 1-1/4 hours.

Punch dough down. Divide in half; shape into two round loaves. Place in prepared pans. Cover and let rise until doubled, about 45 minutes. Bake at 375° for 25-30 minutes or until golden brown. Remove from pans to wire racks to cool.

For herb butter, combine the butter, chives, parsley, lemon juice and pepper in a small mixing bowl. Serve with the bread. Store bread and the butter in the refrigerator. **Yield:** 2 loaves (2/3 cup butter).

*Editor's Note: Warm buttermilk may appear curdled.

---

    6 cups all-purpose flour
Melted butter *or* margarine, optional

In a mixing bowl, dissolve yeast in water. Add milk, butter, oil, sugar, egg and mashed potatoes; mix well. Stir in the salt, baking powder, baking soda and enough flour to form a soft dough. Turn onto a floured surface; knead until smooth and elastic, about 6-8 minutes. Place in a greased bowl, turning once to grease top. Cover and let rise in a warm place until doubled, about 1-1/2 hours.

Punch dough down. Turn onto a lightly floured surface; divide in half. Cover one piece. Shape the other piece into 16 balls. Place 2 in. apart on greased baking sheets. Repeat with the remaining dough. Cover and let rise until doubled, about 30 minutes. Bake at 375° for 15-18 minutes or until golden brown. Brush with butter if desired. **Yield:** 32 rolls.

※※※※※※※※※※
STRAWBERRY BUTTER

Marlene Heimlich, Cardington, Ohio

My taste for strawberries stems from girlhood berry-picking trips around our family farm. Though I must admit, more ended up in my mouth than in the basket! This sweetened butter is one of my favorite recipes using those luscious berries.

  1/2 cup butter (no substitutes), softened
  1/3 cup confectioners' sugar
    1 package (10 ounces) frozen sweetened
      sliced strawberries, thawed and drained

In a mixing bowl, cream butter until light and fluffy; gradually add confectioners' sugar. Slowly add strawberries to creamed mixture; beat well. Serve with French toast, waffles, muffins, biscuits or bagels. **Yield:** 1-1/4 cups.

BUTTERMILK DOUGHNUTS

(Pictured below)

Betty Rauschendorfer, Sidney, Montana

It doesn't take long for a platter of these doughnuts to vanish. Our grandkids go for them in a big way! They're great for munching at breakfast or brunch.

> 4 eggs
> 2 cups sugar
> 1/3 cup butter *or* margarine, melted
> 1 teaspoon vanilla extract
> 5-1/2 to 6 cups all-purpose flour
> 2 teaspoons baking powder
> 2 teaspoons baking soda
> 1 teaspoon salt
> 1 teaspoon ground nutmeg
> 2 cups buttermilk

Oil for deep-fat frying
Additional sugar, cinnamon-sugar *or*
  confectioners' sugar, optional

In a mixing bowl, beat eggs and sugar until light and lemon-colored. Add butter and vanilla; mix well. Combine the flour, baking powder, baking soda, salt and nutmeg; add to egg mixture alternately with buttermilk. Cover and refrigerate for 2-3 hours.

On a lightly floured surface, roll dough to 1/2-in. thickness. Cut with a 3-in. doughnut cutter. In an electric skillet or deep-fat fryer, heat oil to 375°. Fry doughnuts, a few at a time, for 1 minute on each side or until golden. Drain on paper towels. Roll in sugar if desired. **Yield:** 4 dozen.

CORNMEAL YEAST BREAD

Mildred Mikel, Ennis, Texas

This bread goes very well with chili or any kind of soup on a cold winter day.

> 2 packages (1/4 ounce *each*) active dry
>   yeast
> 1/2 cup warm water (110° to 115°)
> 3/4 cup milk
> 1/3 cup sugar
> 1/3 cup butter *or* margarine, melted
> 1 egg
> 3/4 cup cornmeal
> 1 teaspoon salt
> 3-1/2 to 4 cups all-purpose flour

In a mixing bowl, dissolve yeast in warm water. Add milk, sugar, butter, egg, cornmeal and salt. Beat in 1-1/2 cups flour until smooth. Add enough remaining flour to form a soft dough. Turn onto a floured surface; knead until smooth and elastic, about 6-8 minutes. Place in a greased bowl, turning once to grease top.

Cover and let rise in a warm place until doubled, about 45 minutes. Punch dough down. Divide in half and shape into two loaves. Place in greased 8-in. x 4-in. x 2-in. loaf pans. Cover and let rise until doubled, about 30 minutes. Bake at 350° for 35-40 minutes or until golden brown. Remove from pans to cool on wire racks. **Yield:** 2 loaves.

BUTTER-DIPPED BISCUIT SQUARES

Rebekah DeWitt, Star City, Arkansas

These are the easiest and best biscuits I've ever made. They're light and buttery and go well with virtually any meal.

> 2 cups self-rising flour*
> 2 tablespoons sugar
> 1 cup milk
> 1/2 cup butter (no substitutes), melted

All-purpose flour

In a bowl, combine the self-rising flour, sugar and milk; mix well. Turn onto a floured surface; sprinkle with all-purpose flour. Pat dough to 1/2-in. thickness. With a sharp knife dipped in flour, cut into 3-in. x 2-in. pieces. Pour butter into an ungreased 13-in. x 9-in. x 2-in. baking pan. Dip one side of each piece into melted butter. Carefully turn to coat. Bake, uncovered, at 450° for 10 minutes or until golden brown. **Yield:** 15 biscuits.

*Editor's Note: As a substitute for each cup of self-rising flour, place 1-1/2 teaspoons baking powder and 1/2 teaspoon salt in a measuring cup. Add all-purpose flour to measure 1 cup.

RAISIN BUTTERMILK COFFEE CAKE
(Pictured at right)

Lauren Heyn, Oak Creek, Wisconsin

Folks will be lining up in your kitchen while this coffee cake is baking—then they'll come back for more once they've tasted it!

 1 cup packed brown sugar
 1 cup chopped nuts
1/3 cup butter *or* margarine, melted
 2 tablespoons all-purpose flour
 4 teaspoons ground cinnamon
BATTER:
1/2 cup butter *or* margarine, softened
1-1/2 cups sugar
 2 eggs
 3 cups all-purpose flour
 4 teaspoons baking powder
1/2 teaspoon salt
 2 cups buttermilk
 1 cup raisins

In a bowl, combine the first five ingredients until mixture resembles coarse crumbs; set aside. In a mixing bowl, cream butter and sugar. Add eggs, one at a time, beating well after each addition. Combine the dry ingredients; add to creamed mixture alternately with buttermilk. Stir in raisins.

 Spread half of the batter into a greased 13-in. x 9-in. x 2-in. baking pan. Sprinkle with half of the crumb mixture. Carefully spread with remaining batter and sprinkle with remaining crumb mixture. Bake at 350° for 35-40 minutes or until a toothpick inserted near the center comes out clean. **Yield:** 12-15 servings.

CINNAMON RAISIN BREAD
(Pictured above right)

Deanna Patterson, Greenville, Texas

Tasty swirls of cinnamon and rich yeasty flavor make this recipe wonderful. The raisin-dotted bread is sure to rise to any occasion, whether you take it to a gathering, serve it for brunch or offer it as a snack to your family.

 1 package (1/4 ounce) active dry yeast
1/4 cup warm water (110° to 115°)
 2 cups warm milk (110° to 115°)
1/3 cup plus 1/2 cup sugar, *divided*
1/4 cup vegetable oil
 2 teaspoons salt
5-3/4 to 6-1/4 cups all-purpose flour
 2 cups raisins
 1 tablespoon ground cinnamon
 1 tablespoon water
GLAZE:
1/2 cup confectioners' sugar
 1 tablespoon milk

In a mixing bowl, dissolve yeast in warm water. Add milk, 1/3 cup sugar, oil, salt and 2 cups flour. Beat until smooth. Add raisins and enough remaining flour to form a soft dough. Turn onto a floured surface; knead until smooth and elastic, about 6-8 minutes. Place in a greased bowl, turning once to grease top. Cover and let rise in a warm place until doubled, about 1-1/4 hours.

 Punch dough down. On a lightly floured surface, divide in half. Roll each into a 15-in. x 7-in. rectangle. Combine cinnamon and remaining sugar; sprinkle over dough. Sprinkle with water. Starting with a short side, roll up tightly, jelly-roll style. Pinch seams and ends to seal. Place, seam side down, in two greased 9-in. x 5-in. x 3-in. loaf pans. Cover and let rise until doubled, about 1 hour. Bake at 350° for 30-35 minutes or until golden brown. Remove from pans to wire racks to cool completely. Combine glaze ingredients; drizzle over loaves. **Yield:** 2 loaves.

form a soft dough. Place in a greased bowl, turning once to grease top. Refrigerate for 6-8 hours or overnight.

Punch dough down. Turn onto a lightly floured surface. Divide in half; roll each into a 15-in. x 12-in. rectangle. Melt remaining butter; brush over dough. Combine filling ingredients; sprinkle over dough. Roll up, jelly-roll style, beginning with a long side; pinch seam to seal. Cut each roll into 15 slices; place cut side down in two greased 9-in. pie plates. Cover and let rise until doubled, about 45 minutes. Bake at 375° for 20-25 minutes or until golden brown. Combine glaze ingredients; drizzle over warm rolls. Cool in pans on wire racks. **Yield:** 2-1/2 dozen.

MANGO NUT BREAD

Jo Sherley, Kahului, Hawaii

We live on the slopes of Haleakala, where carrots, potatoes, cabbage, bananas, litchis and mangoes are grown. This is my favorite recipe using mangoes.

        2 cups all-purpose flour
  1-1/2 cups sugar
        1 teaspoon baking soda
      1/2 teaspoon salt
      1/2 teaspoon ground cinnamon
        3 eggs
      1/2 cup vegetable oil
        1 teaspoon vanilla extract
        2 cups chopped mangoes
      1/2 cup chopped dates
      1/2 cup chopped walnuts *or* macadamia nuts

In a large bowl, combine the first five ingredients. In another bowl, beat eggs, oil and vanilla. Stir into dry ingredients just until moistened. Fold in mangoes, dates and nuts (batter will be stiff). Spoon into two greased 8-in. x 4-in. x 2-in. loaf pans. Bake at 350° for 50-55 minutes or until a toothpick inserted near the center comes out clean. Cool for 10 minutes before removing from pans to wire racks. **Yield:** 2 loaves.

NO-KNEAD CITRUS ROLLS

(Pictured above)

Margaret Otley, Waverly, Nebraska

These flavorful homemade rolls can come fresh from the oven any morning. Besides the fact that they don't require kneading, the goodies are ideal to start preparing the night before and then bake for breakfast. You won't have to get up at the crack of dawn, either…but they will taste like you did!

      1/4 cup warm water (110° to 115°)
        2 packages (1/4 ounce *each*) active dry
          yeast
        7 tablespoons sugar, *divided*
        1 cup warm whipping cream (110° to
          115°)
        3 egg yolks, beaten
  3-1/2 to 4 cups all-purpose flour
        1 teaspoon salt
      3/4 cup cold butter *or* margarine, *divided*
FILLING:
      1/2 cup sugar
        2 tablespoons grated lemon peel
        2 tablespoons grated orange peel
GLAZE:
  1-1/3 cups confectioners' sugar
        2 tablespoons milk
        1 tablespoon lemon juice
        1 tablespoon orange juice

In a bowl, combine water, yeast and 1 tablespoon sugar. Let stand 5 minutes. Stir in cream and egg yolks; mix well. In another bowl, combine 3-1/2 cups flour, salt and remaining sugar; cut in 1/2 cup butter until crumbly. Add yeast mixture; stir just until moistened. Add enough remaining flour to

TANGERINE MUFFINS

Margaret Yerkes
New Port Richey, Florida

Here's a recipe that deliciously represents our state. I like to use tangerines fresh from the trees when making these muffins.

✓ **Uses less fat, sugar or salt. Includes Nutritional Analysis and Diabetic Exchanges.**

2 cups all-purpose flour
1/2 cup sugar
2 teaspoons baking powder
1 teaspoon baking soda
1/2 teaspoon salt
1 carton (8 ounces) fat-free vanilla yogurt
1/4 cup egg substitute
1/4 cup margarine, melted
2 tablespoons fat-free milk
1 cup diced peeled tangerine
1 tablespoon grated tangerine peel

In a bowl, combine the first five ingredients. In a small bowl, combine the yogurt, egg substitute, margarine and milk until smooth; stir into dry ingredients just until moistened. Stir in tangerine and peel. Fill greased or paper-lined muffin cups two-thirds full. Bake at 400° for 18-20 minutes or until a toothpick comes out clean. Cool for 5 minutes before removing from pan to a wire rack. **Yield:** 1 dozen.

Nutritional Analysis: One muffin equals 172 calories, 352 mg sodium, trace cholesterol, 30 gm carbohydrate, 4 gm protein, 4 gm fat, 1 gm fiber. **Diabetic Exchanges:** 1 starch, 1 fruit, 1 fat.

POTATO PAN ROLLS

Connie Storckman, Evanston, Wyoming

My family loves these tender rolls and requests them often for dinner. But I don't mind making them. The recipe calls for quick-rise yeast so I can prepare a batch in no time.

4-1/2 to 5 cups all-purpose flour
3 tablespoons sugar
2 packages (1/4 ounce *each*) quick-rise yeast
1-1/2 teaspoons salt
1-1/4 cups water
3 tablespoons butter *or* margarine
1/2 cup mashed potatoes (prepared without milk *or* butter)
Additional all-purpose flour

In a mixing bowl, combine 2 cups flour, sugar, yeast and salt. In a saucepan, heat water and butter to 120°-130°. Add to dry ingredients; beat until smooth. Stir in mashed potatoes and enough remaining flour to form a soft dough. Turn onto a floured surface; knead until smooth and elastic, about 6-8 minutes. Cover and let rest for 10 minutes.

Divide into 16 pieces. Shape each into a ball. Place in two greased 8-in. or 9-in. round baking pans. Cover and let rise in a warm place until dou-

bled, about 30 minutes. Sprinkle with additional flour. Bake at 400° for 18-22 minutes or until golden brown. Remove from pans to wire racks to cool. **Yield:** 16 rolls.

CARROT BANANA BREAD

(Pictured below)

Beulah Starkweather, Englewood, Florida

I received this from my mother-in-law, and it's become my favorite banana bread recipe. The carrots add a special touch.

1/3 cup vegetable oil
1 cup sugar
2 eggs
2 cups all-purpose flour
1 teaspoon baking soda
1/2 teaspoon salt
1/2 teaspoon ground cinnamon
1 cup mashed ripe bananas (2 to 3 medium)
1 cup grated carrots
1/2 cup chopped pecans

In a mixing bowl, combine oil and sugar. Add eggs; mix well. Combine flour, baking soda, salt and cinnamon; gradually add to the creamed mixture alternately with bananas. Stir in carrots and pecans. Transfer to a greased 9-in. x 5-in. x 3-in. loaf pan. Bake at 350° for 55-65 minutes or until a toothpick inserted near the center comes out clean. Cool for 10 minutes before removing from pan to a wire rack to cool completely. **Yield:** 1 loaf.

IN THE MOOD *for something sweet? These delicious cakes, cookies and bars are certain to satisfy.*

SWEET SENSATIONS. Clockwise from top left: Frosted Fudge Brownies (p. 100), Out-of-This-World Brownies (p. 99), Macaroon Brownies (p. 99) and Coconut Pecan Blondies (p. 101).

Cakes, Cookies & Bars

OUT-OF-THIS-WORLD BROWNIES
(Pictured at left)

Jeannette Haley, Council, Idaho

Every time there is a bake sale, I bake a batch of these fabulous brownies. Most everyone who tastes them says, "These are the best brownies I have ever eaten!"

> 1 cup butter (no substitutes), softened
> 2 cups sugar
> 4 eggs
> 2 teaspoons vanilla extract
> 2 cups all-purpose flour
> 1/4 cup plus 3 tablespoons baking cocoa
> 1/8 teaspoon salt

BROWN BUTTER FROSTING:
> 1/2 cup butter (no substitutes)
> 4 cups confectioners' sugar
> 1/4 cup plus 2 teaspoons half-and-half cream
> 2 teaspoons vanilla extract

GLAZE:
> 1 square (1 ounce) unsweetened chocolate
> 1 tablespoon butter (no substitutes)

In a mixing bowl, cream butter and sugar. Add the eggs, one at a time, beating well after each addition. Beat in vanilla. Combine flour, cocoa and salt; gradually add to the creamed mixture. Spread into an ungreased 13-in. x 9-in. x 2-in. baking pan. Bake at 350° for 25-30 minutes or until a toothpick inserted near the center comes out clean (do not overbake). Cool on wire rack.

For frosting, in a heavy saucepan, cook and stir butter over medium heat for 5-7 minutes or until golden brown. Pour into a mixing bowl; beat in the confectioners' sugar, cream and vanilla. Frost cooled brownies. For glaze, melt chocolate and butter; drizzle over the frosting. Cut into bars. **Yield:** 3 dozen.

MACAROON BROWNIES
(Pictured at left)

Christine Foust, Stoneboro, Pennsylvania

My mother-in-law made these coconut-filled brownies for my bridal shower and wedding reception.

> 1 cup butter *or* margarine, softened
> 2 cups sugar
> 4 eggs
> 1 teaspoon vanilla extract
> 2 cups all-purpose flour
> 1/2 cup baking cocoa
> 1/2 teaspoon cream of tartar
> 1/2 cup chopped walnuts

MACAROON FILLING:
> 1 package (14 ounces) flaked coconut
> 1 can (14 ounces) sweetened condensed milk
> 2 teaspoons vanilla extract

FROSTING:
> 3/4 cup sugar
> 1/4 cup milk
> 2 tablespoons butter *or* margarine
> 1 cup miniature marshmallows
> 1 cup (6 ounces) semisweet chocolate chips
> 1 teaspoon vanilla extract

In a mixing bowl, cream butter and sugar. Add eggs and vanilla; mix well. Combine flour, cocoa and cream of tartar; gradually add to creamed mixture. Stir in nuts. Spread half into a greased 13-in. x 9-in. x 2-in. baking pan. Combine coconut, condensed milk and vanilla; carefully spread over chocolate layer. Top with the remaining chocolate mixture. Bake at 350° for 40-45 minutes or until a toothpick inserted near the center comes out clean. Cool on a wire rack.

For frosting, combine sugar, milk and butter in a saucepan; cook and stir until sugar is dissolved. Add the remaining ingredients. Cook and stir until marshmallows and chips are melted. Cool until mixture reaches spreading consistency, about 25 minutes. Spread over the cooled brownies. Cut into bars. **Yield:** 4 dozen.

KEEPING COCOA
Store baking cocoa, sealed airtight, in a cool dark place for up to 2 years.

Bars Rate "The Best"

FROSTED Fudge Brownies came to Sue Soderlund of Elgin, Illinois special delivery.

"A neighbor gave our family a trayful, along with the recipe, when I brought our baby daughter home from the hospital," says Sue. "Laurie, now a teenager, still considers these brownies a favorite dessert, as do my husband, Ernie, and son, Eric.

"We celebrate special family occasions with them, plus they're a 'must' for church potlucks, school activities and work parties," she adds.

A batch of her rich made-from-scratch bars is memorable even without the frosting. "Laurie likes them just plain—or with a sprinkle of powdered sugar on top or a dollop of chocolate whipped topping," says Sue.

"Other times, we go all out and add nuts, chocolate bits or holiday candies. For an elegant twist, I spread cherry pie filling on top instead of frosting and add whipped cream and shaved chocolate for a Black Forest variation."

FROSTED FUDGE BROWNIES

(Pictured on page 98)

1 cup plus 3 tablespoons butter *or* margarine
3/4 cup baking cocoa
4 eggs
2 cups sugar
1-1/2 cups all-purpose flour
1 teaspoon baking powder
1 teaspoon salt
1 teaspoon vanilla extract
FROSTING:
6 tablespoons butter *or* margarine, softened
2-2/3 cups confectioners' sugar
1/2 cup baking cocoa
1 teaspoon vanilla extract
1/4 to 1/3 cup milk

In a saucepan, melt butter. Remove from the heat. Stir in cocoa; cool. In a mixing bowl, beat eggs and sugar. Combine flour, baking powder and salt; gradually add to egg mixture. Stir in vanilla and the cooled chocolate mixture; mix well. Spread into a greased 13-in. x 9-in. x 2-in. baking pan. Bake at 350° for 25-28 minutes or until a toothpick inserted near the center comes out clean (do not overbake). Cool on a wire rack.

For frosting, in a mixing bowl, cream butter, confectioners' sugar, cocoa and vanilla. Add enough milk until the frosting achieves spreading consistency. Spread over brownies. Cut into bars. **Yield:** 2 dozen.

CHOCOLATE MAPLE COOKIES

Sheree Gilpin, Lehighton, Pennsylvania

My aunt made these one year for Christmas, and my husband ate about a dozen. Since he liked them so much, I asked for the recipe and have made them often.

1-1/4 cups shortening
1-1/2 cups packed brown sugar
5 eggs
1 teaspoon vanilla extract
1/2 teaspoon maple flavoring
2-1/2 cups all-purpose flour
3/4 teaspoon baking soda
1/2 teaspoon salt
FROSTING:
2 squares (1 ounce *each*) semisweet chocolate
1 tablespoon butter (no substitutes)
1-1/2 cups confectioners' sugar
1/4 cup milk

In a mixing bowl, cream shortening and brown sugar. Add eggs, one at a time, beating well after each addition. Beat in vanilla and maple flavoring. Combine flour, baking soda and salt; gradually add to the creamed mixture. Drop by teaspoonfuls 2 in. apart onto greased baking sheets.

Bake at 350° for 8-10 minutes or until edges begin to brown. Remove to wire racks to cool. For frosting, melt chocolate and butter in a microwave or heavy saucepan. Add sugar and milk; mix well. Frost cooled cookies. **Yield:** 4 dozen.

OLD-FASHIONED RAISIN CAKE

Norma Poole, Auburndale, Florida

This is a wonderful cake for the holidays. It fills the house with a heavenly aroma when it's baking.

1 large navel orange, cut into 8 wedges
1 cup raisins

1/2 cup pecans
1/2 cup butter or margarine, softened
  1 cup sugar
  2 eggs
  1 teaspoon vanilla extract
  2 cups all-purpose flour
  1 teaspoon baking soda
1/2 teaspoon salt
2/3 cup buttermilk

GLAZE:
1/2 cup confectioners' sugar
  2 tablespoons orange juice

In a food processor, combine the orange, raisins and pecans. Cover and process until mixture is finely chopped; set aside. In a mixing bowl, cream butter and sugar. Beat in eggs and vanilla; mix well. Combine the flour, baking soda and salt; add to creamed mixture alternately with buttermilk. Stir in orange
floured 10-

Choc Maple Cookies -p 100 (handwritten)

til a tooth-
lean. Cool
In a small
l smooth;
ely before

crumbs (do not overbake). Cool on a wire rack. Cut into bars. **Yield:** 16 brownies.

DIES

as
at I've en-
ke for the

brown

d and

ose flour

oasted

  4 squares (1 ounce *each*) white baking
    chocolate, coarsely chopped

In a mixing bowl, beat egg and brown sugar for 3 minutes. Add butter and vanilla; mix well. Combine flour, baking soda and salt; gradually add to the brown sugar mixture, beating just until blended. Stir in pecans, coconut and white chocolate. Spread into a greased 8-in. square baking pan. Bake at 325° for 30-40 minutes or until a toothpick inserted near the center comes out with moist

LIME ANGEL FOOD CAKE
(Pictured above)

Nancy Foust, Stoneboro, Pennsylvania

It's fun to start with a purchased angel food cake and turn out a pretty and special dessert. A lovely lime cream frosting is the key to this creation.

  2 eggs
  2 egg yolks
1/2 cup plus 3 tablespoons sugar, *divided*
  6 tablespoons lime juice
  2 teaspoons grated lime peel
1/2 cup cold butter *or* margarine, cubed
  1 cup whipping cream
1/2 teaspoon vanilla extract
  1 prepared angel food cake (10 inches)
  1 cup flaked coconut, toasted

In the top of a double boiler, beat eggs and yolks. Stir in 1/2 cup of sugar, lime juice and peel. Cook over simmering water while gradually whisking in butter. Cook and stir until mixture is thickened and reaches 160°. Strain; refrigerate until completely cool. In a mixing bowl, beat cream and vanilla until stiff peaks form; gradually beat in remaining sugar. Gently fold into lime mixture.

Split cake horizontally into three layers. Place bottom layer on a serving plate. Spread with 2/3 cup lime mixture. Repeat. Place top layer on cake. Frost top and sides with remaining lime mixture. Sprinkle with coconut. Refrigerate for at least 30 minutes before slicing. **Yield:** 12 servings.

Rita Ross, Delta, Ohio

Even those watching their diet can indulge in these light but luscious brownies.

✓ **Uses less fat, sugar or salt. Includes Nutritional Analysis and Diabetic Exchanges.**

    3 egg whites
  3/4 cup 2% cottage cheese
    1 teaspoon vanilla extract
    1 cup sugar
  3/4 cup all-purpose flour
  1/2 teaspoon baking powder
  1/4 teaspoon salt
    3 squares (1 ounce *each*) unsweetened
      chocolate, melted and cooled
    2 teaspoons confectioners' sugar

Place egg whites, cottage cheese and vanilla in a blender or food processor; cover and process until smooth. Combine dry ingredients; add to cottage cheese mixture. Cover and process for 30 seconds. Add chocolate; cover and process just until blended, about 15 seconds. Spread into an 8-in. square baking pan coated with nonstick cooking spray. Bake at 350° for 20-25 minutes or until a toothpick inserted near the center comes out clean (do not overbake). Cool on a wire rack. Dust with confectioners' sugar. **Yield:** 16 brownies.

Nutritional Analysis: One brownie equals 110 calories, 98 mg sodium, 1 mg cholesterol, 19 gm carbohydrate, 3 gm protein, 3 gm fat. **Diabetic Exchanges:** 1 starch, 1/2 fat.

Lemon Cake Roll

(Pictured above)

Dorothy Earl, Lancaster, South Carolina

This cake roll recipe dates back quite a few years. My mother used to make it for me when I was a child, and I'm now in my 70s.

    3 eggs
    1 cup sugar
    3 tablespoons cold water
    1 cup all-purpose flour
    1 teaspoon baking powder
  1/4 teaspoon salt
FILLING:
    1 cup sugar
    3 tablespoons all-purpose flour
    1 egg, lightly beaten
  3/4 cup water
  1/4 cup lemon juice

In a mixing bowl, beat eggs and sugar until thick and smooth. Add water. Combine flour, baking powder and salt; stir into egg mixture just until moistened. Line a greased 15-in. x 10-in. x 1-in. baking pan with waxed paper; grease the paper. Spread batter evenly in pan. Bake at 375° for 12-14 minutes or until cake springs back when lightly touched in center. Cool cake in pan on a wire rack for 5 minutes. Turn cake out onto a kitchen towel. Gently peel off the waxed paper. Beginning with short side, roll up cake, jelly-roll style. Cool completely on a wire rack.

For filling, in a saucepan, combine sugar, flour, egg, water and lemon juice. Cook and stir over medium heat until mixture comes to a boil. Cook and stir 1 minute longer until thickened. Remove from the heat; cool to room temperature. Unroll cake; spread cooled filling to within 1 in. of edges. Roll up again. Cover and chill for 1-2 hours before serving. Store in the refrigerator. **Yield:** 10-12 servings.

Christmas Sandwich Cookies

Elizabeth Klager, St. Catharines, Ontario

My mother-in-law gave me the recipe for these melt-in-your-mouth Christmas cookies.

    1 cup butter (no substitutes), softened
  1/2 cup confectioners' sugar
    2 teaspoons milk
    2 cups all-purpose flour
  1/2 cup cornstarch
  1/8 teaspoon salt
FILLING:
    5 tablespoons raspberry jam
FROSTING:
  1/4 cup butter (no substitutes), softened
    1 cup confectioners' sugar
    1 teaspoon vanilla extract
Green food coloring
Red candied cherries and colored sprinkles

In a mixing bowl, cream butter, confectioners' sugar and milk. Combine flour, cornstarch and salt; add to the creamed mixture, beating just until dough forms a ball. On a lightly floured surface, knead 20 times. Roll out to 3/8-in. thickness. Cut with a 2-in. round cookie cutter. Place 1 in. apart on ungreased baking sheets.

Bake at 350° for 12-13 minutes or until edges are lightly browned. Remove to wire racks to cool. Spread raspberry jam over the bottom of half of the cookies; top with remaining cookies. For frosting, in a mixing bowl, cream butter, confectioners' sugar, vanilla and food coloring. Pipe frosting in tree shapes or other decorations on cookies.

Board's a Winner

IT'S OKAY TO PLAY with your food—when the treat is a cookie checkerboard, that is! So says Awynne Thurstenson of Siloam Springs, Arkansas.

"My husband and I annually join a group of friends to ring in the New Year by playing parlor games and munching on potluck desserts," she explains. "We always have a great time.

"One year, I created a tasty centerpiece for our evening of fun and games by alternating squares of brown- and red-tinted sugar cookie dough.

"This checkerboard takes a bit of time to assemble, but it's not tricky to combine all of the ingredients and put it all together."

The checkers are sweetly coated circles cut out from the same dough.

"I also lined up a set of 'dominoes' by simply adding mini chocolate chips to rectangular shortbread cookies," she reports. "And cubes of pound cake dipped in a white icing, then dotted with melted chocolate made delicious 'dice'."

Adds Awynne, "I decorated my table with playing cards and bingo cards...and laminated playing cards with clear contact paper to use as coasters."

Your gang won't be "board" if you're game to try this winning idea at your next gathering!

COOKIE CHECKERBOARD

3/4 cup butter (no substitutes), softened
3/4 cup sugar
1 egg
1 tablespoon milk
2 teaspoons vanilla extract
2 cups all-purpose flour
1-1/2 teaspoons baking powder
1/4 teaspoon salt
Red paste food coloring
2 squares (1 ounce *each*) semisweet chocolate

CHECKER GLAZE:
1 cup confectioners' sugar
5 to 6 teaspoons water
Red paste food coloring
1 cup (6 ounces) semisweet chocolate chips
1 tablespoon shortening

In a mixing bowl, cream butter and sugar. Beat in egg, milk and vanilla. Combine the flour, baking powder and salt; gradually add to creamed mixture. Divide dough in half. Add red food coloring to one portion; wrap in plastic wrap. Refrigerate for at least 1 hour or until easy to handle.

Melt chocolate in a microwave or heavy saucepan. Stir 1 tablespoon of the remaining dough into chocolate until well mixed. Stir chocolate mixture into remaining plain dough. Wrap and refrigerate for at least 1 hour or until easy to handle.

On a lightly floured surface, roll red dough to 1/4-in. thickness. Cut into 32 squares (1-1/4 in. each) and 12 circles (1-in. diameter); set aside. (Return dough to refrigerator as needed.) Repeat with brown dough. On a parchment- or foil-lined baking sheet, alternate red and brown squares to form a checkerboard with eight rows of eight squares. Gently press seams together. Place circles on baking sheet.

Bake at 350° for 12 minutes or until set. Carefully slide parchment with checkerboard onto a wire rack to cool. For glaze, combine the confectioners' sugar and enough water to achieve a thin glaze. Tint with food coloring. Dip 12 red cookies into red glaze; place on a waxed paper-lined baking sheet and refrigerate until set.

Melt the chocolate chips and shortening in a microwave or heavy saucepan, stirring frequently. Dip 12 brown cookies into chocolate mixture; place on a waxed paper-lined baking sheet and refrigerate until set. **Yield:** 1 checkerboard with 24 checkers.

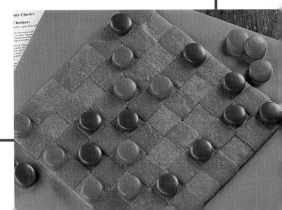

▰▰▰▰▰▰▰▰▰▰▰▰
CARAMEL CASHEW BROWNIES
(Pictured on page 107)

Judy High, Berryville, Arkansas

I always have my eye out for a good recipe, like the one for these marvelous golden brownies. It's hard to eat just one! They're a nice change of pace from the usual chocolate variety.

18 caramels
1/3 cup butter *or* margarine
2 tablespoons milk
3/4 cup sugar
2 eggs
1/2 teaspoon vanilla extract
1 cup all-purpose flour
1/2 teaspoon baking powder
1/4 teaspoon salt
1 cup chopped salted cashews

In a saucepan, cook and stir caramels, butter and milk over low heat until the caramels are melted and mixture is smooth. Remove from the heat; stir in sugar. Combine eggs and vanilla; stir into caramel mixture. Combine flour, baking powder and salt; stir into caramel mixture until blended. Fold in cashews.

Transfer to a greased 9-in. square baking pan. Bake at 350° for 24-28 minutes or until a toothpick inserted near the center comes out clean. Cool on a wire rack. Cut into bars. **Yield:** 25 brownies.

▰▰▰▰▰▰▰▰▰▰▰▰
GLAZED CHOCOLATE CHIP BROWNIES
(Pictured on page 106)

Dawn Berg, Budd Lake, New Jersey

Shortly after we married, my husband asked if I would bake up a pan of brownies for him to take to work. I said, "Sure—I have the best recipe." He liked to cook, too, and said he had the best recipe. To settle the matter, we each baked a batch and let his co-workers decide. My recipe won!

2/3 cup butter *or* margarine, melted
2 eggs, lightly beaten
1 teaspoon vanilla extract
2 cups sugar
1-1/3 cups all-purpose flour
3/4 cup baking cocoa
1/2 teaspoon baking soda
1/4 teaspoon salt
1/2 cup water
1 cup (6 ounces) semisweet chocolate chips

GLAZE:
3/4 cup semisweet chocolate chips
1/4 cup milk
2 tablespoons butter *or* margarine
1-1/4 cups confectioners' sugar
1 teaspoon vanilla extract

In a bowl, combine the butter, eggs and vanilla. Combine the sugar, flour, cocoa, baking soda and salt; add to the butter mixture and mix well. Stir in water and chocolate chips until combined. Pour into a greased 13-in. x 9-in. x 2-in. baking pan. Bake at 350° for 30-35 minutes or until brownies pull away from the sides of the pan. Cool on a wire rack.

In a saucepan, combine the chips, milk and butter until chips and butter are melted. Remove from the heat; whisk in the confectioners' sugar and vanilla until smooth. Cover and refrigerate until frosting is room temperature, about 20 minutes; frost brownies. Cut into bars. **Yield:** 4 dozen.

▰▰▰▰▰▰▰▰▰▰▰▰
FUDGY NUT BROWNIES
(Pictured on page 107)

Ruth Sparer Stern, Shadow Hills, California

I've prepared this special recipe for many an open house and potluck dinner. It came from an old roommate, who is now a grandmother. While in our early 20s, we never imagined we'd be sharing brownie recipes after all these years.

2-1/2 cups semisweet chocolate chips
1 cup butter *or* margarine
1 cup sugar
1/4 teaspoon salt
4 eggs, lightly beaten
2 teaspoons vanilla extract
3/4 cup all-purpose flour
1 cup coarsely chopped hazelnuts *or* almonds, toasted
TOPPING:
12 squares (1 ounce *each*) semisweet chocolate
1 tablespoon shortening
3 squares (1 ounce *each*) white baking chocolate

In a saucepan over low heat, melt the chocolate chips and butter; remove from the heat. Add the sugar and salt; stir until dissolved. Cool for 10 minutes. Stir in the eggs, vanilla, flour and nuts. Spread into a greased 15-in. x 10-in. x 1-in. baking pan.

Bake at 350° for 25-30 minutes or until a toothpick inserted near the center comes out with moist crumbs (do not overbake). Cool completely on a wire rack.

For topping, in a heavy saucepan or microwave, heat semisweet chocolate and shortening just until melted. Spread over brownies. Melt white chocolate. Pour into a small heavy-duty resealable plastic bag; cut a small hole in corner of bag. Pipe thin lines 1 in. apart widthwise. Beginning about 1 in. from a wide side, gently pull a toothpick through the lines to the opposite side. Wipe toothpick clean. Then pull toothpick through lines in opposite direction. Repeat over entire top at 1-in. intervals. Cut into bars. **Yield:** about 2-1/2 dozen.

MACADAMIA CHIP BROWNIES

(Pictured on page 106)

Lucile Cline, Wichita, Kansas

With two kinds of chocolate, plus the macadamia nuts, there's no need to frost these scrumptious bars! I like to make them for special occasions. I'm a retired home economist and love to bake for fun and relaxation. Often, I share goodies with friends and families at our local Ronald McDonald House.

> 1/3 cup butter *or* margarine
> 4 squares (1 ounce *each*) white baking chocolate
> 2 eggs
> 1 cup sugar
> 1 teaspoon vanilla extract
> 1 cup all-purpose flour
> 1/4 teaspoon salt
> 1/2 cup chopped macadamia nuts
> 1/2 cup milk chocolate chips

In a saucepan over low heat, melt butter and white chocolate; remove from the heat. In a bowl, combine the eggs, sugar and vanilla. Add the chocolate mixture, flour and salt; mix well. Stir in nuts and chocolate chips. Pour into a greased 9-in. square baking pan. Bake at 325° for 30-35 minutes or until top is lightly browned. Cool on a wire rack. Cut into bars. **Yield:** 1-1/2 dozen.

ALMOND COCONUT BROWNIES

(Pictured at right)

Wendy Wilkins, Prattville, Alabama

I combined a couple of my favorite brownie recipes and came up with this. My family has always enjoyed brownies, and this has become a special treat.

1-1/2 cups butter (no substitutes)

> 4 squares (1 ounce *each*) unsweetened chocolate
> 2-1/4 cups sugar
> 3 eggs, beaten
> 1 cup all-purpose flour
> 3/4 cup chopped slivered almonds
> 1 teaspoon vanilla extract

FILLING:

> 1 cup sugar
> 1 cup milk
> 24 large marshmallows
> 1 package (14 ounces) flaked coconut

TOPPING:

> 1 cup (6 ounces) semisweet chocolate chips
> 3/4 cup sugar
> 1/4 cup butter (no substitutes)
> 1/4 cup milk
> 1/4 cup chopped slivered almonds, toasted

In a saucepan over low heat, melt butter and chocolate; cool slightly. Add sugar. Stir in the eggs, flour, almonds and vanilla. Transfer to a greased 13-in. x 9-in. x 2-in. baking pan. Bake at 350° for 30 minutes or until a toothpick inserted in the center comes out clean. Cool on a wire rack.

In a large saucepan, combine filling ingredients; bring to a boil. Pour over cooled brownies. In another saucepan, combine chocolate chips, sugar, butter and milk; bring to a boil. Spoon over the filling. Sprinkle with almonds. Chill for 2 hours or until set. Cut into bars. Store in the refrigerator. **Yield:** 4 dozen.

FROM rich and chewy to nutty and gooey, this scrumptious spread of from-scratch brownies is oh-so-delicious!

BRAVO FOR BROWNIES. Clockwise from top right: Treasured Brownies (p. 108), Caramel Cashew Brownies (p. 104), Mint Brownie Cupcakes (p. 108), Fudgy Nut Brownies (p. 104), Glazed Chocolate Chip Brownies (p. 104), Macadamia Chip Brownies (p. 105), Mocha Truffle Brownies (p. 109) and Brownie Baked Alaska (p. 109).

TREASURED BROWNIES

(Pictured on page 107)

Marianne Wolfe, Westlock, Alberta

This terrific treat is included in a book of good-but-easy recipes my sister compiled as a wedding present for me. She refers to them as "money-back guarantee" brownies—they turn out 100% of the time.

    1 cup butter *or* margarine, melted and
      cooled
    3 eggs
1-1/2 teaspoons vanilla extract
    1 cup all-purpose flour
    1 cup sugar
    1 cup packed brown sugar
  3/4 cup baking cocoa
1-1/2 teaspoons baking powder
    1 cup chopped nuts
ICING:
  1/2 cup butter *or* margarine, softened
1-1/4 cups confectioners' sugar
  2/3 cup baking cocoa
    2 tablespoons milk
    2 tablespoons hot brewed coffee
    1 teaspoon vanilla extract

In a mixing bowl, combine butter, eggs and vanilla. Combine the dry ingredients; gradually add to butter mixture. Stir in nuts (do not overmix). Spread into a greased 13-in. x 9-in. x 2-in. baking pan. Bake at 350° for 25-30 minutes or until a toothpick inserted near the center comes out clean. Cool on a wire rack. Combine icing ingredients in a mixing bowl; beat until smooth. Spread over cooled brownies. Cut into bars. **Yield:** 1-1/2 dozen.

APPLE SNACK CAKE

(Pictured below)

Sue Harlow, Manchester, New Hampshire

Our state has many outstanding apple orchards. I've tried many apple recipes, and this is one of my favorites. It's great for company.

    3 eggs
2-1/4 cups sugar
    1 can (5 ounces) evaporated milk
    1 tablespoon vanilla extract
2-1/4 cups all-purpose flour
    1 tablespoon ground cinnamon
2-1/4 teaspoons baking powder
  1/2 teaspoon salt
    2 medium tart apples, peeled and thinly
      sliced
1-1/2 cups chopped walnuts
Whipped topping, optional

In a mixing bowl, combine the eggs, sugar, milk and vanilla. Combine the flour, cinnamon, baking powder and salt; add to egg mixture and mix well. Stir in the apples and walnuts. Transfer to a greased 13-in. x 9-in. x 2-in. baking pan. Bake at 350° for 40-45 minutes or until a toothpick inserted near the center comes out clean. Cool on wire rack. Cut into squares. Serve with whipped topping if desired. **Yield:** 16-20 servings.

MINT BROWNIE CUPCAKES

(Pictured on page 107)

Carol Maertz, Spruce Grove, Alberta

"Are they a brownie or are they a cupcake?" There's no wrong answer to this question, I tell my first-grade students. I found the recipe when I began teaching over 20 years ago.

    1 cup mint chocolate chips*
  1/2 cup butter *or* margarine
  1/2 cup sugar
    2 eggs
  1/2 cup all-purpose flour
    1 teaspoon baking powder
TOPPING:
    4 cups miniature marshmallows
  3/4 cup milk
1-1/2 teaspoons peppermint extract
Green *or* red food coloring, optional
1-1/2 cups whipping cream, whipped
Additional chocolate chips, optional

In a heavy saucepan, melt chips and butter; stir until smooth. Remove from the heat. Stir in sugar and eggs. Combine flour and baking powder; gradually stir into chocolate mixture until smooth. Fill paper-lined muffin cups half full. Bake at 350° for 15-20 minutes or until a toothpick comes out clean (cupcakes will fall in center). Remove to a wire rack.

In a saucepan, cook and stir marshmallows and milk over low heat until smooth. Remove from the heat; stir in extract and food coloring if desired. Cover and refrigerate until cool, about 15 minutes. Fold in whipped cream. Spread over cupcakes or top each with a dollop of topping. Chill for at least 1 hour. Sprinkle with chocolate chips if desired. Store in the refrigerator. **Yield:** 16 cupcakes.

*Editor's Note: If mint chocolate chips are not available, substitute semisweet chocolate chips and add 1/4 teaspoon peppermint extract.

▰▰▰▰▰▰▰▰▰▰▰▰▰

MOCHA TRUFFLE BROWNIES

(Pictured on page 106)

Margaret Roberts, Kuna, Idaho

My husband is a chocolate lover, so I bake brownies about once a week. This mouth-watering variety is one of his favorites and so simple to make.

1-1/4 cups semisweet chocolate chips
1/2 cup butter *or* margarine
1 teaspoon instant coffee granules
2 tablespoons hot water
2 eggs
3/4 cup packed brown sugar
3/4 cup all-purpose flour
1/2 teaspoon baking powder
FILLING:
1 tablespoon instant coffee granules
1 tablespoon hot water
1 package (8 ounces) cream cheese, softened
1/3 cup confectioners' sugar
1 cup (6 ounces) semisweet chocolate chips, melted
GLAZE:
1/4 cup semisweet chocolate chips
1 teaspoon shortening

In a heavy saucepan or microwave, melt chips and butter. Stir until smooth; cool for 5 minutes. Dissolve coffee granules in hot water; set aside. In a mixing bowl, combine eggs and brown sugar; beat on medium for 1 minute. Stir in chocolate mixture and coffee. Combine flour and baking powder; gradually add to chocolate mixture. Transfer to a greased 9-in. square baking pan. Bake at 350° for 30-35 minutes or until a toothpick inserted near the center comes out with moist crumbs. Cool completely on a wire rack.

For filling, dissolve coffee granules in water; set aside. In a mixing bowl, beat cream cheese until smooth. Beat in confectioners' sugar, melted chocolate and coffee. Spread over brownies. For glaze, melt the chips and shortening; stir until smooth. Drizzle over filling. Refrigerate for at least 2 hours before cutting. **Yield:** about 6-1/2 dozen.

▰▰▰▰▰▰▰▰▰▰▰▰▰

BROWNIE BAKED ALASKA

(Pictured on page 106)

Carol Twardzik, Spy Hill, Saskatchewan

Kids of all ages are impressed when I slice into this sweet treat. No one can resist the combination of brownies and two kinds of ice cream with a light meringue topping. This cool and chocolaty dessert looks like I fussed, when really, it's pretty easy to put together.

2 squares (1 ounce *each*) unsweetened chocolate
1/2 cup shortening
1 cup sugar
1 teaspoon vanilla extract
2 eggs
3/4 cup all-purpose flour
1/2 teaspoon baking powder
1/2 teaspoon salt
1 cup chopped walnuts, optional
1 quart strawberry ice cream, slightly softened
1 quart vanilla ice cream, slightly softened
MERINGUE:
5 egg whites
1/2 teaspoon cream of tartar
2/3 cup sugar

In a large saucepan, melt chocolate and shortening; remove from the heat. Stir in sugar and vanilla. Add eggs, one at a time, beating well after each addition. Combine flour, baking powder and salt; stir into chocolate mixture. Add nuts if desired. Spread into a greased 8-in. round baking pan. Bake at 350° for 25-30 minutes or until a toothpick inserted near the center comes out with moist crumbs (do not overbake). Cool for 10 minutes before removing from pan to a wire rack to cool completely.

Meanwhile, line an 8-in. round bowl (1-1/2 qts.) with foil. Quickly spread strawberry ice cream over bottom and up sides of bowl, leaving center hollow; cover and freeze for 30 minutes. Pack vanilla ice cream into center; cover and freeze. To assemble, place the brownie base on a 10-in. ovenproof serving plate. Unmold ice cream onto brownie. Return to freezer while preparing meringue.

In a double boiler, beat eggs whites and cream of tartar with a portable mixer until soft peaks form. Beat in sugar, 1 tablespoon at a time, until stiff peaks form and meringue reaches 160°, about 5 minutes. Watch carefully. Quickly spread over ice cream and brownie. Return to freezer until ready to serve. Bake at 500° for 2-3 minutes or until meringue is lightly browned. Serve immediately. **Yield:** 12 servings.

Brownies In Brief

CRAVING something chocolaty? These yummy creations can be ready for mmm…munching in just a little over 30 minutes!

░░░░░░░░░░░░

MICROWAVE BROWNIES

(Pictured below)

Marie Peart, Hagersville, Ontario

When I need to make a treat on a moment's notice, this is the recipe I reach for. The brownies cook up quickly in the microwave.

     1 cup sugar
     2 eggs
     1 teaspoon vanilla extract
 1/2 teaspoon salt
 1/2 cup butter *or* margarine, melted
 3/4 cup all-purpose flour
 1/2 cup baking cocoa
     1 cup chopped walnuts

In a mixing bowl, beat sugar, eggs, vanilla and salt on medium speed for 1 minute. Add butter; beat until blended. Combine flour and cocoa. Gradually add to sugar mixture; mix well. Stir in walnuts. Transfer to a greased microwave-safe 8-in. square dish. Microwave, uncovered, on high for 5-6 minutes, rotating every 2 minutes or until a moist area about 1-1/4 in. in diameter remains in the center (when touched, brownie will cling to your finger while area underneath will be almost dry). Cool on a wire rack. Cut into bars. **Yield:** 9-12 brownies.

   Editor's Note: This recipe was tested in an 850-watt microwave.

░░░░░░░░░░░░

PEANUT BUTTER BROWNIES

Linda Wales, Millerton, Pennsylvania

A friend shared this peanutty brownie recipe with me when I was a teen, and I've been making them ever since. They're scrumptious!

 2/3 cup butter *or* margarine, softened
 2/3 cup peanut butter
     2 cups sugar
     2 teaspoons vanilla extract

4 eggs
1 cup all-purpose flour
2/3 cup baking cocoa
2 teaspoons baking powder

In a mixing bowl, cream butter, peanut butter, sugar and vanilla. Add eggs, one at a time, beating well after each addition. Combine flour, cocoa and baking powder; add to creamed mixture just until blended. Pour into a greased 13-in. x 9-in. x 2-in. baking pan. Bake at 350° for 22-28 minutes or until a toothpick inserted near the center comes out with moist crumbs (do not overbake). Cool on a wire rack. Cut into bars. **Yield:** about 2 dozen.

CASHEW BLONDIES

Kathey Skarie, Vergas, Minnesota

These easy-to-make white chocolate brownies are a hit at potlucks and other gatherings—I always come home with an empty plate and lots of compliments.

2 eggs
2/3 cup sugar
1 teaspoon vanilla extract
8 squares (1 ounce *each*) white baking chocolate, melted and cooled
1/3 cup butter *or* margarine, melted
1-1/2 cups all-purpose flour
1-1/2 teaspoons baking powder
1/4 teaspoon salt
1/2 to 1 cup chopped salted cashews *or* pecans

In a mixing bowl, beat eggs, sugar and vanilla on medium speed for 1 minute. Beat in chocolate and butter. Combine the flour, baking powder and salt; gradually add to chocolate mixture. Stir in cashews. Spread into a greased 9-in. square baking pan. Bake at 350° for 25-30 minutes or until a toothpick inserted near the center comes out clean. Cool on a wire rack. Cut into bars. **Yield:** 2 dozen.

PECAN BROWNIES

Karen Batchelor, Bellevue, Nebraska

It's hard to eat just one of these nutty treats…good thing a batch can bake up in a matter of minutes!

1/2 cup butter *or* margarine
2 squares (1 ounce *each*) unsweetened chocolate

1 cup sugar
2 eggs, lightly beaten
1 teaspoon vanilla extract
3/4 cup all-purpose flour
1/2 to 1 cup chopped pecans

In a saucepan over low heat, melt butter and chocolate. Stir in sugar; cool slightly. Add eggs and vanilla; mix well. Stir in flour and pecans. Spread into a greased 8-in. square baking pan. Bake at 350° for 15-20 minutes or until a toothpick inserted near the center comes out clean. Cool on a wire rack. Cut into bars. **Yield:** 16 brownies.

FAST FUDGY BROWNIES

Mary Sprick, New Haven, Missouri

The addition of baking soda and chocolate chips makes these brownies doubly delicious.

1 cup vegetable oil
4 eggs
1 teaspoon vanilla extract
2 cups sugar
1-1/3 cups all-purpose flour
1/2 cup baking cocoa
1 teaspoon salt
1 cup (6 ounces) semisweet chocolate chips
1/2 cup chopped maraschino cherries *or* nuts, optional

In a mixing bowl, beat oil, eggs and vanilla on medium speed for 1 minute. Combine the sugar, flour, cocoa and salt; add to egg mixture just until blended. Stir in chocolate chips and cherries if desired. Pour into a greased 13-in. x 9-in. x 2-in. baking pan. Bake at 350° for 30-35 minutes or until a toothpick inserted near the center comes out with moist crumbs (do not overbake). Cool on a wire rack. Cut into bars. **Yield:** 2 dozen.

CUTTING BROWNIES

To easily cut brownies without scratching your expensive baking pans, line the baking pan with foil, leaving 3 inches hanging over each end. Grease foil if the recipe instructs. After the baked brownies have cooled, use the foil to lift them out. Cut into bars and discard the foil.

CHOCOLATE COOKIE TORTE
(Pictured above)

Irene Bigler, New Cumberland, Pennsylvania

This recipe has been used many times in our family for get-togethers. It's easy to make and beautiful when served.

> 1/2 cup butter *or* margarine, softened
> 1 cup sugar
> 1 egg
> 1 egg yolk
> 1/2 teaspoon vanilla extract
> 2 cups all-purpose flour
> 1 teaspoon baking powder
> 1/2 teaspoon salt

Additional sugar
FROSTING:

> 2 cups (12 ounces) semisweet chocolate chips
> 1/2 cup half-and-half cream
> 2 cups whipping cream, whipped
> 2 teaspoons vanilla extract

Chocolate sprinkles

In a mixing bowl, cream butter and sugar. Beat in the egg, yolk and vanilla. Combine flour, baking powder and salt; gradually add to the creamed mixture and mix well. Form into a long log; cut into eight equal pieces. Shape each into a ball; wrap in plastic wrap. Refrigerate for 1 hour.

Roll balls in additional sugar; place between two sheets of waxed paper. Roll each into a 6-in. circle. Remove top sheet of waxed paper; flip the circles onto ungreased baking sheets. Remove waxed paper; prick dough with a fork. Bake at 350° for 10-12 minutes or until lightly browned. Carefully loosen cookies and cool on paper towels.

For frosting, melt chocolate chips with half-and-half in a heavy saucepan, stirring occasionally. Cool. Combine whipped cream and vanilla; fold into chocolate mixture. Layer cookies, spreading

1/4 cup frosting between each layer. Spread remaining frosting over sides and top. Decorate with chocolate sprinkles. Refrigerate overnight before cutting. **Yield:** 8-10 servings.

OLD-FASHIONED RAISIN COOKIES

Darlene Markel, Stayton, Oregon

My mother has been making these morsels for the past 40 years, much to the delight of all in our family.

> 1/2 cup sugar
> 1-1/2 teaspoons cornstarch
> 1/4 teaspoon ground cinnamon
> 1 cup chopped dates
> 1/2 cup raisins
> 1/2 cup water

DOUGH:

> 1 cup butter (no substitutes), softened
> 2 cups sugar
> 3 eggs
> 1 teaspoon vanilla extract
> 4 cups all-purpose flour
> 1/2 teaspoon salt

In a saucepan, combine the first six ingredients. Cook and stir over medium heat until thickened and bubbly. Cool. In a mixing bowl, cream butter and sugar. Add eggs, one at a time, beating well after each addition. Beat in vanilla. Combine flour and salt; gradually add to the creamed mixture. Cover and refrigerate for 2-3 hours or until easy to handle.

On a lightly floured surface, roll half of the dough to 1/8-in. thickness. Cut with a 2-in. round cookie cutter. Place 1 in. apart on ungreased baking sheets. Place 1 teaspoon of raisin filling in the center of each cookie. Roll out remaining dough. Cut with a 2-in. cookie cutter. With a 1-in. round cookie cutter, cut a hole in the center of each; place over filling. With a fork, press edges to seal. Bake at 400° for 10-12 minutes or until edges begin to brown. **Yield:** about 4 dozen.

POTLUCK CHOCOLATE CAKE

Ann Shorey, Sutherlin, Oregon

This rich cake with fudgy icing and a sprinkling of nuts is a proven potluck winner. It's often the most anticipated part of the meal.

> 1 cup butter *or* margarine
> 1 cup water

1/4 cup baking cocoa
2 cups all-purpose flour
2 cups sugar
1/2 teaspoon salt
1/2 cup sour cream
2 eggs
1 teaspoon baking soda

FROSTING:
1/2 cup butter *or* margarine, softened
3-3/4 cups confectioners' sugar
1/4 cup baking cocoa
1 teaspoon vanilla extract
6 to 7 tablespoons milk
1/2 cup chopped walnuts *or* pecans, toasted

In a saucepan, bring butter, water and cocoa to a boil; whisk until smooth. Cool to room temperature. In a mixing bowl, combine flour, sugar and salt. Add cocoa mixture; beat on low speed just until combined. Add sour cream, eggs and baking soda; blend until smooth. Pour into a greased 13-in. x 9-in. x 2-in. baking pan. Bake at 350° for 35-40 minutes or until a toothpick comes out clean. Cool on a wire rack.

For frosting, in a mixing bowl, cream butter. Combine the confectioners' sugar and cocoa; gradually add to butter. Beat in the vanilla and enough milk to achieve spreading consistency. Frost the cake. Sprinkle with nuts. Refrigerate until serving. **Yield:** 12-16 servings.

Brownies Hit the Spot

ON THE SPOT about what to serve for dessert? You needn't be. Just bake up a batch of Holstein Brownies!

"Everyone loves my cow treats," says Jodie Rush from her home in rural Perkins, Oklahoma. "Our grandson's the one who named them. When I first made a batch, he said, 'Oh, look—black and white brownies. They must be Holsteins!' "

To make her fudgy bars resemble that breed, Jodie tops them with rich marshmallow creme and splotches of chocolate glaze.

Mooved to make some for your clan? Jodie's generously shared her recipe here. But if you do stir up a batch, get set for a stampede of requests for more!

HOLSTEIN BROWNIES

2/3 cup butter *or* margarine, softened
2 cups sugar
1/2 cup water
2 eggs

2 teaspoons vanilla extract
1-1/2 cups all-purpose flour
3/4 cup baking cocoa
1/2 teaspoon baking soda
1/4 teaspoon salt
2 cups (12 ounces) semisweet chocolate chips
1/2 cup chopped pecans
1 jar (7 ounces) marshmallow creme

GLAZE:
3/4 cup confectioners' sugar
2 tablespoons baking cocoa
2 tablespoons butter *or* margarine, melted
2 tablespoons milk

In a mixing bowl, cream butter and sugar. Add water, eggs and vanilla; mix well. Combine the dry ingredients; gradually add to creamed mixture. Stir in chocolate chips and pecans. Spread into a greased 13-in. x 9-in. x 2-in. baking pan. Bake at 350° for 35-40 minutes or until a toothpick inserted near the center comes out clean. Cool on a wire rack for 5-10 minutes.

Place marshmallow creme in a microwave-safe bowl. Microwave on high for 20-30 seconds or until warm; spread over warm brownies. Cool completely on a wire rack. For glaze, combine confectioners' sugar, cocoa and butter in a small bowl; stir in enough milk to achieve drizzling consistency. With the tip of a spoon, use glaze to form irregular shapes resembling Holstein spots. Cut into bars. **Yield:** 3 dozen.

Editor's Note: This recipe was tested in an 850-watt microwave.

HOLIDAY BROWNIES

(Pictured below)

Erna Madsen, Bothell, Washington

Folks always ask for this recipe whenever I make these brownies. I make batches and batches of this tasty treat before the holidays and give them as gifts.

    1/2 cup butter (no substitutes)
      4 squares (1 ounce *each*) unsweetened
          chocolate
      2 cups sugar
 1-1/4 cups all-purpose flour
      2 teaspoons ground cinnamon
    1/2 teaspoon salt
      4 eggs, beaten
      1 teaspoon vanilla extract
 1-1/2 cups halved red *and/or* green candied
          cherries, *divided*
      1 cup chopped walnuts

In a heavy saucepan, melt butter and chocolate over low heat. Cool for 10 minutes. In a bowl, combine the sugar, flour, cinnamon and salt. Stir in the cooled chocolate mixture, eggs and vanilla until smooth. Fold in 1-1/4 cups cherries and the walnuts. Transfer to a greased 13-in. x 9-in. x 2-in. baking pan. Arrange remaining cherries over top. Bake at 350° for 35 minutes or until a toothpick inserted near the center comes out clean. Cool on a wire rack. Cut into bars. **Yield:** 2 dozen.

CHEWY OATMEAL COOKIES

Olga Austin, Lodi, New Jersey

With just a few simple ingredients from the pantry, you can whip up a batch of these sweet morsels in no time! It's such a yummy recipe. Not only is it easy, it makes dozens without much fuss.

      3 cups butter *or* margarine, softened
      3 cups packed brown sugar
      3 cups all-purpose flour
      1 tablespoon baking soda
      6 cups quick-cooking oats
    1/2 cup sugar

In a large mixing bowl, cream butter and brown sugar. Combine flour and baking soda; gradually add to creamed mixture. Transfer to a large bowl; knead in oats. Shape into 1-1/2-in. balls, then roll in sugar. Place 2 in. apart on ungreased baking sheets. Flatten with a glass. Bake at 350° for 10-12 minutes or until golden brown. Remove to wire racks to cool. **Yield:** about 8 dozen.

ORANGE DATE POUND CAKE

Ruth Bartz, Suring, Wisconsin

Loaded with chewy dates and crunchy pecans, this cake is a "must" to take to family gatherings. The sweet and zesty orange sauce tops it off just right. This cake slices nicely and looks so appetizing served on a pretty plate.

      1 cup butter *or* margarine, softened
      3 cups sugar, *divided*
      4 eggs
      1 tablespoon orange peel, *divided*
      3 cups all-purpose flour
      1 teaspoon baking soda
 1-1/3 cups buttermilk
      1 pound chopped dates
      1 cup coarsely chopped pecans
    1/2 cup orange juice

In a mixing bowl, cream butter and 2 cups sugar. Add the eggs, one at a time, beating well after each addition. Add 2 teaspoons orange peel. Combine flour and baking soda; add to the creamed mixture alternately with buttermilk. Stir in dates and pecans. Pour into a greased and floured 10-in. tube pan; spread evenly.

Bake at 325° for 70-75 minutes or until a toothpick inserted near the center comes out clean. Combine the orange juice and remaining sugar and orange peel; pour over cake. Cool for 30 minutes before removing from pan to a wire rack to cool completely. **Yield:** 12-16 servings.

Brownie Basics

• When traveling, I place pans of brownies in 1-gallon resealable plastic bags. The bags keep them moist and can then be used for other things when the brownies are gone. —*Jo Ann Ford*
Hamlin, Texas

• To "dress up" brownies in a hurry, place a pretty doily or a stencil cut from thin cardboard on top of the brownies, then sprinkle with confectioners' sugar. —*Edwinna Burch*
New Philadelphia, Ohio

• If your recipe calls for caramels, they'll be much easier to unwrap if they are placed in the freezer for an hour or so first. —*Marg Kerr*
Edmonton, Alberta

• For an attractive treat, drizzle a dessert plate with raspberry sauce... then top with a brownie and dust with confectioners' sugar.
—*Brandy Ashcraft*
Silver Star, Montana

• Make an easy rocky road frosting by stirring 1 cup of miniature marshmallows and nuts into your favorite chocolate frosting when it is just slightly warm. —*Debbi Sherer*
Spanaway, Washington

• When your favorite brownie recipe calls for chocolate chips or nuts to be stirred into the batter or sprinkled over the top before baking, try using other flavored chips or varying the nuts for a different taste.
—*Kim Northenscold*
Maple Lake, Minnesota

• To make fudge-like brownies from a mix, stir batter with a wooden spoon. For cake-like brownies, use an electric mixer. —*Cindy Deal*
Cayuga, New York

• For kids who don't care for nuts, try adding crisp rice cereal to chocolate frosting instead. —*Karen Nerud*
New Prague, Minnesota

• Looking for a refreshing summer treat? Spread cooled brownies with a half gallon of softened ice cream. Cover and return pan to freezer until serving. Cut into squares and top with your favorite ice cream topping if desired.
—*Darlene Bares*
Youngsville, Louisiana

• To keep thick brownie dough from sticking to your fingers as you press it into the pan, butter your fingers first.
—*Holly Hutchison*
Las Vegas, Nevada

• To make an instant glaze, simply sprinkle chocolate chips over the brownies when they come out of the oven. Cover with a baking sheet. Let stand for 3 minutes or until the chips are glossy, then spread with a metal spatula. —*Kay Henriksen*
Sioux Falls, South Dakota

• Topping brownie batter with seasonal colored M&M's (red and green for Christmas, pastels for Easter, etc.) is a simple way to make your brownies special for holidays throughout the year. —*Marce Kern*
Brookfield, Wisconsin

WHETHER your family prefers pie, cobbler, ice cream or something else for dessert, you'll find plenty here to suit their tastes.

TAKE YOUR PICK. From top: Peach Ice Cream (p. 117), Apricot Peach Cobbler (p. 118) and Golden Peach Pie (p. 117).

Pies & Desserts

GOLDEN PEACH PIE

(Pictured at left)

Shirley Olson, Polson, Montana

I entered this beautiful lattice-top pie in the Park County Fair in Livingston. It won a first-place blue ribbon plus a purple ribbon for "Best All Around"! My large family and many friends agree with the judges that it's very delicious.

    Pastry for double-crust pie (9 inches)
    1 cup sugar
    1/4 cup cornstarch
    1/4 teaspoon ground nutmeg
    1/8 teaspoon salt
    2 teaspoons lemon juice
    1/2 teaspoon grated orange peel
    1/8 teaspoon almond extract
    5 cups sliced peeled fresh peaches (about
       5 medium)
    2 tablespoons butter *or* margarine
    Milk

Line a 9-in. pie plate with bottom pastry; trim even with edge of plate. Set aside. In a bowl, combine sugar, cornstarch, nutmeg and salt; stir in lemon juice, orange peel and extract. Add the peaches; toss gently. Pour into crust; dot with butter. Roll out remaining pastry to make a lattice crust or to fit top of pie; make decorative cutouts in pastry. Set cutouts aside.

Place top crust over filling. Trim, seal and flute edges. Brush pastry and cutouts with milk; place cutouts on top of pie. Cover the edges loosely with foil. Bake at 400° for 40 minutes. Remove foil; bake 10-15 minutes longer or until crust is golden brown and filling is bubbly. Cool on a wire rack. **Yield:** 6-8 servings.

PEACH ICE CREAM

(Pictured at left)

Lisa Tenbarge, Haubstadt, Indiana

Adding peaches to a mouth-watering vanilla ice cream recipe I got from my mother-in-law resulted in this fabulous flavor. My boys say it's the greatest.

    1 cup sugar
    1 cup milk
    1 egg, beaten
    3-1/3 cups whipping cream
    1/4 cup instant vanilla pudding mix
    1-1/2 cups finely chopped fresh *or* frozen
       peaches, thawed
    2 teaspoons vanilla extract

In a saucepan, combine sugar, milk and egg. Cook and stir over medium heat until the mixture reaches 160° or is thick enough to coat a metal spoon. Remove from the heat. Cover and refrigerate several hours or overnight. When ready to freeze, stir in the cream, pudding mix, peaches and vanilla. Pour into the cylinder of an ice cream freezer. Freeze according to manufacturer's directions. Allow to ripen in ice cream freezer or firm up in refrigerator freezer for 2-4 hours before serving. **Yield:** 1-1/4 quarts.

Editor's Note: This recipe may need to be frozen in batches.

APPLE RHUBARB CRUMBLE

Liz Bachilas, Shelburne, Vermont

Here in Vermont, we enjoy a bounty of rhubarb, apples and maple syrup. These ingredients inspired me to create this dessert.

    3 cups chopped fresh *or* frozen rhubarb
    2 medium tart apples, peeled and chopped
    1 egg
    3/4 cup sugar
    1/4 cup maple syrup
    1/4 to 1/2 teaspoon ground nutmeg
    1/4 teaspoon ground cinnamon
    1 cup all-purpose flour
    1/2 cup packed brown sugar
    Pinch salt
    1/2 cup cold butter *or* margarine

In a bowl, combine the rhubarb, apples, egg, sugar, syrup, nutmeg and cinnamon. Pour into a greased 2-qt. baking dish. In another bowl, combine the flour, brown sugar and salt. Cut in butter until the mixture resembles coarse crumbs; sprinkle over fruit mixture. Bake at 350° for 45-55 minutes or until bubbly. **Yield:** 4-6 servings.

NORTHERN CHERRY PUFFS
(Pictured above)

Barbara Hanmer, Benzonia, Michigan

Michigan is the top cherry-producing state in the country. This is one of my family's favorite cherry recipes.

> 1 cup fresh *or* frozen pitted dark sweet cherries, thawed and drained
> 1 tablespoon lemon juice
> 1-1/2 teaspoons almond extract, *divided*
> 1/4 teaspoon red food coloring, optional
> 1/3 cup shortening
> 2/3 cup sugar
> 1 egg
> 1 cup all-purpose flour
> 1/2 teaspoon salt
> 1/2 teaspoon baking powder
> 1/3 cup milk

SAUCE:
> 1/2 cup sugar
> 4-1/2 teaspoons cornstarch
> 1/4 cup water
> 2 cups fresh *or* frozen pitted dark sweet cherries
> 1/4 teaspoon red food coloring, optional
> Whipped cream *or* ice cream

In a bowl, combine cherries, lemon juice, 1/2 teaspoon extract and food coloring if desired; toss to coat. Spoon into four greased 10-oz. custard cups. In a mixing bowl, cream shortening and sugar. Beat in egg and remaining extract. Combine flour, salt and baking powder; add to the creamed mixture alternately with milk. Spoon over cherry mixture. Bake at 375° for 20-25 minutes or until golden brown. Cool in cups for 10 minutes.

Meanwhile, in a saucepan, combine sugar and cornstarch. Stir in water, cherries and food coloring if desired until blended. Bring to a boil over medium heat; cook and stir for 2 minutes or until thickened. Invert puffs onto dessert plates; top with warm cherry sauce and whipped cream. **Yield:** 4 servings.

APRICOT PEACH COBBLER
(Pictured on page 116)

Tobi Breternitz, Bay Port, Michigan

Whenever I'm baking with apricots, I recall picking them fresh from my aunt's tree more than 25 years ago. They were so juicy and sweet! This comforting cobbler has a crumb topping that is super.

> 1 can (29 ounces) sliced peaches
> 1 can (15 ounces) apricot halves
> 1/2 cup sugar
> 2 tablespoons cornstarch
> 1/2 teaspoon ground cinnamon
> 1/4 teaspoon ground nutmeg
> 1 tablespoon butter *or* margarine

TOPPING:
> 1/2 cup all-purpose flour
> 1/2 cup sugar
> 3/4 teaspoon baking powder
> 1/4 teaspoon salt
> 1 egg
> 2 tablespoons butter *or* margarine, softened

HONEY CREAM:
> 1 cup whipping cream
> 2 tablespoons honey
> 1/2 teaspoon ground cinnamon

Drain peaches, reserving 1/2 cup syrup. Drain apricots, reserving 1/2 cup syrup. Cut apricots in half; set fruit aside. In a saucepan, combine sugar, cornstarch, cinnamon, nutmeg and reserved syrups until smooth. Bring to a boil; cook and stir for 2 minutes or until thickened. Remove from the heat; stir in butter until melted. Stir in peaches and apricots. Transfer to a greased 8-in. square baking dish.

For topping, combine the flour, sugar, baking powder and salt in a bowl. Add egg and butter; mix well. Spoon over fruit. Bake at 350° for 40-45 minutes or until golden brown. In a mixing bowl, beat cream, honey and cinnamon until stiff peaks form. Serve with warm cobbler. **Yield:** 6-8 servings.

PRETTY PLUM PARFAITS
(Pictured on front cover)

Norma Reynolds, York, Pennsylvania

With a plum tree in our backyard, I'm always eager to try new plum recipes. But none of them have beat this wonderful dessert! It's light and refreshing.

> 9 to 12 medium ripe red *or* purple plums (about 2 pounds), sliced

1/2 cup currant jelly
1/2 cup packed brown sugar
  1 orange peel strip (1 to 3 inches)
  1 cinnamon stick (3 inches)
  1 cup whipping cream
  1 tablespoon confectioners' sugar
1/2 teaspoon vanilla extract
Fancy cookies and additional whipped cream and
  plum slices, optional

In a heavy saucepan, combine plums, jelly, brown sugar, orange peel and cinnamon stick. Bring to a boil; reduce heat. Simmer, uncovered, for 10-15 minutes or until plums are tender, stirring occasionally. Remove from the heat; cool slightly. Discard orange peel and cinnamon stick; coarsely mash plums. Cover and refrigerate.

Just before serving, beat cream, confectioners' sugar and vanilla in a mixing bowl until stiff peaks form. Place about 1/4 cup plum mixture each in four chilled parfait glasses; top with 1/4 cup whipped cream. Repeat layers. Top with remaining plum mixture. Garnish with a cookie, dollop of whipped cream and plum slice if desired. **Yield:** 4 servings.

PECAN PUMPKIN DESSERT

Sue Williams, Mt. Holly, North Carolina

I always fix this dessert for Thanksgiving. The recipe was given to me by a friend, and I've shared it with many others over the years.

  2 cans (15 ounces *each*) solid-pack
    pumpkin
  1 can (12 ounces) evaporated milk
  1 cup sugar
  3 eggs
  1 teaspoon vanilla extract
  1 package (18-1/4 ounces) yellow cake
    mix
  1 cup butter *or* margarine, melted
1-1/2 cups chopped pecans
FROSTING:
  1 package (8 ounces) cream cheese,
    softened
1-1/2 cups confectioners' sugar
  1 teaspoon vanilla extract
  1 carton (12 ounces) frozen whipped
    topping, thawed

Line a 13-in. x 9-in. x 2-in. baking pan with waxed paper and coat the paper with nonstick cooking spray; set aside. In a mixing bowl, combine pumpkin, milk and sugar. Beat in eggs and vanilla. Pour into prepared pan. Sprinkle with dry cake mix and drizzle with butter. Sprinkle with

pecans. Bake at 350° for 1 hour or until golden brown. Cool completely in pan on a wire rack. Invert onto a large serving platter; carefully remove waxed paper. In a mixing bowl, beat cream cheese, confectioners' sugar and vanilla until smooth. Fold in whipped topping. Frost dessert. Store in the refrigerator. **Yield:** 16 servings.

COCONUT ICE CREAM
(Pictured below)

Tamra Kriedeman, Enderlin, North Dakota

This is a refreshing dessert that can cap off a warm summer evening. It has a nice coconut flavor without being too strong.

1-3/4 cups sugar
  1/2 teaspoon salt
    4 cups milk
1-1/2 cups flaked coconut, *divided*
    4 cups whipping cream
    1 tablespoon vanilla extract
Toasted flaked coconut, optional

In a saucepan, combine the sugar, salt and milk; cook and stir over medium heat just until mixture begins to boil. Stir in 1/2 cup coconut. Remove from the heat; let stand for 30 minutes. Strain, discarding coconut. Place milk mixture in a large bowl; add cream, vanilla and remaining coconut.

Freeze in an ice cream freezer according to manufacturer's directions. Transfer to a 2-qt. freezer container. Cover and freeze for at least 4 hours before serving. Garnish with toasted coconut if desired. **Yield:** 2 quarts.

pan. Let stand at room temperature for 30 minutes before cutting. If desired, pipe whipped topping around edges and dust with cocoa; garnish with berries and mint. Store in the refrigerator. **Yield:** 6-8 servings.

AUNT ROSE'S PEACH COBBLER

Lyllus McHargue, Monroe, Michigan

I like to serve this comforting cobbler warm from the oven with ice cream on top.

    2 cans (29 ounces *each*) sliced peaches,
      drained
    7 slices white bread, crusts removed
1-1/2 cups sugar
    2 tablespoons all-purpose flour
  1/2 cup butter *or* margarine, melted
    1 egg
TOPPING:
    1 tablespoon sugar
  1/4 teaspoon ground cinnamon
Vanilla ice cream

Place the peaches in a greased 11-in. x 7-in. x 2-in. baking dish. Cut each slice of bread into four strips; place over peaches. In a bowl, combine the sugar, flour, butter and egg; mix well. Spread over bread. Combine sugar and cinnamon; sprinkle over the top. Bake at 350° for 40-45 minutes or until golden brown. Serve warm with ice cream. **Yield:** 6-8 servings.

MOCHA CHEESECAKE

(Pictured above)

Jane Manges, Cameron Park, California

I've relied on this dessert many times when company comes calling, and it's never let me down. It's simple to make, which is a big plus.

1-1/4 cups confectioners' sugar
    1 cup all-purpose flour
  1/2 cup baking cocoa
  1/4 teaspoon baking soda
Dash salt
  1/2 cup butter *or* margarine, melted
FILLING:
    1 package (8 ounces) cream cheese,
      softened
    1 can (14 ounces) sweetened condensed
      milk
    2 eggs
    1 tablespoon hot water
    2 to 3 teaspoons instant coffee granules
**Whipped topping, baking cocoa, fresh
  raspberries and mint, optional**

In a bowl, combine the first five ingredients. Stir in butter. Press onto the bottom and 1 in. up the sides of a greased 9-in. springform pan. Bake at 350° for 12-15 minutes or until the edges are browned. In a mixing bowl, beat cream cheese and milk until smooth. Add eggs, beating on low speed, just until combined. In a small bowl, combine water and coffee granules; let stand for 1 minute. Add to the creamed mixture; beat just until mixed. Pour into crust.

Bake at 350° for 20 minutes or until center is almost set. Cool on a wire rack for 10 minutes. Carefully run a knife around edge of pan to loosen; cool 1 hour longer. Chill overnight. Remove sides of

---

GRANNY'S RHUBARB PIE

Blanche Baninski, Minto, North Dakota

This recipe originated with my grandmother, who baked many different rhubarb desserts. This was always a favorite of mine.

    3 cups all-purpose flour
1-1/2 teaspoons salt
    1 cup shortening
    5 tablespoons water
    1 egg
    1 teaspoon vinegar
FILLING:
    3 cups cut fresh *or* frozen rhubarb
      (1/2-inch pieces)
    2 cups sliced peeled tart apples
    1 can (8 ounces) crushed pineapple,
      drained
  1/4 cup honey
    1 tablespoon lemon juice
    1 cup sugar

3 tablespoons all-purpose flour
1 tablespoon butter *or* margarine

In a bowl, combine flour and salt; cut in shortening until the mixture resembles coarse crumbs. Combine the water, egg and vinegar; stir into flour mixture until a ball forms. Divide dough in half. Roll out one portion on a lightly floured surface; transfer to a 9-in. pie plate. Trim pastry even with edge. In a bowl, combine the rhubarb, apples, pineapple, honey and lemon juice. Combine sugar and flour; add to rhubarb mixture. Pour into crust. Dot with butter. Roll out remaining pastry to fit top of pie. Place over filling; trim, seal and flute edges. Cut slits in pastry. Bake at 350° for 1-1/4 hours or until the pastry is golden brown and the the apples are tender. **Yield:** 6-8 servings.

Dessert Reels In Raves

CASTING ABOUT for a fun new way to wrap up a meal? Give this fishy treat a try—it's sure to lure "mmm's" from every angle!

Fresh from Becky Vroon of Charlotte, North Carolina, the fish-shaped fruit pizza is a snap to make.

"The base is refrigerated cookie dough you roll out, shape into a fish and bake," she describes. Then simply spread on a layer of sweetened cream cheese and arrange fruit on top.

"I served it at a banquet," adds Becky. "The theme was tropical—and this sweet treat caught everyone's eye!"

Want to hook one for a get-together? Simply follow Becky's directions here.

Feel free to use your imagination to change the fish's dimensions. For instance, the body could be longer and skinnier, the fins larger or smaller, etc. You may find it's easier to shape the fish freehand, with no measurements at all. Have fun!

▪▪▪▪▪▪▪▪▪▪▪▪▪▪▪▪

FRUITED FISH

1 tube (18 ounces) refrigerated sugar cookie dough
2 packages (8 ounces *each*) cream cheese, softened
1/2 cup confectioners' sugar
1 teaspoon vanilla extract
1 pint fresh strawberries, sliced
3 kiwifruit, peeled, halved and sliced
1 can (15 ounces) mandarin oranges, drained
1/2 cup blueberries *or* halved red grapes

Cut dough into three pieces: 6-1/2 in., 2 in. and 1-1/2 in. long. On a greased baking sheet, pat or roll the 6-1/2-in. piece into an oval, about 1/3 in. thick, for fish's body. (See diagrams below for dimensions.) On a lightly floured surface, roll the 2-in. piece into a circle; cut in half. Position the half circles at end of body for tail; press to seal edges. Roll the remaining piece into a square; cut in half diagonally. Place the triangles above and below body for fins; press to seal edges. Bake at 350° for 13-15 minutes or until golden brown. Cool on the baking sheet for 5 minutes before carefully removing to a wire rack to cool completely.

In a mixing bowl, beat cream cheese, sugar and vanilla until fluffy. Transfer fish to a serving platter. With a sharp knife, cut out a small triangle for mouth. Spread cream cheese mixture over entire fish. Arrange fruit as shown in photo. Refrigerate until serving. **Yield:** 12 servings.

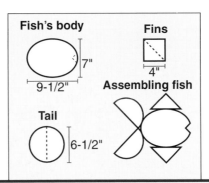

CANDY BAR PIE

(Pictured below)

Mary Ann Smith, Groton, New York

Here's a very rich and creamy pie that tastes terrific. A small sliver is all most folks can handle.

  5 Snickers candy bars (2.07 ounces
     each), cut into 1/4-inch pieces
  1 pastry shell (9 inches), baked
 12 ounces cream cheese, softened
1/2 cup sugar
  2 eggs
1/3 cup sour cream
1/3 cup peanut butter
2/3 cup semisweet chocolate chips
  2 tablespoons whipping cream

Place candy bar pieces in the pastry shell; set aside. In a mixing bowl, beat cream cheese and sugar until smooth. Add eggs, sour cream and peanut butter; beat on low speed just until combined. Pour into pastry shell. Bake at 325° for 35-40 minutes or until set. Cool on a wire rack. In a small heavy saucepan, melt chocolate chips with cream over low heat until smooth. Spread over filling. Refrigerate for 2 hours or overnight. Cut with a warm knife. **Yield:** 8-10 servings.

ORANGE PEACH PIE

Jeanette Zee, Darlington, Wisconsin

When our children still lived at home, I made this light and fruity pie for Sunday dinners. Slices were gobbled up in no time.

 Uses less fat, sugar or salt. Includes Nutritional Analysis and Diabetic Exchanges.

  3 tablespoons plus 1-1/2 teaspoons
     cornstarch
1/4 teaspoon salt
  1 cup water
Artificial sweetener equivalent to 1/2 cup
  sugar
  2 packages (.3 ounce *each*) sugar-free
     orange gelatin
  5 cups diced peeled fresh *or* frozen
     unsweetened peaches, thawed and
     drained
  1 reduced-fat graham cracker crust
     (8 inches)
  1 cup nonfat whipped topping

In a saucepan, combine the cornstarch, salt and water until smooth. Bring to a boil; cook and stir for 2 minutes or until thickened. Stir in sweetener and gelatin. Cool. Fold in peaches. Pour into the crust. Refrigerate for 2 hours or until serving. Garnish with whipped topping. **Yield:** 8 servings.

   Nutritional Analysis: One serving equals 189 calories, 285 mg sodium, 0 cholesterol, 36 gm carbohydrate, 3 gm protein, 4 gm fat, 2 gm fiber. **Diabetic Exchanges:** 1-1/2 starch, 1 fruit.

COCONUT CREAM MERINGUE PIE

Joyce Reece, Mena, Arkansas

Every fifth Sunday at our country church, we have a hymn sing and potluck dinner. I always bring this pie, and it goes fast. It's definitely a favorite.

  1 unbaked pastry shell (9 inches)
  6 tablespoons sugar
  5 tablespoons all-purpose flour
1/4 teaspoon salt
  2 cups milk
  3 egg yolks, lightly beaten
  2 teaspoons vanilla extract
  1 cup flaked coconut
MERINGUE:
  3 egg whites
1/4 teaspoon cream of tartar
  6 tablespoons sugar
1/2 cup flaked coconut

Line unpricked pastry shell with a double thickness of heavy-duty foil. Bake at 450° for 8 minutes. Remove foil; bake 5 minutes longer. Cool on a wire rack. Meanwhile, in a saucepan, combine the sugar, flour and salt. Gradually add milk. Cook and stir over medium-high heat until bubbly. Reduce heat; cook and stir for 2 minutes or until thickened. Remove from the heat. Stir a small amount of hot milk mixture into egg yolks; return all to the pan, stirring constantly. Bring to a gentle boil; cook and stir for 2 minutes. Remove from the heat; stir in vanilla and coconut. Pour into pastry shell.

For meringue, in a mixing bowl, beat egg whites and cream of tartar on medium speed until soft peaks form. Gradually beat in sugar, 1 tablespoon at a time, on high until stiff peaks form. Spread over hot filling, sealing edges to crust. Sprinkle with coconut. Bake at 350° for 12-15 minutes or until golden. Cool on a wire rack for 1 hour. Chill for 1-2 hours before serving. Store in the refrigerator. **Yield:** 6-8 servings.

HONEY FRUIT DESSERT

Deborah Bitz, Medicine Hat, Alberta

Fresh fruit gets even more flavor when it's baked and drizzled with honey. It makes a fantastic dessert.

> 2 medium ripe nectarines *or* peaches *or* 4
>   apricots, halved and pitted
> 4 plums, halved and pitted
> 2 tablespoons honey
> Vanilla ice cream
> 1/4 cup chopped cashews *or* peanuts,
>   optional

Line a 13-in. x 9-in. x 2-in. baking pan with foil; coat foil with nonstick cooking spray. Place fruit, cut side up, in pan. Bake, uncovered, at 425° for 18-20 minutes or until tender. Drizzle with honey; bake 2-3 minutes longer or until golden brown. Serve warm with ice cream and nuts if desired. **Yield:** 4-6 servings.

MARSHMALLOW CREAM WITH CUSTARD SAUCE

(Pictured above right)

Penny Klusman, Richmond, Indiana

This dessert has always been a favorite of my husband and children. The original recipe came from my great-grandmother and has been passed down through the generations. I'm sure I'll pass it on to my own kids someday, too.

> 2 egg whites
> 1/4 cup sugar
> Pinch salt
> 1/4 teaspoon vanilla extract
> CUSTARD SAUCE:
> 1-1/2 cups milk
> 2 egg yolks
> 1 egg
> 1/4 cup sugar
> 2 teaspoons vanilla extract
> Fresh raspberries

In the top of a double boiler over simmering water, combine the egg whites, sugar, salt and vanilla. Beat with a portable mixer on high speed until mixture reaches 160°. Beat until stiff peaks form, about 1 minute. Spoon into dessert glasses; refrigerate until chilled.

For the custard sauce, heat milk in a small saucepan over medium heat until small bubbles form around side of pan. Remove from the heat. Combine egg yolks, egg and sugar in a bowl. Stir a small amount of hot milk into egg mixture; return all to the pan, stirring constantly. Cook and stir on low until mixture reaches 160° and coats a spoon, about 20 minutes. Remove from the heat; stir in vanilla. Refrigerate for at least 1 hour. Serve custard over marshmallow cream; top with raspberries. **Yield:** 6 servings.

RASPBERRY MERINGUE PIE

(Pictured above)

Mrs. Anton Sohrwiede, McGraw, New York

We have raspberry bushes, so I'm always looking for recipes using this delicious fruit. This is one of our favorites.

- 1 cup all-purpose flour
- 1/3 cup sugar
- 1 teaspoon baking powder
- 1/4 teaspoon salt
- 2 tablespoons cold butter *or* margarine
- 1 egg, beaten
- 2 tablespoons milk

TOPPING:
- 2 egg whites
- 1/2 cup sugar
- 2 cups unsweetened raspberries

In a bowl, combine the flour, sugar, baking powder and salt; cut in butter. Combine egg and milk; stir into flour mixture (dough will be sticky). Press into the bottom and up the sides of a greased 9-in. pie plate; set aside. In a mixing bowl, beat egg whites on medium speed until soft peaks form. Gradually beat in sugar, 1 tablespoon at a time, until stiff peaks form. Fold in raspberries. Spoon over the crust. Bake at 350° for 30-35 minutes or until browned. Cool on a wire rack. Refrigerate leftovers. **Yield:** 6-8 servings.

OLD-FASHIONED CHESS PIE

Christine Batts, Murray, Kentucky

This recipe dates back many years and has certainly stood the test of time. It's very rich, so small servings might be in order.

- 1 cup butter (no substitutes), softened
- 2 cups sugar
- 6 egg yolks
- 1 egg
- 1/3 cup cornmeal
- 1/4 cup all-purpose flour
- 1/3 cup milk
- 1 teaspoon vanilla extract
- 1 unbaked deep-dish pastry shell (9 inches)

TOPPING:
- 2 cups sugar, *divided*
- 2/3 cup milk
- 1/2 cup butter (no substitutes)

In a mixing bowl, cream butter and sugar. Beat in egg yolks and egg. Add the cornmeal and flour; mix well. Beat in milk and vanilla (do not overbeat). Pour into the pastry shell. Bake at 325° for 55-65 minutes or until the filling is almost set. Cool on a wire rack.

In a heavy saucepan, heat 1/2 cup sugar over low heat without stirring until partially melted, about 5 minutes. Cook and stir with a metal spoon until syrup is completely melted and golden, about 5 minutes. Stir in milk, butter and remaining sugar (mixture will be lumpy). Cook over medium heat, stirring until a candy thermometer reads 234° (soft-ball stage). Remove from the heat. Pour into a mixing bowl without stirring. Cool, without stirring, to 190°. Beat on high speed until mixture turns light brown and creamy and a candy thermometer reads 130°-137°, about 5 minutes. Immediately spread over pie. Store in the refrigerator. **Yield:** 8-10 servings.

SOUR CREAM RAISIN PIE

Patricia Kile, Greentown, Pennsylvania

A hint of lemon gives extra zing to the creamy pudding-and-raisin filling in this homey dessert. Topped off with sweetened sour cream, it's sure to be a hit at your house.

- 1-3/4 cups water
- 1 cup raisins
- 1 package (3 ounces) cook-and-serve vanilla pudding mix
- 2 tablespoons sugar
- 1/4 teaspoon salt
- 1 tablespoon butter *or* margarine
- 2 teaspoons lemon juice
- 1 teaspoon grated lemon peel
- 1 pastry shell (9 inches), baked
- 1 cup (8 ounces) sour cream

1/4 cup confectioners' sugar
1/4 teaspoon ground nutmeg

In a saucepan, combine the first five ingredients. Cook and stir until mixture comes to a boil and is thickened and bubbly. Remove from the heat; stir in butter, lemon juice and peel. Cool for 5 minutes, stirring twice. Pour into pastry shell. Press a piece of plastic wrap or waxed paper on top of filling; refrigerate overnight. Remove waxed paper. In a bowl, combine the sour cream, confectioners' sugar and nutmeg. Spread over pie. Store in the refrigerator. **Yield:** 6-8 servings.

🔳🔳🔳🔳🔳

PEACH CAKE DESSERT

Virginia Slater, West Sunbury, Pennsylvania

You can name just about any fruit (except citrus), and it's grown here in northwestern Pennsylvania. This dessert is good served with whipped cream or ice cream.

    1 cup sugar
    1 tablespoon all-purpose flour
    1 to 2 teaspoons ground cinnamon
    5 medium fresh peaches, peeled and sliced
CAKE:
    1/4 cup butter *or* margarine, softened
    1/2 cup sugar
    1 egg
    1 cup all-purpose flour
    2 teaspoons baking powder
    1/4 teaspoon salt
    1/4 cup milk

In a bowl, combine sugar, flour and cinnamon. Add peaches and toss to coat. Transfer to a greased 8-in. square baking pan. In a mixing bowl, cream butter and sugar. Beat in egg. Combine flour, baking powder and salt; add to the creamed mixture alternately with milk. Drop by spoonfuls onto peaches; spread evenly. Bake at 350° for 40-45 minutes or until a toothpick inserted near the center comes out clean. Serve warm. **Yield:** 6 servings.

🔳🔳🔳🔳🔳

 ## MACAROON CHERRY PIE
(Pictured at right)

Lori Daniels, Beverly, West Virginia

I use homegrown cherries in this bountiful pie with its unique crunchy coconut topping. But I've found that purchased tart cherries yield a dessert that's nearly as

delicious. I always bake this pie around Presidents' Day or Valentine's Day, but it's popular with my family in any season.

Pastry for single-crust pie (9 inches)
    3 cans (14-1/2 ounces *each*) pitted tart cherries
    1 cup sugar
    1/3 cup cornstarch
    1/2 teaspoon ground cinnamon
    1/4 teaspoon red food coloring, optional
TOPPING:
    1 egg, lightly beaten
    2 tablespoons milk
    1 tablespoon butter *or* margarine, melted
    1/4 teaspoon almond extract
    1/4 cup sugar
    1/8 teaspoon salt
    1 cup flaked coconut
    1/2 cup sliced almonds

Line a 9-in. deep-dish pie plate with pastry. Trim to 1/2 in. beyond edge of plate; flute edges. Bake at 400° for 6 minutes; set aside. Drain cherries, reserving 1 cup juice. Set cherries aside. In a saucepan, combine sugar and cornstarch; gradually stir in cherry juice until blended. Bring to a boil over medium heat; cook and stir for 2 minutes or until thickened. Remove from the heat; stir in cinnamon and food coloring if desired. Gently fold in cherries. Pour into crust.

Cover edges loosely with foil. Bake at 400° for 20 minutes. Meanwhile, in a bowl, combine the first six topping ingredients. Stir in coconut and almonds. Remove foil from pie; spoon topping over pie. Bake at 350° for 20 minutes or until topping is lightly browned. Cool on a wire rack for 1 hour. Chill for 4 hours or overnight before cutting. **Yield:** 6-8 servings.

CHERRY BERRY PIE
(Pictured above)

Wanda Van Voorhis, Plain City, Ohio

Every time I bake this dessert a neighbor shared with me, folks rave about it. I'm always looking for new treats to serve my husband and daughter. This one's definitely a keeper.

- 1-1/2 cups sugar
- 1/4 cup plus 2 teaspoons quick-cooking tapioca
- 1/8 teaspoon salt
- 2-1/2 cups fresh *or* frozen pitted tart cherries, thawed
- 1-1/2 cups fresh *or* frozen unsweetened raspberries, thawed
- 1 teaspoon lemon juice
- Pastry for double-crust pie (9 inches)
- 1 tablespoon butter *or* margarine

In a bowl, combine sugar, tapioca and salt. Add the cherries, raspberries and lemon juice; toss gently. Let stand for 15 minutes. Line a 9-in. pie plate with bottom pastry. Trim to 1 in. beyond edge of pie plate. Pour filling into crust; dot with butter. Roll out remaining pastry; make a lattice crust. Trim, seal and flute high edges. Cover edges loosely with foil. Bake at 400° for 30 minutes. Remove foil; bake 5-10 minutes longer or until crust is golden brown and filling is bubbly. Cool on a wire rack. **Yield:** 6-8 servings.

HARVEST APPLE CHEESECAKE

Bonnie Jost, Manitowoc, Wisconsin

Slices of this creamy cake bring tempting fall taste plus delightfully different textures. The crust is on the tender side, since it absorbs the apple juice. Yet the fruit is slightly crunchy.

- 2-1/4 cups graham cracker crumbs (about 36 squares)
- 1/3 cup sugar
- 1/2 cup butter (no substitutes), melted

FILLING:

- 4 packages (8 ounces *each*) cream cheese, softened
- 1-1/4 cups sugar, *divided*
- 4 eggs
- 2 tablespoons lemon juice
- 4 teaspoons ground cinnamon, *divided*
- 1-1/2 teaspoons vanilla extract
- 3 cups thinly sliced peeled tart apples
- Red, green and yellow liquid food coloring

In a small bowl, combine cracker crumbs and sugar; stir in butter. Press onto the bottom and 1-1/2 in. up the sides of a greased 9-in. springform pan. Bake at 325° for 10 minutes. Cool on a wire rack. In a mixing bowl, beat cream cheese and 1 cup sugar until smooth. Add eggs; beat on low speed just until combined. Add the lemon juice, 3 teaspoons cinnamon and vanilla; beat just until blended. In a bowl, toss the apples with the remaining sugar and cinnamon. Arrange apples over crust. Place 1 teaspoon of cream cheese filling each in three bowls; tint one red, one green and one orange (mixing red and yellow). Spread remaining filling over apples. Place each color of filling in a separate pastry or plastic bag; cut a small hole in the corner of bag. Pipe one leaf of each color in the center of cheesecake.

Bake at 325° for 60-65 minutes or until center is almost set. Cool on a wire rack for 10 minutes. Carefully run a knife around the edge of the pan to loosen; cool 1 hour longer. Refrigerate overnight. Remove sides of pan. Let stand at room temperature for 30 minutes before cutting. Store in refrigerator. **Yield:** 12-16 servings.

Editor's Note: Even a tight-fitting springform pan may leak. To prevent drips, place the filled pan on a baking sheet in the oven.

Fruitful Tips

• When baking pies and cobblers with tart pie cherries, add a few drops of red food coloring to give your cherry filling a more vibrant look.
—*Sally Ferguson*
Jamestown, New York

• I've found that adding 1/4 teaspoon almond extract to peaches or cherries when cooking them enhances their natural flavor. —*Elsie Keith*
Trion, Georgia

• If your peaches need ripening, place them on trays or baking sheets with a little space in between them to let the air circulate. Then slide each tray into a brown paper bag and close it. Turn the fruit occasionally until ripened, removing any peach that shows signs of spoilage. Peaches ripen best at room temperature.
—*Margaret Johns*
Arva, Ontario

• When fruit is in season, I measure and freeze the amounts called for in my favorite recipes in plastic containers or freezer bags. Then I label each with the volume, date frozen and recipe title. —*Myrl Solum*
Rudyard, Montana

• When selecting fresh peaches and nectarines, choose those that have a fruity fragrance and are slightly soft when gently pressed near the stem end of the fruit. —*Jo Baker*
Litchfield, Illinois

• You can easily remove the pit from peaches and nectarines by cutting in half along the natural indentation of the fruit. Then twist the halves in the opposite direction and gently pull apart. When pitting plums, cut across the natural indentation, then twist apart. —*Pat Yaeger*
Naples, Florida

• I like to liven up the flavor of a traditional peach pie by adding some slices of fresh plums. —*Roni Dean*
Troy, Pennsylvania

• Folding drained and chopped maraschino cherries into angel food cake batter gives a colorful and flavorful change of pace. —*Shirley Robertson*
Versailles, Missouri

• I add chopped fresh peaches and lemon zest when making my favorite bread pudding. —*Cheryl Roger*
Ames, Iowa

Meals in Minutes

Set any of these hearty homemade meals on the dinner table—in less than 30 minutes!

Family-Pleasing Pork Chop Dinner Made Pronto

ONE OF the best "fast food" spots for miles around Baldwin, New York is Edith Ruth Muldoon's kitchen!

"With four generations of family who enjoy visiting me, I've developed a taste for fast-to-fix dinners," the amiable widow says. "Besides, easy recipes give me time to sit down and catch up with my children, grandkids and great-grandchildren."

The family favorites featured here consistently coax kudos from Edith Ruth's appreciative brood.

"Pork Chops with Herbed Cream Sauce is perfect for a spur-of-the-moment lunch or as a no-fuss entree for a special Sunday dinner," she affirms. "The meat cooks up moist and tender, and the bouillon lends instant flavor to the gravy.

"You won't waste a second making Pasta Veggie Medley," she adds. "Cook the pasta while you're sauteing the vegetables, and they'll be done at the same time."

Raspberry Cupcake Dessert is a hit with kids of all ages. "When I'm in a hurry, store-bought cupcakes work fine," Edith Ruth says. "And while I prefer homemade whipped cream, purchased whipped topping is an easy option."

PORK CHOPS WITH HERBED CREAM SAUCE

- 4 pork chops (1/2 inch thick)
- 2 tablespoons vegetable oil
- 1 tablespoon all-purpose flour
- 1/2 teaspoon beef bouillon granules
- 1 tablespoon minced fresh parsley
- 1/2 teaspoon dried basil, thyme *or* tarragon
- 2/3 cup milk *or* half-and-half cream

- 2 tablespoons water
- 1/8 to 1/4 teaspoon pepper

In a skillet, cook pork chops in oil until the juices run clear. Remove and keep warm; drain. Add flour, bouillon, parsley and basil to the skillet. Gradually stir in milk, water and pepper until smooth. Bring to a boil; cook and stir for 2 minutes or until thickened and bubbly. Spoon over chops. **Yield:** 4 servings.

PASTA VEGGIE MEDLEY

- 1 package (8 ounces) medium tube pasta
- 1 medium onion, chopped
- 2 tablespoons vegetable oil
- 2 small zucchini, julienned
- 2 medium carrots, julienned
- 2 tablespoons grated Parmesan cheese

Cook pasta according to package directions. Meanwhile, in a skillet, saute onion in oil until tender. Add zucchini and carrots; stir-fry until carrots are tender. Drain pasta; place in a serving bowl. Add vegetables and toss gently. Sprinkle with Parmesan cheese. **Yield:** 4-6 servings.

RASPBERRY CUPCAKE DESSERT

- 2 creamed-filled chocolate cupcakes,* cut in half
- 1 to 2 cups whipping cream
- 3 tablespoons confectioners' sugar
- 1/2 teaspoon vanilla extract
- 1 to 1-1/2 cups fresh *or* frozen raspberries, thawed and drained

Additional raspberries, optional

Place one cupcake half each in four dessert dishes. In a mixing bowl, beat cream until soft peaks form. Beat in sugar and vanilla until stiff peaks form. Fold in raspberries. Spoon over cupcakes. Garnish with additional berries if desired. Refrigerate until serving. **Yield:** 4 servings.

*Editor's Note: This recipe was prepared with Hostess brand cupcakes.

Speedy Seafood Fare Scores With Family

SPEEDY RECIPES are the name of the game for farm wife Louise Fauth from Foremost, Alberta. In fact, to have a sporting chance in her active family, she relies on fast-to-fix dinners.

"With son Josh playing hockey and daughter Jessica rodeoing, I get my exercise," relates the lively wife, mother and full-time fan with a smile. "Making quick and nutritious meals for them, plus my husband, Mike, and son Chad, is a daily challenge."

The family favorites featured here always score big with Louise's hungry home team.

"Our brood loves seafood, and Crab Melt Loaf is a nice switch from more traditional sandwiches," Louise affirms. "I've served big slices of the bread for lunch, Sunday brunch and as a field meal for Mike.

"Instead of crab," she suggests, "use canned tuna or salmon. Cheddar cheese can replace the mozzarella...and you can substitute a toasted bun or croissant for the French bread."

Romaine with Oranges and Almonds complements most any entree, especially the seafood sandwiches. "The fruit contributes color, the almonds provide crunch and the dressing lends a lightly sweet flavor," details Louise.

The salad can also be varied by adding chopped apples and sunflower kernels, which add a nice crunch.

Not one to trifle with her crew's sweet tooth, Louise makes Brownie Mocha Trifle for both a snack and a memorable mealtime finale.

"By using instant pudding and a convenient box of brownie mix, there's nothing to the preparation," she notes. "The result is moist and chewy. And the layers look so pretty spooned into a glass trifle bowl."

For a different flavored trifle, layer white cake, lemon pudding and whipped topping. For another look, serve in individual dessert cups with grated chocolate on top.

As the family chauffeur, head cheerleader and grain farm "gofer", Louise finds fuss-free dishes like these are a must.

And although she leaves the skating and barrel racing to the youngsters, she clearly leads the competition at beating the clock in the kitchen!

CRAB MELT LOAF

1 pound imitation crabmeat, chopped
1/2 cup mayonnaise
1/4 cup thinly sliced green onions
1/4 cup diced celery
2 cups (8 ounces) shredded mozzarella cheese
1/8 teaspoon salt
1/8 teaspoon pepper
1 loaf (1 pound) unsliced French bread, halved lengthwise

In a bowl, combine the first four ingredients. Stir in cheese, salt and pepper. Spread over bottom of bread; replace top. Wrap in a large piece of heavy-duty aluminum foil. Bake at 400° for 20 minutes or until heated through. Cut into slices. **Yield:** 8 servings.

ROMAINE WITH ORANGES AND ALMONDS

8 cups torn romaine
1 can (11 ounces) mandarin oranges, drained
2 green onions, thinly sliced
1/4 cup slivered almonds, toasted
1/4 cup sugar
1/4 cup vegetable oil
1/4 cup vinegar

In a bowl, toss the first four ingredients. In a jar with tight-fitting lid, combine sugar, oil and vinegar; shake well. Drizzle over salad and toss to coat. **Yield:** 8 servings.

BROWNIE MOCHA TRIFLE

1 package brownie mix (8-inch-square pan size)
1-3/4 cups cold milk
2 packages (3.4 ounces *each*) instant vanilla pudding mix
1/4 cup cold brewed coffee
2 cups whipped topping
1 Heath candy bar (1.4 ounces), crushed

Prepare and bake brownies according to package directions. Cool and cut into 1-in. pieces. In a mixing bowl, beat milk and pudding mix for 2 minutes or until thickened. Add coffee; mix well. Fold in whipped topping. In a trifle bowl or 2-qt. glass bowl, layer a third of the brownie pieces, pudding mixture and candy. Repeat layers twice. Refrigerate until serving. **Yield:** 8 servings.

Time-Saving Supper Is a Triple Treat

QUICK AS one…two…three, Christi Gillentine from Tulsa, Oklahoma has come to depend on speedy meals—for a trio of lively little reasons.

"Our son Tyler and twins Colton and Dana have turned my husband, Clint, and me into efficiency experts," Christi cheerfully confirms. "With three babies all going in different directions at once, I find myself heading straight for my fast-to-fix recipe file."

In no time, Christi's growing brood will exchange high-chair fare for the sure-to-please favorites featured here. But for now, she and her husband often rely on the recipes, which can be made in under half an hour.

"Tangy Broiled Chicken Slices are ideal for a hurry-up supper or a special dinner with friends," Christy affirms. "The leftover slices stay flavorful reheated or tossed into a cold salad.

"Turkey breast is a perfect stand-in for the chicken," she suggests. "You can also grill this entree by putting the meat on skewers."

The chicken is perfect paired with brown rice, rice pilaf or potatoes. "But we like it best served with Tex-Mex Bean Salad.

"My father-in-law's recipe, this salad is both pretty and packed with protein. It's also convenient since it uses a variety of canned beans," she reports. "It's even more flavorful when prepared the night before."

Christi's shortcut Banana Split Shortcake uses purchased pound or sponge cake instead of from-scratch biscuits. "By varying the fruits, it's a treat for any season," she offers. "Kids enjoy adding their choice of sundae toppings."

For a deliciously different dessert, try another flavor of ice cream…or choose a fruit such as fresh boysenberries, peaches or pears. You'll be pleased with the scrumptious results.

Away from the kitchen, Christi pilots a triple stroller to a baby play group and to meetings of Mothers of Multiples. She's often delivered this meal to a new mom…on the double.

"Considering how our kids love to be in the kitchen with me, I'm sure I'll soon have some excellent helpers," Christi smiles. Stirring up these satisfying time-saving recipes then will surely be three times the fun!

BROILED CHICKEN SLICES

1/2 cup cider *or* red wine vinegar
1/4 cup soy sauce
  4 garlic cloves, minced
  1 pound boneless skinless chicken breasts, cut into 1-inch slices
Hot cooked rice, optional

In a heavy-duty resealable plastic bag, combine vinegar, soy sauce and garlic. Add chicken; turn to coat. Seal and refrigerate for 15 minutes. Drain and discard marinade. Broil chicken 4 in. from the heat for 10-12 minutes or until juices run clear, turning frequently. Serve over rice if desired. **Yield:** 4 servings.

TEX-MEX BEAN SALAD

  1 can (16 ounces) kidney beans, rinsed and drained
  1 can (15-1/2 ounces) red beans, rinsed and drained
  1 can (15-1/2 ounces) black-eyed peas, rinsed and drained
1/4 cup minced fresh cilantro *or* parsley
  1 jalapeno pepper, seeded and chopped*
  4 green onions, sliced
1/4 cup olive *or* vegetable oil
1/4 cup cider *or* red wine vinegar
1/2 teaspoon garlic salt
1/2 teaspoon pepper
Lettuce leaves, optional

In a bowl, combine the beans, peas, cilantro, jalapeno pepper, onions, oil, vinegar, garlic salt and pepper. Toss to blend. Cover and refrigerate until serving. Serve with a slotted spoon on lettuce leaves if desired. **Yield:** 6 servings.

*Editor's Note: When cutting or seeding hot peppers, use rubber or plastic gloves to protect your hands. Avoid touching your face.

BANANA SPLIT SHORTCAKE

  8 slices pound cake (1/2 inch thick) *or* 4 individual round sponge cakes
  2 medium firm bananas, cut into 1/4-inch slices
  4 scoops vanilla ice cream
1/4 cup chocolate sauce

Place cake slices on four dessert plates. Top each with bananas and ice cream. Drizzle with chocolate sauce. **Yield:** 4 servings.

Meat Loaf Meal Is Easy as Pie To Make

AN EMPTY NEST has left Judy Foye of Freeport, Maine busier than ever. Luckily, her recipe file is filled to the brim with ready-in-minutes menus.

"When the youngest of my three sons left for college, I got moving, too," she enthuses. "I'm a teacher's aide in the morning, and I work at a candy shop all afternoon. In the evening, I take a little time out for cooking."

With almost no effort, Judy can serve one or feed a bunch with the fast-to-fix favorites featured here.

"Everybody enjoys my Meat Loaf Pie—a tasty cross between meat loaf and pizza," she offers. "Often, I divide it into two pans, bake one for me and freeze the other. That way, I'm ready for drop-in company or potluck suppers.

"Tomato paste or spaghetti sauce can be substituted for ketchup in my meat pie," says Judy. "Cheese lovers might want to add mozzarella to the topping as well.

"Lemony Tossed Salad is simple to toss together with garden-fresh tomatoes and cucumbers," she explains. "The vinaigrette dressing is light and lemony—a refreshing start to any meal, plain or fancy."

The salad can be dressed up with various vegetables, such as onions and peppers, croutons or other toppings.

For dessert, Judy stirs up quick Pear Apple Crisp. "By using canned fruit, I eliminate time-consuming peeling and slicing," she confides. "Usually, I slide it in the oven right next to the meat dish. The oven-fresh crisp is ready to eat when we're done with dinner.

"To make the fruit crisp extra-special, scoop your favorite ice cream or whipped cream on top," Judy suggests.

"I've shared many of these recipes with other members of my Empty-Nest Mothers' Group," Judy adds with a smile. "The time we save on meal-making, we spend baking cookies and putting together care packages for our college kids."

In additon, Judy crafts, makes baskets, gardens and loves to take walks by the ocean.

"One place you won't find me, though, is at a fast-food drive-thru," she concludes. "My own kitchen is quicker."

MEAT LOAF PIE

1 can (5 ounces) evaporated milk
1/2 cup dry bread crumbs
1/2 teaspoon garlic salt
1 pound lean ground beef
1/3 cup ketchup
1 cup (4 ounces) shredded cheddar cheese
1/2 teaspoon dried oregano
1 tablespoon grated Parmesan cheese

In a bowl, combine milk, bread crumbs and garlic salt. Add beef; mix well. Press meat mixture onto the bottom and 1 in. up the sides of a greased 9-in. pie plate. Bake, uncovered, at 350° for 20 minutes; drain. Spread with ketchup. Sprinkle with cheddar cheese, oregano and Parmesan cheese. Bake 3-5 minutes longer or until meat is no longer pink and cheese is melted. **Yield:** 4 servings.

LEMONY TOSSED SALAD

4 cups ready-to-serve salad greens
2 medium tomatoes, cut into wedges
3/4 cup sliced cucumber
1/2 cup olive *or* vegetable oil
1/4 cup lemon juice
1 garlic clove, minced
1 teaspoon sugar
1 teaspoon dried oregano *or* mint flakes
Salt and pepper to taste

In a salad bowl, combine salad greens, tomatoes and cucumber. In a jar with a tight-fitting lid, combine the remaining ingredients; shake well. Drizzle over salad and toss to coat. **Yield:** 4 servings.

PEAR APPLE CRISP

1 can (21 ounces) apple pie filling
1 can (8-1/2 ounces) sliced pears, drained
1/2 cup packed brown sugar
1/2 cup all-purpose flour
1/4 cup quick-cooking oats
1/2 teaspoon ground cinnamon
6 tablespoons cold butter *or* margarine
Ice cream, optional

In a greased 9-in. baking dish, combine pie filling and pears; set aside. In a small bowl, combine brown sugar, flour, oats and cinnamon; cut in butter until mixture resembles coarse crumbs. Sprinkle over fruit. Bake at 350° for 23-25 minutes or until golden brown. Serve with ice cream if desired. **Yield:** 4 servings.

Italian-Style Dinner Ideal for Drop-In Guests

GOOD FOOD travels fast in Marilyn Janssen's kitchen in Dawson Creek, British Columbia. Her scrumptious supply of quick-to-fix meals keeps pace with the hungry demand.

"With six grown children, 16 grandkids and a student boarder, I almost always have company for dinner," Marilyn shares. "My quick-and-easy recipes let me spend time with my guests while not wasting a moment worrying about how the meal will turn out.

"I always have a package of frozen chicken breasts on hand for making Chicken with Fettuccine," Marilyn confirms. "But leftover chicken or turkey also works fine."

The sauce for the chicken can be livened up by adding yogurt or sour cream. Or you can replace the fettuccine with spaghetti or linguine.

"Tomato Bean Salad is packed with tasty surprises," she reports. "Since it's dressed before serving, it's ideal for a help-yourself buffet."

Marilyn tops off her speedy supper with Saucy Chocolate Cake, which was passed along by her mother. "I get the cake in the oven first so it can bake while we're eating," she notes. "It's wonderful served warm."

CHICKEN WITH FETTUCCINE

6 boneless skinless chicken breast halves
1 tablespoon butter *or* margarine
1 tablespoon vegetable oil
1 medium onion, coarsely chopped
1/2 cup minced fresh basil *or* 1 tablespoon dried basil
4 garlic cloves, minced
1/2 teaspoon salt
1/4 teaspoon pepper
3/4 cup chicken broth
1/2 cup whipping cream
2 tablespoons dried parsley flakes
2 large tomatoes, diced
1 pound fettuccine

Flatten chicken to 1/2-in. thickness. In a skillet, brown chicken on both sides in butter and oil; remove and set aside. In the same skillet, saute onion until tender. Add basil, garlic, salt and pep-

per; cook and stir for 2-3 minutes. Stir in broth, cream, parsley and tomatoes. Return chicken to pan. Cover and simmer for 15 minutes or until chicken juices run clear. Meanwhile, cook fettuccine according to package directions; drain. Arrange chicken over fettuccine; top with sauce. **Yield:** 6 servings.

TOMATO BEAN SALAD

1 cup canned kidney beans, rinsed and drained
1 large tomato, diced
1 celery rib, sliced
4 green onions, sliced
1/2 cup mayonnaise *or* salad dressing
1/4 cup ranch salad dressing
1 teaspoon dill weed
1/4 teaspoon garlic powder
3 cups torn leaf lettuce

In a bowl, combine the first four ingredients. In another bowl, combine mayonnaise, ranch dressing, dill and garlic powder. Pour over vegetables and toss to coat. Place lettuce in a serving bowl; add vegetable mixture. Toss just before serving. **Yield:** 6 servings.

SAUCY CHOCOLATE CAKE

1 cup sugar, *divided*
3 tablespoons baking cocoa, *divided*
1-1/2 cups boiling water
2 tablespoons butter *or* margarine, softened
1 teaspoon vanilla extract
1 cup all-purpose flour
2 teaspoons baking powder
1/2 teaspoon salt
1/2 cup milk
Ice cream *or* whipped topping
Maraschino cherries, optional

In a saucepan, combine 1/2 cup sugar and 1 tablespoon cocoa. Stir in boiling water until smooth. Simmer, uncovered, for 5 minutes. Meanwhile, in a mixing bowl, cream butter, vanilla and remaining sugar. Combine flour, baking powder, salt and remaining cocoa; add to creamed mixture alternately with milk. Beat well.

Pour the chocolate sauce into a greased 1-1/2-qt. baking dish. Drop batter by rounded teaspoonfuls onto sauce. Bake, uncovered, at 375° for 25 minutes or until a toothpick inserted in the center comes out clean. Serve warm with ice cream. Garnish with cherries if desired. **Yield:** 4-6 servings.

Flair for Fast Food Runs in The Family

KITCHEN EFFICIENCY is relatively easy for on-the-go Texan Tabitha Allen. After all, it runs in her family.

"I come from a long line of busy cooks," informs the mother of two who works full-time in Cypress. "When one of us finds a speedy recipe, we immediately send it out on the family grapevine for all to try."

In fact, the fast favorites featured here were rapidly relayed to Tabitha by an aunt and her grandmother.

"Canned corn and tomato sauce get Maw-Maw Allen's hearty noodle-based Beef Skillet Supper off to a quick start," she offers. "Sometimes, I'll make extra to guarantee leftovers. It's a great take-along main dish for work or school.

"Trim calories from the entree by substituting ground turkey for the beef and low-fat cheese," says Tabitha. "For variety, use pasta with a novel shape.

"To hurry up my aunt's Bean Tossed Salad, I assemble it ahead of time and add the corn chips and salad dressing just before serving."

You can adapt her salad by adding kidney beans, various cheeses and croutons or crushed tortillas instead of corn chips.

As for her version of her grandma's dessert, Tabitha peels off Banana Delight in no time. "Thanks to my fruit-loving son, Noah, I have bunches of ingredients on hand," Tabitha laughs. "My daughter, Shayna, is a whiz at crushing the cookies and scooping the ice cream.

"Turn the dessert into a mini banana split by drizzling on warm butterscotch sauce, plus chopped walnuts and a cherry," Tabitha suggests.

"This easy meal is so eye-pleasing, I often serve it as a no-fuss lunch...or even as a special sit-down supper," she adds. "For an appetizing accent, I trim the edges of my plates with cilantro and garnish with colored tostado chips."

Her artistic appetite also keeps Tabitha active with quilting and woodcrafts. She often presents these handmades for her family's annual holiday gift exchange and buffet.

"It's a wonderful opportunity to catch up with the relatives," Tabitha affirms—not to mention getting up to speed on their fast-to-fix recipes!

BEEF SKILLET SUPPER

1 package (8 ounces) medium egg noodles
1-1/2 pounds ground beef
1 medium onion, chopped
1 can (8 ounces) tomato sauce
1/2 cup water
1 can (11 ounces) Mexicorn, drained
1/2 teaspoon salt
1/4 teaspoon pepper
1 cup (4 ounces) shredded cheddar cheese

Cook the egg noodles according to package directions. Meanwhile, in a large skillet, cook the beef and onion over medium heat until meat is no longer pink; drain. Add the tomato sauce and water. Cover and cook for 8 minutes. Drain the noodles; add to beef mixture. Add the corn, salt and pepper. Sprinkle with cheese; cover and cook until heated through and the cheese is melted. **Yield:** 8-10 servings.

BEAN TOSSED SALAD

1/2 head iceberg lettuce, torn
1 cup (4 ounces) shredded cheddar cheese
1 cup ranch-style beans, rinsed and drained
1/2 medium tomato, chopped
1/2 cup chopped onion
1/4 cup chopped green pepper
1/2 to 1 cup tortilla *or* corn chips
1/3 cup Catalina salad dressing

In a salad bowl, combine the lettuce, cheese, beans, tomato, onion and green pepper. Just before serving, add chips and salad dressing; toss to coat. **Yield:** 8 servings.

BANANA DELIGHT

20 vanilla wafers, crushed
1/2 cup sugar
1/2 teaspoon ground cinnamon
8 medium firm bananas, cut into 1/2-inch slices
1/3 cup butter *or* margarine
Vanilla ice cream

In a small bowl, combine wafer crumbs, sugar and cinnamon; set aside. In a large skillet, saute the bananas in butter over medium heat for 1 minute. Sprinkle with crumb mixture; cook for 3 minutes or until heated through. Serve warm over ice cream. **Yield:** 8 servings.

Our Most Memorable Meals

Mealtime will be memorable when you gather your family around the table for any of these down-home menus.

Fare Has Been Pleasing Families For Years

THESE DELICIOUS DISHES passed down through the generations are sure to delight your own family.

"Herbed Pork Roast was our family's celebration roast," recalls Ruth Bethurum of Ozan, Arkansas. "Mother served it on birthdays and holidays. The combination of herbs enhances the drippings as well, so I use it to make gravy."

During Phyllis Jean Sheeley's teen years, she lived on her aunt's farm. "Onion Pie was one of her satisfying dishes, and one of many I enjoyed," attests this Altoona, Illinois resident. "It's a wonderful side dish to complement any meat entree."

Dorothy Pritchett of Wills Point, Texas discovered the recipe for Spinach Pecan Bake while on a hunt for a different kind of vegetable dish. "I tried it and declared it a winner," says Dorothy. "The guests I first served this to also raved."

The recipe for Chewy Ginger Drop Cookies originated with Lois Furcron's grandmother. "My mom, an excellent baker, also made these cookies," states Lois from her home in Coudersport, Pennsylvania.

HERBED PORK ROAST

  1 boneless pork loin roast (3-1/2 to 4 pounds)
1/2 teaspoon salt
1/2 teaspoon pepper
1/2 cup water
1/2 cup chicken broth
1/4 cup ketchup
  1 garlic clove, minced
1/4 teaspoon ground mustard

1/4 teaspoon *each* dried marjoram, thyme and rosemary, crushed
  2 large onions, sliced
  1 bay leaf
  1 can (8-3/4 ounces) mushroom stems and pieces, undrained

In a Dutch oven coated with nonstick cooking spray, brown roast over medium heat. Sprinkle with salt and pepper. Combine water, broth, ketchup, garlic and seasonings; pour over roast. Add onions and bay leaf. Cover and simmer over medium heat for 1-1/2 hours or until a meat thermometer reads 160°. Add mushrooms; heat through. Discard bay leaf. Let stand 10 minutes before slicing. Serve with onions and mushrooms. Thicken pan drippings for gravy if desired. **Yield:** 8-10 servings.

ONION PIE

  3 large onions, sliced
  1 tablespoon butter *or* margarine
  3 eggs
  2 cups half-and-half cream
Salt and pepper to taste
Pastry for double-crust pie (9 inches)
  4 bacon strips, cooked and crumbled
1/2 cup shredded cheddar cheese

In a skillet, saute onions in butter until golden brown. In a bowl, beat eggs and cream. Add the onions, salt and pepper. Line a deep-dish 9-in. pie plate with bottom pastry. Add egg mixture; sprinkle with bacon and cheese. Roll out remaining pastry to fit top of pie; place over filling. Seal and flute the edges; cut slits in top. Bake at 350° for 55-60 minutes or until crust is golden brown. Let stand 15 minutes before cutting. Refrigerate leftovers. **Yield:** 6-8 servings.

SPINACH PECAN BAKE

  1 medium onion, finely chopped
1/4 cup butter *or* margarine

3 packages (10 ounces *each*) frozen leaf
spinach, thawed and drained
1/2 cup half-and-half cream
1/2 cup coarsely chopped pecans
1/3 cup dry bread crumbs
1 teaspoon salt
1/2 teaspoon ground nutmeg
1/8 teaspoon pepper

TOPPING:
1/4 cup dry bread crumbs
2 tablespoons butter *or* margarine, melted

In a skillet, saute onion in butter until tender. In a
large bowl, combine onion, spinach, cream, pecans,
bread crumbs, salt, nutmeg and pepper; mix well.
Transfer to a greased 1-1/2-qt. baking dish. Combine topping ingredients; sprinkle over the spinach
mixture. Bake, uncovered, at 350° for 30 minutes
or until lightly browned. **Yield:** 6-8 servings.

CHEWY GINGER DROP COOKIES

1/2 cup shortening
1/2 cup sugar
2 cups all-purpose flour
1/2 teaspoon baking soda
1/2 teaspoon ground ginger
1/4 teaspoon salt
1/2 cup molasses
1/4 cup water

In a mixing bowl, cream shortening and sugar. Combine flour, baking soda, ginger and salt. Combine
molasses and water. Add dry ingredients to the
creamed mixture alternately with molasses mixture.
Drop by teaspoonfuls 2 in. apart onto greased baking sheets. Sprinkle with additional sugar. Bake at
350° for 13-15 minutes or until edges are set. Remove to wire racks to cool. **Yield:** about 2-1/2 dozen.

Fresh and Flavorful Ideas for a Satisfying Supper

IF YOU'RE TIRED of serving your family the same thing for supper, try the refreshing selections here. They're sure to satisfy.

Marion Lowery's Baked Lemon Chicken is as good cold as it is right out of the oven. "It's moist, tender and lemony with a nice crunch," says this Medford, Oregon cook. "It's a delicious picnic entree as well as a wonderful meal with scalloped or baked potatoes and a fresh green salad on the side."

Green Beans with Cherry Tomatoes is a tasty combination of flavors, especially in summer, when the ingredients can be garden fresh. Shirley Heare of Fayetteville, North Carolina likes to serve this pretty vegetable side dish when entertaining. "It's so colorful," Shirley shares.

Sweet, light and versatile all describe Fresh Fruit Medley from Patricia Ford of Creve Coeur, Illinois. "Many different combinations of fruit can be used," explains Patricia. "I've even tossed in chopped lettuce and—to lure the grandkids—miniature marshmallows!"

Lisa Ann DiNunzio comes from a family of cooks and was inspired to cook and bake ever since she was young. "Mother and Grandmom were always in the kitchen cooking up something delicious," recalls Lisa Ann from her home in Vineland, New Jersey. "The recipe for Maple Carrot Cupcakes is handed down from Grandmom and is always requested at special gatherings."

BAKED LEMON CHICKEN

    3 tablespoons butter *or* margarine, melted
    2 tablespoons lemon juice
    1 garlic clove, minced
  1/2 teaspoon salt
  1/4 teaspoon pepper
  1/2 cup seasoned bread crumbs
    4 boneless skinless chicken breast halves

In a shallow dish, combine the first five ingredients. Place bread crumbs in another dish. Dip chicken in butter mixture, then coat with crumbs. Place in a greased 13-in. x 9-in. x 2-in. baking pan. Drizzle with remaining butter mixture. Bake, uncovered, at 350° for 25-30 minutes or until juices run clear. **Yield:** 4 servings.

GREEN BEANS WITH CHERRY TOMATOES

1-1/2 pounds fresh green beans, cut into 2-inch pieces
1-1/2 cups water
  1/4 cup butter *or* margarine
    1 tablespoon sugar
1-1/2 teaspoons dried basil
  1/2 teaspoon garlic salt
  1/4 teaspoon salt
  1/8 teaspoon pepper
    2 cups halved cherry tomatoes
    3 fresh basil leaves

Place beans and water in a saucepan; bring to a boil. Reduce heat; cover and simmer for 12-15 minutes or until crisp-tender. Meanwhile, melt butter in a skillet; stir in sugar, basil, garlic salt, salt and pepper. Add tomatoes; saute until tender. Drain beans; top with tomato mixture. Garnish with basil. **Yield:** 6-8 servings.

FRESH FRUIT MEDLEY

    1 medium ripe banana, sliced, *divided*
    2 tablespoons mayonnaise
    1 teaspoon sugar
    1 kiwifruit, peeled, sliced and quartered
    1 medium pear, cubed
    1 small apple, cubed
   12 seedless green grapes, halved

In a large bowl, mash half of the banana slices. Stir in mayonnaise and sugar. Add kiwi, pear, apple, grapes and remaining banana slices; toss gently. Serve immediately. **Yield:** 3-4 servings.

MAPLE CARROT CUPCAKES

    2 cups all-purpose flour
    1 cup sugar
    1 teaspoon baking powder
    1 teaspoon baking soda
    1 teaspoon ground cinnamon
  1/2 teaspoon salt

          4 eggs
          1 cup vegetable oil
      1/2 cup maple syrup
          3 cups grated carrots (about 6 medium)
FROSTING:
          1 package (8 ounces) cream cheese,
              softened
      1/4 cup butter *or* margarine, softened
      1/4 cup maple syrup
          1 teaspoon vanilla extract
Chopped walnuts, optional

In a large bowl, combine the first six ingredients. In another bowl, beat eggs, oil and syrup. Stir into dry ingredients just until moistened. Fold in carrots. Fill greased or paper-lined muffin cups two-thirds full. Bake at 350° for 20-25 minutes or until a toothpick comes out clean. Cool for 5 minutes before removing from pans to wire racks.

For frosting, combine cream cheese, butter, syrup and vanilla in a mixing bowl; beat until smooth. Frost cooled cupcakes. Sprinkle with nuts if desired. **Yield:** 1-1/2 dozen.

Cook Up Fancy-Looking Foods Fit for Company

LOOKING for something special to serve company? This elegant fare will be the talk of the dinner table.

Braised Beef Rolls is a great dish for guests because it can be fixed ahead of time. Mary Kay Ankney of Springfield, Oregon, who shares the recipe, says that everyone who tries the rolls enjoys the old-fashioned sweet-and-sour flavor.

Shares Anne Kulick from Phillipsburg, New Jersey, "My daughter-in-law served Cream of Mushroom Soup as a first course for Thanksgiving dinner one year. She'd gotten the recipe from her mom and graciously shared it with me."

Growing up on a farm, Ruby Miguez of Crowley, Louisiana had access to fresh vegetables most of the year. "Mother served Special Brussels Sprouts twice a week," remembers Ruby. "Fresh from the garden, they were sweet and tender. Now I make this recipe all year using frozen sprouts."

Charleston, Illinois resident Juanita Sherwood also lived on a farm while growing up and enjoyed lots of fruit trees. "Since Dad loved fruit," says Juanita, "Mother prepared it often in many different ways. Blackberries or blueberries can also be used in George Washington Cherry Cobbler."

BRAISED BEEF ROLLS

2 to 3 pounds London broil *or* flank
   steak rolls
1/2 teaspoon salt
1/4 teaspoon pepper
2 tablespoons vegetable oil
1-3/4 cups water, *divided*
1/2 cup packed brown sugar
1/2 cup raisins
1 medium onion, cut into wedges
2 tablespoons vinegar
2 tablespoons lemon juice
1 teaspoon ground mustard
1 bay leaf, optional
2 tablespoons all-purpose flour
Hot cooked rice

Sprinkle meat with salt and pepper. In a Dutch oven over medium heat, brown the meat on both sides in oil; drain. In a saucepan, combine 1-1/2 cups of water, brown sugar, raisins, onion, vinegar, lemon juice, mustard and bay leaf if desired. Bring to a boil. Combine flour and remaining water until smooth; stir into raisin sauce. Bring to a boil; cook and stir for 2 minutes or until thickened. Pour over the meat rolls. Cover and bake at 325° for 1-1/2 hours or until the meat is tender. Discard bay leaf. Serve over rice. **Yield:** 4-6 servings.

CREAM OF MUSHROOM SOUP

1/4 cup chopped onion
2 tablespoons butter *or* margarine
3 cups sliced fresh mushrooms
6 tablespoons all-purpose flour
2 cans (14-1/2 ounces *each*) chicken broth
1 cup half-and-half cream
1/2 teaspoon salt
1/8 teaspoon pepper

In a large saucepan, saute onion in butter until tender. Add mushrooms and saute until tender. Combine flour and broth until smooth; stir into the mushroom mixture. Bring to a boil; cook and stir for 2 minutes or until thickened. Reduce heat. Stir in the cream, salt and pepper. Simmer, uncovered, for 15 minutes, stirring often. **Yield:** 4-6 servings.

SPECIAL BRUSSELS SPROUTS

1/4 cup sliced almonds
1 tablespoon butter *or* margarine
1 package (16 ounces) frozen brussels
   sprouts
1 chicken bouillon cube
1 can (10-3/4 ounces) condensed cream
   of chicken soup, undiluted
2 tablespoons milk
1 jar (2 ounces) chopped pimientos,
   drained
1/4 teaspoon pepper
1/8 teaspoon dried thyme

In a small skillet, saute almonds in butter until lightly browned; set aside. In a saucepan, cook brussels sprouts according to package directions, adding the bouillon cube to the water. Meanwhile, in another saucepan, combine the soup, milk, pimientos, pepper and thyme. Cook until heated through. Drain sprouts; top with the cream sauce and stir gently. Sprinkle with almonds. **Yield:** 4-6 servings.

▰▰▰▰▰▰▰▰▰▰▰

GEORGE WASHINGTON
CHERRY COBBLER

    1/2 cup sugar
      2 tablespoons cornstarch
    1/4 teaspoon ground cinnamon
    3/4 cup water
      1 package (12 ounces) frozen dark sweet
         cherries, thawed
      1 tablespoon butter *or* margarine
TOPPING:
      1 cup all-purpose flour
      4 tablespoons sugar, *divided*
      2 teaspoons baking powder
    1/2 teaspoon salt

      3 tablespoons shortening
    1/2 cup milk
Ice cream, optional

In a saucepan, combine sugar, cornstarch and cin-namon. Stir in water until smooth. Add cherries and butter. Bring to a boil over medium heat, stirring fre-quently. Cook and stir for 2 minutes or until thick-ened. Pour into an 8-in. square baking pan.

In a bowl, combine flour, 2 tablespoons sugar, bak-ing powder and salt. Cut in shortening until mixture resembles coarse crumbs. Stir in milk just until moist-ened. Drop by spoonfuls over the cherries; sprinkle with remaining sugar. Bake at 400° for 30-35 min-utes or until golden brown. Serve warm with ice cream if desired. **Yield:** 8 servings.

Meat and Potatoes Shine in Home-Style Supper

EXPERIMENTING in the kitchen led to the creation of the crowd pleasers featured here.

Bernadine Dirmeyer of Harpster, Ohio created the recipe for Deluxe Bacon Burgers and won a red ribbon for it in a 1976 cookbook contest. "When I prepared this for dinner," relates Bernadine, "I always felt my family was well fed. It's like meat loaf in a bun, so it's very hearty."

When Bay City, Texas cook Mildred Sherrer had a large vegetable garden, she had fun creating new recipes, depending on what was ready for picking. Colorful Vegetable Salad is one such garden-fresh recipe.

Patty Kile's best recipes come from friends and family. "Homemade Potato Salad is from my aunt," credits this Greentown, Pennsylvania resident. "I learned to cook by watching and helping her in the kitchen.

"I have so many family favorites that I created my own cookbook," continues Patty.

Coffee Ice Cream is the concoction of Theresa Hansen, who lives in Pensacola, Florida. "I combined two recipes—one for vanilla ice cream and the other for a special coffee sauce—to come up with this one," Theresa explains.

"I serve it plain, just scooped into a dessert dish, so the mild creamy coffee flavor can be enjoyed to the fullest."

DELUXE BACON BURGERS

    2 large carrots, grated
    1 large onion, grated
    1 cup mashed potato flakes
    2 eggs, lightly beaten
    1 garlic clove, minced
    1 teaspoon salt
Pepper to taste
    2 pounds ground beef
    8 bacon strips
    8 hamburger buns, optional
    8 lettuce leaves, optional

In a large bowl, combine the first seven ingredients. Crumble beef over mixture and mix gently. Shape into eight patties. Wrap a bacon strip around each patty; secure with toothpicks. In a large skillet, cook burgers until meat is no longer pink and bacon is crisp. Remove toothpicks. Serve on lettuce-lined buns if desired. **Yield:** 8 servings.

COLORFUL VEGETABLE SALAD

    3 cups canned or frozen corn, thawed
    1 can (15 ounces) black beans, rinsed and
      drained
    3 medium tomatoes, seeded and diced
    1 cup chopped green pepper
    1 cup chopped sweet red pepper
DRESSING:
    1/4 cup olive or vegetable oil
    3 tablespoons lime juice
    2 tablespoons minced fresh cilantro or
      parsley
    1 garlic clove, minced
    1 teaspoon salt
    1/2 teaspoon pepper

In a large bowl, combine the first five ingredients. In a jar with a tight-fitting lid, combine the dressing ingredients; shake well. Pour over vegetables and toss to coat. Cover and refrigerate for at least 2 hours before serving. **Yield:** 8 servings.

HOMEMADE POTATO SALAD

    1 tablespoon sugar
    2 teaspoons all-purpose flour
    1/4 teaspoon ground mustard
Pinch salt
    1 egg, beaten
    1/3 cup water
    1 tablespoon vinegar
    3/4 cup mayonnaise or salad dressing
    5 large potatoes, peeled and cubed
    4 hard-cooked eggs, chopped
    1 cup chopped celery
    1/4 cup chopped green onions
Salt and pepper to taste

In a small saucepan, combine the sugar, flour, mustard and salt. Combine egg, water and vinegar; stir into dry ingredients until smooth. Bring to a boil over medium heat, stirring constantly. Cook and stir for 2 minutes. Remove from the heat; cool slightly. Stir in mayonnaise. In a bowl, combine the potatoes, hard-cooked eggs, celery, onions, salt and pepper. Add the dressing and toss gently to coat. Refrigerate until ready to serve. **Yield:** 8-10 servings.

▰▰▰▰▰▰▰▰▰▰▰▰▰
COFFEE ICE CREAM

1/4 cup sugar
  1 tablespoon cornstarch
  1 tablespoon instant coffee granules
  2 tablespoons butter *or* margarine, melted
  1 cup milk
  1 teaspoon vanilla extract
  1 can (14 ounces) sweetened condensed
    milk

2 cups whipping cream

In a saucepan, stir sugar, cornstarch, coffee and butter until blended. Stir in milk. Bring to a boil over medium heat; cook and stir for 2 minutes or until thickened. Remove from the heat; stir in vanilla. Cool completely. Stir in condensed milk. In a mixing bowl, beat cream until stiff peaks form; fold into milk mixture. Pour into a 9-in. square pan. Cover and freeze for 6 hours or until firm. **Yield:** 1-1/2 quarts.

Hearty Meal Is Full of Autumn Appeal

A HARVEST of good eating awaits when you prepare this bounty of family favorites.

Over 10 years ago, Pat Habiger of Spearville, Kansas entered Swiss Steak with Dumplings in a recipe contest and won. "It's one of our workers' favorites during harvesttime," says Pat.

Rosalie Rizzolo-Wright's Italian grandmother grew all her own produce in a backyard garden. "So many of Grandma's recipes made good use of her bountiful fresh vegetables," shares Rosalie from San Jose, California. "Garden Tossed Salad is refreshing with any main course."

Golden Gelatin Salad is one of Mrs. Daniel Leaman's favorites her grandmother used to make almost 40 years ago. "I always looked forward to going to her house because her food was so good," says this Lancaster, Pennsylvania resident. "I make it often in the fall. The color and flavor seem to pair well with the season."

Sally Green of Mobile, Alabama got the recipe for Chocolate Sweet Potato Cake from her mom in 1940. "Mother had lost all of her recipes in a house fire, so her friends gave her a recipe party," says Sally. "Among the recipes was this cake, which is one of our family's favorites."

SWISS STEAK WITH DUMPLINGS

- 2 pounds round steak (3/4 inch thick), trimmed
- 1/3 cup all-purpose flour
- 2 tablespoons vegetable oil
- 2 cans (10-3/4 ounces *each*) condensed cream of chicken soup, undiluted
- 1-1/3 cups water
- 1/2 teaspoon salt
- 1/8 teaspoon pepper

DUMPLINGS:
- 1/2 cup dry bread crumbs
- 5 tablespoons butter *or* margarine, melted, *divided*
- 1-1/3 cups all-purpose flour
- 2 teaspoons baking powder
- 1/4 teaspoon poultry seasoning
- 1/2 teaspoon salt
- 2/3 cup milk

Cut the steak into six or eight pieces; dredge in flour. In a large skillet, brown meat on both sides in oil. Transfer to a greased 2-1/2-qt. baking dish. In the same skillet, combine the soup, water, salt and pepper; bring to a boil, stirring occasionally. Pour over steak. Cover and bake at 350° for 50-60 minutes or until meat is tender.

For dumplings, combine bread crumbs and 2 tablespoons butter in a small bowl; set aside. In another bowl, combine the flour, baking powder, poultry seasoning and salt. Stir in milk and remaining butter just until moistened. Drop by rounded tablespoonfuls into the crumb mixture; roll until coated. Place dumplings over steak. Bake, uncovered, at 425° for 20-30 minutes or until dumplings are lightly browned and a toothpick comes out clean. **Yield:** 6-8 servings.

GARDEN TOSSED SALAD

- 8 cups torn salad greens
- 1/2 cup sliced fresh mushrooms
- 1/2 cup chopped celery
- 2 medium tomatoes, cut into wedges
- 1/2 medium green pepper, sliced
- 1 teaspoon minced fresh basil *or* 1/4 teaspoon dried basil

DRESSING:
- 1/4 cup olive *or* vegetable oil
- 4-1/2 teaspoons cider *or* red wine vinegar
- 1/4 teaspoon dried oregano
- 1/8 teaspoon garlic powder
- Salt and pepper to taste
- Parmesan cheese

Combine the first six ingredients in a large salad bowl. In a jar with a tight-fitting lid, combine the oil, vinegar, oregano, garlic powder, salt and pepper; shake well. Drizzle over salad; toss to coat. Sprinkle with Parmesan cheese. **Yield:** 8 servings.

GOLDEN GELATIN SALAD

(Not pictured)

- 1 envelope unflavored gelatin
- 1/4 cup cold water
- 1 can (20 ounces) crushed pineapple
- 1/4 cup sugar
- 1/4 teaspoon salt
- 1/2 cup orange juice
- 1/4 cup vinegar
- 1 cup grated carrots

In a bowl, sprinkle gelatin over cold water; let stand for 1 minute. Drain pineapple, reserving 1 cup juice

(discard remaining juice or save for another use). Set the pineapple aside. In a saucepan, bring reserved juice to a boil. Remove from the heat. Stir in sugar, salt and gelatin mixture until dissolved. Add orange juice and vinegar.

Refrigerate for 2 hours or until partially set. Fold in the carrots and pineapple. Transfer to a 4-cup mold coated with nonstick cooking spray. Refrigerate until firm. Unmold onto a serving platter. **Yield:** 8 servings.

▪▪▪▪▪▪▪▪▪▪▪▪
CHOCOLATE SWEET POTATO CAKE

2/3 cup butter *or* margarine, softened
  2 cups sugar
  4 eggs
  2 cups all-purpose flour
  1 tablespoon baking cocoa
  1 teaspoon baking soda
  1 teaspoon baking powder
  1 teaspoon *each* ground cinnamon,
    nutmeg, allspice and cloves
1/2 cup milk
  2 medium sweet potatoes, peeled, cooked,
    mashed and cooled
  1 teaspoon vanilla extract
  2 cups chopped pecans
1/2 cup raisins
Confectioners' sugar, optional

In a mixing bowl, cream butter and sugar. Add eggs, one at a time, beating well after each addition. Combine the dry ingredients; add to creamed mixture alternately with milk. Stir in sweet potatoes and vanilla; mix well. Add the pecans and raisins.

Transfer to a greased and floured 10-in. fluted tube pan. Bake at 350° for 70-80 minutes or until a toothpick inserted near the center comes out clean. Cool for 10 minutes before removing from pan to a wire rack to cool completely. Dust with confectioners' sugar if desired. **Yield:** 12-16 servings.

Make the Holidays Merry with Festive Food

CELEBRATE the season with family and friends by presenting appetizers and punch.

Cranberry Meatballs is a versatile recipe to be used either as a main dish or as an appetizer. You simply adjust the size of the meatballs.

"I like to serve it during the holidays as an appetizer," says Frances Venator of Ottumwa, Iowa, who shares the recipe. "It works well to curb appetites while your guests await the main meal."

Diane Hixon first tasted Zippy Cheese Dip in a cooking class at a local Niceville, Florida supermarket. "It isn't necessary to add the eggs," explains Diane, "but they give the dip a thicker consistency."

Rosy Fruit Punch goes a long way to satisfy the thirst of your guests. All the flavors of the holiday season are in this colorful and refreshing punch from Joyce Brown of Genesee, Idaho.

Marcella Kulp's family has enjoyed Ham Salad Spread for years. "It came to be an expected leftover every time we had ham for a special dinner," says this Quakertown, Pennsylvania cook. "Recently, I decided to measure the ingredients, write down the recipe and pass it on to my daughter and daughter-in-law."

CRANBERRY MEATBALLS

- 2 eggs, lightly beaten
- 1 cup crushed saltines (about 15 crackers)
- 1 medium onion, finely chopped
- 2 teaspoons salt
- 1/4 teaspoon pepper
- 1 pound ground beef
- 1 pound ground pork
- 2 cans (16 ounces *each*) whole-berry cranberry sauce
- 2 cans (10-3/4 ounces *each*) condensed tomato soup, undiluted
- 1 teaspoon prepared mustard

In a bowl, combine the first five ingredients. Add beef and pork; mix well. Shape into 1-in. meatballs. Place on a rack in a 15-in. x 10-in. x 1-in. baking pan. Bake at 400° for 15 minutes. Meanwhile, combine the cranberry sauce, soup and mustard in a large saucepan. Bring to a boil. Reduce heat; add the meatballs. Simmer, uncovered, for 10 minutes. **Yield:** 5 dozen.

Editor's Note: To serve the meatballs as a main dish instead of an appetizer, make 1-1/4-inch balls and bake for 20 minutes.

ZIPPY CHEESE DIP

- 1/4 cup chopped onion
- 1 tablespoon butter *or* margarine
- 1 can (14-1/2 ounces) diced tomatoes, drained
- 1 pound process American cheese, cubed
- 1 teaspoon Worcestershire sauce
- 1/2 teaspoon paprika
- 1/4 teaspoon salt
- 2 drops hot pepper sauce
- 2 eggs, beaten

Crackers

In a saucepan, saute onion in butter until tender. Add tomatoes, cheese, Worcestershire sauce, paprika, salt and hot pepper sauce. Cook and stir over medium heat until cheese is melted. Remove from the heat. Stir a small amount of hot mixture into eggs. Return all to the pan, stirring constantly. Cook and stir until mixture reaches 160°. Serve warm with crackers. Store leftovers in the refrigerator. **Yield:** 3-1/2 cups.

ROSY FRUIT PUNCH

- 1 bottle (128 ounces) cranberry juice, chilled
- 1 carton (64 ounces) orange juice, chilled
- 6 cups cold water
- 3 cups pineapple juice, chilled
- 3 cups sugar
- 3/4 cup lemon juice

In a large punch bowl, combine all ingredients; stir until sugar is dissolved. **Yield:** about 8-1/2 quarts.

HAM SALAD SPREAD

- 3 cups ground fully cooked ham
- 1 hard-cooked egg, chopped
- 2 tablespoons finely chopped celery
- 2 teaspoons finely chopped onion
- 2 teaspoons sweet pickle relish

3/4 cup mayonnaise
    1 tablespoon prepared mustard
Assorted crackers

In a bowl, combine the first five ingredients.
Combine mayonnaise and mustard; add to ham
mixture and mix well. Refrigerate until serving.
Serve with crackers. **Yield:** 3 cups.

MAKING MEATBALLS

Use an ice cream scoop to make meatballs of
uniform size. Dampen your hands with cold
water before rolling mixture into balls.

Cooking for Two

*Small-quantity recipes that are big on taste fit the bill
when you're cooking for just the two of you.*

MINI TUNA CASSEROLES

Rebecca Reese, Jacksboro, Texas

*I can whip up this dish in a hurry, and it's perfect for
a light supper or luncheon for two. I always have a can
of tuna on my pantry shelf, and when I prepare it, I
feel I've served us a satisfying meal.*

```
1/2  cup chopped green onions
  2  tablespoons butter or margarine
  2  tablespoons all-purpose flour
3/4  cup milk
  1  can (6 ounces) tuna, drained
  1  cup crushed potato chips, divided
1/4  teaspoon pepper
```

In a saucepan, saute onions in butter. Stir in
flour until blended. Gradually stir in milk. Bring
to a boil over medium heat; cook and stir for 2
minutes or until thickened. Remove from the
heat. Stir in the tuna, 1/2 cup of potato chips
and pepper. Pour into two greased 8-oz. baking
dishes. Sprinkle with remaining potato chips.
Bake, uncovered, at 350° for 20-25 minutes or until hot and bubbly. **Yield:** 2 servings.

COLORFUL CABBAGE SKILLET

Bernice Knutson, Soldier, Iowa

*Crunchy and colorful, this side dish has the flavor and
texture of creamy coleslaw, but it's served warm. It's
a nice change from typical vegetable dishes. I serve it
often with any meat entree.*

```
  1  cup coarsely shredded cabbage
1/3  cup sliced celery
1/3  cup julienned carrot
  2  tablespoons chopped onion
  2  tablespoons butter or margarine
1/2  teaspoon salt
Dash pepper
  3  tablespoons half-and-half cream
Minced fresh parsley
```

In a skillet, saute the cabbage, celery, carrot and
onion in butter for 12 minutes or until crisp-tender.

Sprinkle with salt and pepper. Reduce heat; stir in
cream. Cook and stir for 3 minutes or until heated
through. Sprinkle with parsley. **Yield:** 2 servings.

DILLED NOODLES

Anna Prenni, Saltsburg, Pennsylvania

*This recipe is as simple as it is delicious. I tried it the
first year I had an herb garden, when I was looking for
recipes that called for fresh herbs. The noodles are
compatible with many main dishes.*

```
1-1/2  cups medium egg noodles
  1/2  cup small-curd cottage cheese
    1  to 2 tablespoons snipped fresh dill or 1
       to 2 teaspoons dill weed
  1/4  teaspoon salt
Dash pepper
```

In a saucepan, cook noodles according to package directions. Meanwhile, combine the remaining ingredients. Drain noodles; add to cottage
cheese mixture and toss gently. Serve immediately. **Yield:** 2 servings.

RASPBERRY CREAM

Christl Bennett, Burlington, Kentucky

*I have a passion for trying new recipes, the kind that
bring joy to my eyes as well as my stomach! I discovered this recipe over 40 years ago. If you need a great-
looking, tasty treat to end a meal, this is it.*

```
  1  package (3 ounces) raspberry gelatin
1/2  cup boiling water
  1  package (10 ounces) frozen sweetened
     raspberries
  1  cup vanilla ice cream, softened
Whipped cream
```

In a bowl, dissolve gelatin in boiling water. Stir in
raspberries and ice cream until blended. Spoon into two dessert dishes. Cover and refrigerate for at
least 1 hour. Top with a dollop of whipped cream.
Yield: 2 servings.

BROCCOLI-STUFFED CHICKEN

Donald Laugherty, Connellsville, Pennsylvania

I was born in 1936 to a family of eight. Much of our food came from our garden and the henhouse at the back of our city lot. Mother served fried chicken every Sunday, but sometimes she liked to surprise us with this creation.

     2 boneless skinless chicken breast halves
       (about 6 ounces *each*)
     1 teaspoon poultry seasoning
   1/2 teaspoon white pepper
   1/2 teaspoon curry powder
   1/2 teaspoon garlic powder
   1/4 teaspoon salt
     1 cup finely chopped fresh broccoli
   1/2 cup shredded cheddar cheese
   1/2 cup chicken broth
Hot cooked rice, optional

Flatten chicken to 1/4-in. thickness. Combine poultry seasoning, pepper, curry powder, garlic powder and salt; sprinkle over chicken. Combine broccoli and cheese; place half in the center of each chicken breast. Fold long sides over filling; fold ends up and secure with a toothpick.

Place, seam side down, in an 8-in. square baking pan. Add broth. Cover pan loosely with foil. Bake at 350° for 30 minutes. Remove foil; baste the chicken with pan juices. Bake, uncovered, 10 minutes longer or until meat juices run clear. Remove toothpicks before serving. Thicken pan juices for gravy if desired. Serve with rice if desired. **Yield:** 2 servings.

POPOVERS FOR TWO

Alpha Wilson, Roswell, New Mexico

This recipe has been handed down through my family, and I've had it for almost 50 years. My husband and I especially like these popovers for a late breakfast, but they're great with soup or salad. Simply served with butter and honey, they're delicious anytime.

   1/2 cup milk
     1 egg
   1/2 cup all-purpose flour
   1/4 teaspoon salt
   1/4 teaspoon poultry seasoning, optional

Let milk and egg stand at room temperature for 30 minutes. Combine all ingredients in a mixing bowl; beat just until smooth. Pour into four greased 6-oz. custard cups; place on a baking sheet. Bake at 425° for 15 minutes. Reduce heat to 350° (do not open door). Bake 15-20 minutes longer or until popovers are deep golden brown (do not underbake). Serve warm. **Yield:** 4 popovers.

CRANBERRY PEAR SALAD

Edna Hoffman, Hebron, Indiana

I've had this recipe for as long as my husband and I have been married—more than 50 years! I like to serve the salad on a bed of green or red leaf lettuce and sometimes garnish it with dates. We like it as much now as we did all those years ago.

     1 can (8 ounces) pear halves
Lettuce leaves
   1/2 cup whole-berry cranberry sauce
Toasted sliced almonds, optional

Drain pears, reserving 1 tablespoon juice (discard remaining juice or refrigerate for another use). Place pears, cut side up, on a lettuce-lined plate. Combine the cranberry sauce and reserved pear juice; spoon over pears. Sprinkle with almonds if desired. **Yield:** 2 servings.

MINTY BAKED ALASKA

Brenda Mast, Clearwater, Florida

I've made this dessert on a few special occasions for my husband and me. He just loves it. It's so easy, but it looks and tastes like you spent all day in the kitchen. Crushed peppermint candy adds a special taste and decorative touch. It never fails to impress.

     2 egg whites
   1/4 cup sugar
   1/4 teaspoon cream of tartar
   1/4 teaspoon vanilla extract
Dash salt
     1 tablespoon crushed peppermint candy
   2/3 cup mint chocolate chip ice cream
     2 individual round sponge cakes

In a double boiler, combine the egg whites, sugar and cream of tartar; with a portable mixer, beat on low speed for 1 minute. Continue beating over low heat until mixture reaches 160°, about 12 minutes. Remove from the heat. Add vanilla and salt; beat until stiff peaks form, about 2 minutes. Fold in peppermint candy.

Place sponge cakes on an ungreased foil-lined baking sheet; top each with 1/3 cup ice cream. Immediately spread meringue over ice cream and cake, sealing meringue to the foil. Broil 8 in. from the heat for 3-5 minutes or until lightly browned. Serve immediately. **Yield:** 2 servings.

HAM STEW FOR TWO

Judy Hall, Lockport, Illinois

This dish is one my husband and I enjoy any time of the year, and if I don't have leftover ham, I buy a thick slice and use that. Served with a salad and rolls, it's a quick meal for two, but it's also easily adapted for a larger number.

    2 medium potatoes, peeled and cut into
      3/4-inch cubes
    2 medium carrots, sliced
1-1/2 cups cubed fully cooked ham
    1 cup water
    1 small onion, chopped
    1 bay leaf
  1/2 teaspoon salt
  1/4 teaspoon dried savory
  1/8 teaspoon pepper
    3 tablespoons all-purpose flour
    1 cup milk

In a saucepan, combine the first nine ingredients. Bring to a boil. Reduce heat; cover and simmer until vegetables are tender. In a small bowl, combine the flour and milk until smooth. Stir into stew. Bring to a boil; cook and stir for 2 minutes or until thickened. Discard bay leaf before serving. **Yield:** 2 servings.

BUTTERMILK CORN BREAD

Elizabeth Cooper, Madison, Alabama

My grandmother would refer to this recipe as "comfort food", made from ingredients available on the farm or staples found in her pantry. She always cooked the corn bread in her "seasoned" black skillet, and it turned out slick as butter every time.

    1 tablespoon vegetable oil
    1 cup cornmeal
  1/4 cup all-purpose flour
1-1/2 teaspoons baking powder
  1/2 teaspoon salt
  1/2 teaspoon baking soda
    1 egg
    1 cup buttermilk

Place oil in an 8-in. ovenproof skillet; tilt to coat bottom and sides. Place in a 425° oven for 10 minutes. In a bowl, combine cornmeal, flour, baking powder, salt and baking soda. Beat egg and buttermilk; add to dry ingredients just until moistened. Pour into the hot skillet. Bake for 15 minutes or until golden brown and a toothpick comes out clean. **Yield:** 2-4 servings.

EGG RICE SALAD

Flois Price, Morgan, Texas

The first time I tried this salad, I knew it was a keeper. Using rice as the basic ingredient is a refreshing change. I serve it as a luncheon salad or a side dish for a main meal. Garnished with olives and tomato wedges, it makes a colorful addition to the table.

  1/2 cup cooked rice, room temperature
    1 hard-cooked egg, chopped
  1/4 cup chopped celery
    1 green onion, chopped
    2 to 3 tablespoons mayonnaise
    1 tablespoon sweet pickle relish
Salt and pepper to taste
Lettuce leaves

In a bowl, combine the rice, egg, celery and onion. In another bowl, combine the mayonnaise, pickle relish, salt and pepper. Add to rice mixture and toss to coat. Transfer to two custard cups or a 1/2-cup mold. Cover and refrigerate until chilled. Just before serving, unmold onto lettuce-lined plates. **Yield:** 2 servings.

CREAMY CHOCOLATE PUDDING

Nora Reidy, Montoursville, Pennsylvania

Here's a recipe that satisfies a sweet tooth without any fuss. This wonderful chocolate pudding can be served plain or topped with whipped cream for a more elaborate finish.

    6 tablespoons sugar
  1/4 cup baking cocoa
    2 tablespoons cornstarch
1-1/2 cups milk
  1/2 teaspoon vanilla extract
Whipped topping, optional

In a saucepan, combine the sugar, cocoa and cornstarch. Gradually stir in milk until smooth. Bring to a boil over low heat, stirring constantly. Cook and stir for 2 minutes or until thickened. Remove from the heat; stir in vanilla. Pour into two serving dishes. Cover and refrigerate until chilled. Garnish with whipped topping if desired. **Yield:** 2 servings.

PUDDING TOPPERS
Tastefully top off pudding with strawberry slices, coconut or chopped nuts.

CHICKEN VEGETABLE POTPIE

Marva Vandivier, Battle Ground, Washington

I actually created this recipe when I was a young girl. Since then, I've found it's a good way to use up the second pastry when I make a one-crust pie. When I tell my husband, "It's chicken potpie for supper tonight," he lights up and thinks I've worked in the kitchen all day!

  2 medium carrots, sliced
  1 medium potato, peeled and cubed
  1 small onion, chopped
  1 celery rib, chopped
  1 cup water
1/2 cup frozen peas, thawed
  1 cup cubed cooked chicken
  1 can (10-3/4 ounces) condensed cream
    of chicken soup, undiluted
Pastry for single-crust pie (9 inches)

In a saucepan, cook the carrots, potato, onion and celery in water for 10 minutes or until tender; drain. Stir in the peas, chicken and soup. Pour into a greased 1-1/2-qt. deep baking dish. Roll out pastry to fit top of dish; place over filling. Trim, seal and flute edges. Cut slits in pastry. Bake at 350° for 50 minutes or until crust is golden and filling is bubbly. **Yield:** 2 servings.

WHOLE WHEAT BISCUITS

Edna Hoffman, Hebron, Indiana

I've had this biscuit recipe in my file for a long time. I love cooking and baking and am always creating something new by experimenting with recipes. I thought the substitution of whole wheat flour gave these biscuits a little different taste. They're great served alongside any meal.

1/3 cup all-purpose flour
1/3 cup whole wheat flour
  1 tablespoon sugar
3/4 teaspoon baking powder
1/4 teaspoon baking soda
1/4 teaspoon salt
  2 tablespoons cold butter *or* margarine
1/4 cup buttermilk

In a bowl, combine the all-purpose and whole wheat flours, sugar, baking powder, baking soda and salt. Cut in butter until crumbly. Stir in buttermilk just until moistened. Turn onto a floured surface; knead 6-8 times. Pat to 1-in. thickness; cut with a 2-1/2-in. biscuit cutter. Place on a greased baking sheet. Bake at 375° for 18-20 minutes or until lightly browned. **Yield:** 4 biscuits.

CRUNCHY MACARONI SALAD

Ruth Griggs, South Hill, Virginia

This pasta salad is ideal for one or two people, but I've often increased the recipe to take to potlucks. For variety, I'll sometimes add chopped pickles or shredded cheese. In summer, fresh tomatoes add color and flavor. However I choose to serve this versatile pasta salad, it's always well received.

  1 cup cooked elbow macaroni
  1 hard-cooked egg, chopped
  2 tablespoons chopped celery
  2 tablespoons chopped onion
  3 tablespoons mayonnaise *or* salad
    dressing
  1 teaspoon sugar
  1 teaspoon vinegar
1/2 teaspoon prepared mustard
1/4 teaspoon salt
Pinch pepper

In a bowl, combine the macaroni, egg, celery and onion. In another bowl, combine the remaining ingredients. Pour over macaroni mixture and toss gently. Cover and chill for 2 hours before serving. **Yield:** 2 servings.

PEAR CRUMBLE

Kezia Sullivan, Sackets Harbor, New York

Originally a pear crumble pie, I shortened this recipe to a crumble when I often was too short on time to make a pie crust from scratch. I've also found canned pears work as well as fresh, so that makes it even easier to prepare. The crumble is a very comforting, down-home dessert.

  3 medium pears, peeled, cored and sliced
  2 teaspoons lemon juice
  3 tablespoons sugar
  3 tablespoons old-fashioned oats
  2 tablespoons all-purpose flour
1/8 teaspoon ground cinnamon
1/8 teaspoon ground ginger
Dash ground nutmeg
  1 tablespoon cold butter *or* margarine
  2 tablespoons chopped nuts
Ice cream, optional

Place pear slices in a greased 1-qt. baking dish. Sprinkle with lemon juice. In a bowl, combine the sugar, oats, flour, cinnamon, ginger and nutmeg. Cut in butter until crumbly; add nuts. Sprinkle over pears. Bake at 350° for 25-30 minutes or until bubbly. Serve warm with ice cream if desired. **Yield:** 2 servings.

ANNIVERSARY CHOWDER

Barbara Harrison, Ringoes, New Jersey

We celebrated our 35th wedding anniversary with dinner at a lovely pre-Revolutionary War restaurant in Pennsylvania, where I enjoyed a wonderful salmon chowder. I wanted to duplicate it, so I put this recipe together, using salmon we had purchased in Alaska. It's a thick hearty soup.

    2 small red potatoes, cubed
  1/2 medium carrot, finely chopped
  1/4 cup finely chopped onion
    2 tablespoons butter *or* margarine
    2 cups half-and-half cream
    1 can (6 ounces) boneless skinless
        salmon, drained and flaked
  1/2 cup fresh or frozen corn
  1/4 teaspoon dried rosemary, crushed
  1/4 teaspoon dried parsley flakes
  1/4 teaspoon salt
  1/8 teaspoon pepper
  1/8 teaspoon rubbed sage
  1/8 teaspoon dried thyme

In a large saucepan, saute the potatoes, carrot and onion in butter until tender. Reduce heat; stir in remaining ingredients. Cook and stir for 10 minutes or until heated through. **Yield:** 2 servings.

CREAMY BASIL DRESSING

Shirley Awood Glaab, Hattiesburg, Mississippi

When I was growing up, our supper was not complete without a green salad and my dad's homemade dressing. He never had a written recipe, but the basic ingredients didn't vary. Making the salad was a ritual, and we would watch the process with great anticipation.

✓ **Uses less fat, sugar or salt. Includes Nutritional Analysis and Diabetic Exchanges.**

    2 tablespoons reduced-fat mayonnaise
    2 tablespoons fat-free plain yogurt
    2 teaspoons minced green onion *or* chives
  1/2 teaspoon dried basil
  1/4 teaspoon salt, optional
Salad greens and tomato wedges

In a small bowl, combine the mayonnaise, yogurt, onion, basil and salt if desired; mix well. Serve over greens and tomatoes. **Yield:** 1/4 cup.

Nutritional Analysis: 2 tablespoons of dressing (prepared without salt) equals 76 calories, 430 mg sodium, 5 mg cholesterol, 5 gm carbohydrate, 2 gm protein, 5 gm fat. **Diabetic Exchanges:** 1/2 starch, 1/2 fat.

CHOCOLATE SNACK CAKE

Debi Peschka, Broken Arrow, Oklahoma

This is a moist delicious snack cake, so good that icing is not necessary. Sometimes my husband puts a scoop of vanilla ice cream on top with a drizzle of chocolate syrup. Either way, it always satisfies our sweet tooth.

    1 cup boiling water
  1/4 cup butter *or* margarine
    1 egg
    1 teaspoon vanilla extract
    1 cup all-purpose flour
    1 cup sugar
    3 tablespoons baking cocoa
    1 teaspoon baking powder
  1/2 teaspoon baking soda
  1/4 teaspoon salt
Confectioners' sugar

In a mixing bowl, beat water and butter until butter is melted. Beat in egg and vanilla. Combine flour, sugar, cocoa, baking powder, baking soda and salt; add to the egg mixture. Beat for 2 minutes. Pour into a greased 8-in. square baking pan. Bake at 350° for 25-30 minutes or until a toothpick inserted near the center comes out clean. Cool on a wire rack. Dust with confectioners' sugar. **Yield:** 9 servings.

Editor's Note: Pieces of cake can be wrapped individually and frozen for a quick dessert.

ZIPPY EGG SALAD

(Not pictured)

Annemarie Pietila, Farmington Hills, Michigan

Egg salad is a refreshing, tasty change from lunch meat or peanut butter sandwiches. Everyone raves about this version with its added zip. It's the touch of mustard and lemon juice that does it.

    3 tablespoons mayonnaise
1-1/2 teaspoons prepared mustard
  1/8 teaspoon salt
  1/8 teaspoon pepper
  1/8 teaspoon lemon juice
    3 hard-cooked eggs, coarsely chopped
    1 tablespoon minced green onion
Bread *or* crackers
Sliced tomato, optional

In a small bowl, combine the mayonnaise, mustard, salt, pepper and lemon juice. Stir in the eggs and onion. Serve on bread or crackers; top with tomato if desired. **Yield:** 2 servings.

CUBE STEAK SKILLET SUPPER

Karen Rodgers, Verona, Virginia

I first made this delicious main dish in the '70s for a progressive dinner party. It was so easy to prepare. This fast recipe came in handy while I was a working mom, too. I still like to make the cube steaks often to this day.

1/4 cup all-purpose flour
1/4 teaspoon salt
Dash pepper
2 cube steaks
1 to 2 tablespoons vegetable oil
1 small onion, sliced
1 can (15 ounces) sliced potatoes, drained
1 can (14-1/2 ounces) French-style green beans, drained
1 can (10-3/4 ounces) condensed golden mushroom soup, undiluted
Paprika

In a large resealable plastic bag, combine the flour, salt and pepper. Add cube steaks and shake to coat. In a skillet, brown steaks on both sides in oil. Set aside and keep warm. Add onion, potatoes and green beans to skillet; stir in soup. Return steaks to skillet. Cover and simmer for 15 minutes or until meat is tender. Sprinkle with paprika. **Yield:** 2 servings.

FRENCH ONION SOUP

Barbara Brunner, Steelton, Pennsylvania

I adapted a basic recipe to copy the onion soup served at my favorite restaurant. No matter what my entree, I always ordered the soup. Now I can make it at home. It's a meal in itself or an impressive beginning to a full-course meal.

2 medium onions, chopped
1 teaspoon sugar
6 tablespoons butter *or* margarine, *divided*
1 tablespoon all-purpose flour
1/8 teaspoon pepper
Dash ground nutmeg
2-1/2 cups beef broth
2 tablespoons grated Parmesan cheese
2 slices French bread (1 inch thick)
4 slices provolone cheese

In a saucepan, saute onions and sugar in 3 tablespoons of butter until golden brown. Stir in the flour, pepper and nutmeg until blended. Gradually stir in broth. Bring to a boil; cook and stir for

2 minutes. Reduce heat; cover and simmer for 30 minutes. Stir in the Parmesan cheese.

Meanwhile, in a skillet, melt the remaining butter; add French bread. Cook until golden brown on both sides. Ladle soup into two oven-proof bowls. Place a slice of provolone cheese in each bowl; top with bread and remaining cheese. Bake at 375° for 10 minutes or until the cheese is bubbly. **Yield:** 2 servings.

ORANGE BANANA SALAD

Mary Paulson, Hopkins, Minnesota

I came up with this salad when an unexpected guest showed up for lunch and I had to "make do" with what was on hand. I thought it would complement my homemade ginger chicken soup, and it did! It's a wonderful make-ahead salad and very attractive.

1 medium navel orange, peeled and sliced
1 to 2 tablespoons honey
1 teaspoon whole cloves
2 cups torn salad greens
1 medium firm banana, sliced
1 to 2 teaspoons flaked coconut, toasted

Place orange slices in a bowl. Combine honey and cloves; pour over oranges. Cover and refrigerate for at least 1 hour. Discard cloves. Arrange greens on salad plates. Top with orange and banana slices. Drizzle with honey mixture. Sprinkle with coconut. **Yield:** 2 servings.

APPLE GRAHAM DESSERT

Rita Ferro, Alameda, California

My favorite after-school snack was applesauce with graham crackers. I started cooking and baking when I was a very young child, and as far as I can remember, this cake was my creation. It deliciously combines my favorite schooltime treats.

6 cinnamon graham crackers (4-3/4 inches x 2-1/2 inches)
1 cup applesauce
1 cup whipped topping
Chopped walnuts, optional

Place one graham cracker on a serving plate. Spread with 2 heaping tablespoons of applesauce. Repeat layers five more times, ending with applesauce. Spread whipped topping over top and sides. Sprinkle with nuts if desired. Refrigerate for 2 hours before slicing. **Yield:** 2 servings.

MEAT LOAF PATTIE

Dorothy Hunt, Waltham, Massachusetts

With this recipe, we can have a hearty meat loaf dinner without leftovers. That delights both my husband and me. He never liked the creative ways I used up leftover meat loaf!

  1/3 cup seasoned bread crumbs
    3 tablespoons milk
    1 teaspoon Worcestershire sauce
    1 teaspoon finely chopped onion
  1/4 teaspoon salt
  1/2 pound lean ground beef
Ketchup

In a bowl, combine the first five ingredients. Crumble beef over mixture and mix well. Shape into a large pattie. Place in a shallow microwave-safe dish. Microwave, uncovered, on high for 3-4 minutes. Let stand for 3 minutes or until a meat thermometer reads 160°. Serve with ketchup. **Yield:** 2 servings.

    Editor's Note: This recipe was tested in an 850-watt microwave. Meat loaf may also be baked at 350° for 20 minutes or until a meat thermometer reads 160°.

OLIVE-CHEESE ZUCCHINI BOATS

Dorothy Pritchett, Wills Point, Texas

I was anxious the first time I tried this recipe, wondering if my family would like it. It was a big hit, though, and I was happy to find another idea for serving this prolific garden vegetable.

    1 medium zucchini
  1/4 cup water
  1/8 teaspoon salt
    1 tablespoon butter *or* margarine
  1/4 cup soft bread crumbs
    2 tablespoons chopped stuffed olives
    2 tablespoons shredded cheddar cheese

Cut zucchini in half lengthwise; scoop out and reserve pulp, leaving 1/4-in. shells. Place zucchini shells, cut side down, in a skillet. Add water. Bring to a boil; reduce heat. Cover and simmer for 5-6 minutes or until tender; drain. Turn shells cut side up; sprinkle with salt.

    Chop the zucchini pulp; saute in a small saucepan in butter for 5 minutes or until tender. Stir in the bread crumbs and olives. Spoon into the zucchini shells; sprinkle with cheddar cheese. Cover and cook over medium heat (with no added water) for 5 minutes or until the cheese is melted. **Yield:** 2 servings.

CUCUMBER POTATO SALAD

Martha Campbell, Belton, South Carolina

This salad is just the right size for my husband and me. When I use the microwave to cook the potatoes, I can serve it up in no time.

    2 medium red potatoes, cooked and cubed
  2 to 3 tablespoons mayonnaise
    1 tablespoon dill pickle relish
    1 tablespoon diced pimientos
  1/2 teaspoon celery seed
  1/2 teaspoon dill weed
  1/4 teaspoon salt
    1 medium cucumber, sliced
    2 tablespoons chopped pecans, toasted

In a bowl, combine the first seven ingredients. Place cucumber slices in a fan shape on two salad plates; top with potato salad. Sprinkle with pecans. **Yield:** 2 servings.

DEEP-DISH BLACKBERRY PIE

Dorothy Lilliquist, Brooklyn Center, Minnesota

When I make this dessert, I think back to 1942. We grew extra large and juicy blackberries that year, and Mother canned 400 quarts.

    3 cups fresh *or* frozen blackberries,
      thawed and drained
  1/2 cup sugar
    2 tablespoons cornstarch
    1 teaspoon lemon juice
  1/4 teaspoon ground cinnamon
TOPPING:
  3/4 cup all-purpose flour
    3 teaspoons sugar, *divided*
  1/4 teaspoon salt
    3 tablespoons cold butter *or* margarine
    1 tablespoon shortening
    3 tablespoons cold water
    1 egg white, beaten

Place blackberries in a bowl. Combine sugar and cornstarch; sprinkle over berries. Add lemon juice and cinnamon; toss to coat. Spoon into a greased 1-qt. baking dish. In a bowl, combine the flour, 1 teaspoon sugar and salt. Cut in butter and shortening until mixture resembles coarse crumbs. Add water; toss with a fork until a ball forms.

    Roll out pastry; make a lattice crust over filling. Crimp edges. Brush with egg white; sprinkle with remaining sugar. Bake at 375° for 40-45 minutes or until crust is golden brown and filling is bubbly. **Yield:** 2 servings.

PASTA PRIMAVERA

Clara DelVitto, Venice, Florida

Since I eat very little meat, I'm always on the look-out for vegetarian and low-fat recipes. I came up with this recipe after a lot of experimenting.

  1/2 cup sliced onion
  1/2 cup julienned green *or* sweet red pepper
    2 teaspoons olive *or* vegetable oil
  1/2 cup sliced zucchini
  1/2 cup sliced yellow summer squash
    2 medium fresh mushrooms, sliced
  3/4 cup stewed tomatoes
  1/4 to 1/2 teaspoon dried basil
    2 cups hot cooked pasta
Shredded Parmesan cheese, optional

In a skillet, saute onion and green pepper in oil until crisp-tender. Add zucchini, yellow squash and mushrooms; saute for 1 minute. Add tomatoes and basil. Bring to a boil; reduce heat. Cover and simmer for 8-10 minutes or until vegetables are tender. Toss with pasta; sprinkle with cheese if desired. **Yield:** 2 servings.

COFFEE MALLOW DESSERT

Helen Davis, Waterbury, Vermont

This is one of my favorite summertime desserts, cool and soothing on a hot, humid day. The mild coffee flavor is most refreshing.

    8 cream-filled chocolate cookies, crushed
    2 tablespoons butter *or* margarine, melted
  1/2 cup hot brewed coffee
  16 marshmallows
  1/2 cup whipping cream
    1 tablespoon confectioners' sugar
  1/2 teaspoon vanilla extract

Combine cookie crumbs and butter; set aside 1 tablespoon for topping. Press remaining crumb mixture onto the bottom and up the sides of two lightly greased 10-oz. custard cups; set aside. Place coffee and eight marshmallows in a blender; cover and process until smooth. Add the remaining marshmallows; cover and process until smooth. Cover and refrigerate in the blender for 2 hours or until cold. Process again until smooth; transfer to a bowl. In a mixing bowl, beat whipping cream until soft peaks form. Gradually add sugar and vanilla, beating until stiff peaks form. Gently fold into coffee mixture. Spoon into prepared cups; sprinkle with reserved crumbs. Refrigerate for at least 1-2 hours before serving. **Yield:** 2 servings.

SALSA CORN MUFFINS

Pat Akers, Stillwater, Oklahoma

My mother was a great cook and loved to try anything new. At 89, she was still winning ribbons at our county fair. We operate an independent-living retirement home. Mother helped out with the cooking, and these muffins were a frequent request from residents.

    1 cup all-purpose flour
  1/2 cup cornmeal
    2 tablespoons sugar
    1 teaspoon baking powder
  1/4 teaspoon baking soda
Pinch salt
    1 egg, beaten
  1/2 cup fresh *or* frozen corn
  1/2 cup buttermilk
  1/4 cup vegetable oil
  1/4 cup shredded cheddar cheese
    4 teaspoons diced pimientos
    4 teaspoons salsa

In a large bowl, combine the flour, cornmeal, sugar, baking powder, baking soda and salt. In another bowl, combine the remaining ingredients. Stir into dry ingredients just until moistened. Fill paper-lined or greased muffin cups two-thirds full. Bake at 375° for 20-22 minutes or until a toothpick comes out clean. Cool for 5 minutes before removing to a wire rack. **Yield:** 8 muffins.

TROPICAL FRUIT DIP

Jane Mason, Galesburg, Illinois

My husband's Aunt Marilyn gave me this recipe years ago. I have tasted a lot of fruit dips, but this is the best, especially when all the fresh summer fruit is available. I also have doubled the recipe and used it as a delicious filling between lemon or orange cake layers.

  1/4 cup sugar
1-1/2 teaspoons all-purpose flour
    1 egg, beaten
  1/4 cup pineapple juice
    2 tablespoons orange juice
2-1/4 teaspoons lemon juice
1-1/2 cups whipped topping
Assorted fresh fruit

In a small saucepan, combine the sugar and flour. Stir in egg and juices. Cook and stir over low heat until mixture is thickened and reaches 160°. Cover and refrigerate until chilled. Just before serving, fold in whipped topping. Serve with fruit. **Yield:** 1-3/4 cups.

STUFFED PORK CHOPS

Bessie Hulett, Shively, Kentucky

Any time I want the meal to be extra special—for dinner parties with friends, birthdays, anniversaries or holiday meals—I prepare these pork chops.

    2 tablespoons chopped celery leaves
    1 tablespoon chopped onion
    2 tablespoons butter *or* margarine, *divided*
 3/4 cup dry bread crumbs
 2/3 cup chicken broth, *divided*
    1 tablespoon minced fresh parsley *or* 1
        teaspoon dried parsley flakes
 1/2 teaspoon salt
 1/2 teaspoon paprika
 1/2 teaspoon rubbed sage
 1/4 teaspoon pepper
 1/4 teaspoon dried thyme
    2 pork loin chops (1-1/4 inches thick)

In a skillet, saute celery leaves and onion in 1 tablespoon of butter until soft. Remove from the heat; stir in bread crumbs, 1/3 cup broth and the seasonings; mix well. Cut a pocket in each pork chop by slicing from the fat side almost to the bone. Spoon about 1/2 cup stuffing into each pocket. Secure with string or toothpicks.

Melt remaining butter in a skillet. Brown the chops on both sides. Place in a greased 11-in. x 7-in. x 2-in. baking dish; pour remaining broth over the chops. Cover and bake at 350° for 40-50 minutes or until juices run clear. Remove string or toothpicks before serving. Thicken pan juices if desired. **Yield:** 2 servings.

BROCCOLI SQUASH BAKE

Mildred Sherrer, Bay City, Texas

My grandmother made this when she cooked for our farmhands years ago. I've cut her recipe down to serve fewer people.

    2 cups broccoli florets
    3 tablespoons butter *or* margarine
    2 cups sliced yellow summer squash
    1 egg
 1/2 cup shredded Swiss cheese
 1/4 cup milk
 1/4 teaspoon ground mustard
Dash cayenne pepper
    2 tablespoons grated Parmesan cheese

In a skillet, stir-fry broccoli in butter for 3 minutes. Add squash. Cook 3 minutes longer or until the vegetables are tender. Transfer to a greased 1-qt. baking dish. In a bowl, combine the egg,

Swiss cheese, milk, mustard and cayenne; mix well. Pour over vegetables. Sprinkle with Parmesan cheese. Bake, uncovered, at 350° for 15-20 minutes or until set. **Yield:** 2-4 servings.

CRUMB-COATED TOMATOES

Connie Simon, Cleveland, Ohio

This recipe brings back many memories of my grandmother. It was her favorite dish for family get-togethers. It's easy to make and takes little time to prepare.

 1/2 cup crushed butter-flavored crackers
        (about 13)
 1/2 teaspoon salt
 1/4 teaspoon pepper
    1 medium tomato, cut into 1/4-inch slices
    1 egg, beaten
    2 tablespoons butter *or* margarine

In a shallow bowl, combine the cracker crumbs, salt and pepper. Dip tomato slices into egg, then into crumbs. In a skillet, cook tomatoes in butter for 2 minutes on each side or until golden brown. Serve immediately. **Yield:** 2 servings.

COCONUT CHOCOLATE CHIP COOKIES

(Not pictured)

Laura Bankard, Manchester, Maryland

Here is a delicious twist on traditional chocolate chip cookies. They're great for coconut lovers. My whole family agrees this recipe is a winner.

 1/2 cup butter *or* margarine, softened
 3/4 cup sugar
    1 egg
 1/2 teaspoon coconut extract
    1 cup plus 2 tablespoons all-purpose flour
 1/2 teaspoon baking soda
 1/2 teaspoon salt
    1 cup (6 ounces) semisweet chocolate
        chips
 1/2 cup flaked coconut

In a mixing bowl, cream butter and sugar. Beat in egg and coconut extract; mix well. Combine the flour, baking soda and salt; add to the creamed mixture. Stir in chocolate chips and coconut. Drop by rounded tablespoonfuls 2 in. apart onto ungreased baking sheets. Bake at 375° for 11-13 minutes or until golden brown. Remove to wire racks to cool. **Yield:** about 1-1/4 dozen.

▰▰▰▰▰▰▰▰▰▰▰▰
SAUSAGE SPINACH BAKE

Monna McConnell, Beaver Falls, Pennsylvania

My family wouldn't eat spinach until I found this recipe. Then it became a dish they frequently requested. It's a meal in itself, but it also adds color to any menu.

- 1/4 pound bulk pork sausage
- 1/2 cup chopped onion
- 1/2 cup chopped celery
- 1 package (10 ounces) frozen chopped spinach, thawed and drained
- 1 egg, beaten
- 1/2 cup dry bread crumbs
- 1/4 cup shredded cheddar cheese
- 1/4 teaspoon salt
- 1 tablespoon grated Parmesan cheese

In a skillet, cook sausage, onion and celery over medium heat until meat is no longer pink and vegetables are tender. Drain; remove from the heat. Add spinach, egg, crumbs, cheddar cheese and salt. Transfer to a greased shallow 1-qt. baking dish. Sprinkle with Parmesan cheese. Cover and bake at 350° for 20 minutes or until heated through. **Yield:** 2 servings.

▰▰▰▰▰▰▰▰▰▰▰▰
CITRUS FROST

John Eberhardt, Jamestown, North Dakota

This creamy drink is refreshing any time of the year, but especially on hot and humid days. It's easy to prepare and very flavorful.

- 1 can (8 ounces) crushed pineapple, undrained
- 1 cup orange juice
- 1/3 cup sugar
- 2 tablespoons lime juice
- 2 tablespoons lemon juice
- 1-1/4 cups vanilla ice cream

Place the first five ingredients in a blender; cover and process on high speed until smooth. Add ice cream and process until blended. Pour into chilled glasses. Serve immediately. **Yield:** 2 servings.

▰▰▰▰▰▰▰▰▰▰▰▰
QUICK CHEESE PUFFS

Janet Scherffius, Mountain Home, Arkansas

This recipe is one of my favorites for a luncheon dish or a quick and easy meatless meal. For extra flavor,

I'll sometimes use homemade bread or a specialty bread such as Italian, French or sourdough.

- 2 tablespoons butter *or* margarine, softened
- 3 slices white bread
- 2 eggs
- 1 cup milk
- 1/2 cup shredded cheddar cheese
- 1/4 teaspoon onion salt
- 8 to 10 drops hot pepper sauce

Spread butter on one side of each slice of bread. Cut bread into strips; place strips, buttered side down, on the bottom and around the sides of two greased 10-oz. baking dishes. In a bowl, beat eggs and milk. Add cheese, onion salt and hot pepper sauce. Pour over bread. Place the dishes on a baking sheet. Bake, uncovered, at 350° for 30-35 minutes or until puffed and golden brown. Serve immediately. **Yield:** 2 servings.

▰▰▰▰▰▰▰▰▰▰▰▰
APPLE CRISP FOR TWO

(Not pictured)

Emma Crowder, Anaheim, California

I like to make this dessert in fall, when the apple crop is fresh and delicious. It's perfect for the two of us and a wonderful ending to any meal.

- 2 medium tart apples, peeled and sliced
- 3 tablespoons water
- 3 tablespoons graham cracker crumbs
- 3 tablespoons sugar
- 1/4 teaspoon ground cinnamon
- 2 tablespoons cold butter *or* margarine
- Whipped topping and additional cinnamon, optional

Place apples in a greased 1-qt. baking dish; pour water over apples. In a bowl, combine the graham cracker crumbs, sugar and cinnamon. Cut in butter until crumbly. Sprinkle over apples. Bake, uncovered, at 350° for 25-30 minutes or until apples are tender. Garnish with whipped topping and cinnamon if desired. **Yield:** 2 servings.

TOPPING CRISPS WITH CHEESE

For a tasty variation, add a slice of cheddar cheese to a serving of apple crisp before warming. When the cheese is melted, top with vanilla ice cream and a sprinkling of cinnamon.

PRIME RIB AND POTATOES

Richard Fairchild, Tustin, California

I've discovered a variety of small roasts that work well for two, without creating leftovers for the rest of the week. This prime rib is perfect for a holiday meal when company isn't coming. The portion for each is generous, and the flavor is unsurpassed.

- 1 tablespoon olive *or* vegetable oil
- 1 small garlic clove, minced
- 1 standing beef rib roast (about 3 pounds and 2 ribs)
- 2 large baking potatoes

Combine the oil and garlic; rub evenly over roast. Place roast, fat side up, in a small roasting pan. Place a potato on each side of roast. Bake, uncovered, at 325° for 2 to 2-1/2 hours until meat reaches desired doneness (for rare, a meat thermometer should read 140°; medium, 160°; well-done, 170°). Let stand for 10 minutes before carving. **Yield:** 2 servings.

WARM BACON SPINACH SALAD

Patty Kile, Greentown, Pennsylvania

This was what the Pennsylvania Germans called "wilted salad". It was one of the first recipes I was taught to make. When the dressing is warm, I pour it over the greens and set it aside while I prepare the rest of the meal. The heat wilts the greens, which are still slightly warm when served.

- 3 bacon strips, diced
- 1 tablespoon all-purpose flour
- 1 egg
- 6 tablespoons water
- 2 tablespoons vinegar
- 1 tablespoon sugar
- Salt and pepper to taste
- 3 cups torn fresh spinach
- 1/2 cup seasoned croutons

In a skillet, cook the bacon until crisp. Remove bacon to paper towels. Drain, reserving 1 tablespoon of the drippings. Stir flour into drippings until smooth. In a large bowl, beat the egg; add the water, vinegar, sugar, salt and pepper. Slowly pour into skillet. Bring to a boil; boil for 2 minutes, stirring constantly.

Place spinach in a bowl. Remove dressing from the heat; stir in reserved bacon. Immediately spoon desired amount over spinach; add croutons and toss to coat. Serve warm. Store leftover dressing in the refrigerator for up to 2 days. Before

serving, reheat over low heat just until heated through. **Yield:** 2 servings.

MAPLE-GLAZED CARROTS

Sharon Bickett, Chester, South Carolina

I like to make this side dish when I want to add some color to my meal. The touch of maple syrup is a nice surprise and so compatible with the carrot flavor.

- 1-1/2 cups baby carrots *or* sliced carrots
- 1/2 cup water
- 1 tablespoon butter *or* margarine
- 2 tablespoons maple syrup
- 1/4 cup chopped pecans

In a small saucepan, bring carrots and water to a boil. Reduce heat; cover and cook for 10 minutes or until tender. Drain. Stir in butter, syrup and pecans until the butter is melted. **Yield:** 2 servings.

PUMPKIN STREUSEL CUSTARD

Maxine Smith, Owanka, South Dakota

This is a delectable dessert for chilly fall and winter days. The streusel topping complements the smooth, spicy custard to perfection. I adjusted a dessert recipe in my files to come up with this two-serving version.

- 1 egg
- 1/4 cup packed brown sugar
- 1/4 teaspoon vanilla extract
- 1/4 teaspoon salt
- 1/4 teaspoon ground cinnamon
- 1/8 teaspoon *each* ground allspice, ginger and nutmeg
- 2/3 cup cooked *or* canned pumpkin
- 1/2 cup evaporated milk

TOPPING:
- 1 tablespoon brown sugar
- 2 teaspoons all-purpose flour
- 1/4 teaspoon ground cinnamon
- 1 teaspoon cold butter *or* margarine
- 2 tablespoons chopped pecans

In a mixing bowl, beat the egg. Add brown sugar, vanilla, salt and spices. Stir in pumpkin and milk. Pour into two greased 8- or 10-oz. custard cups. Bake at 325° for 20 minutes. Meanwhile, for topping, combine brown sugar, flour and cinnamon in a small bowl. Cut in the butter until crumbly; stir in pecans. Sprinkle over custard. Bake 15 minutes longer or until a knife inserted near the center comes out clean. **Yield:** 2 servings.

Turkey Turnovers

Julie Wagner, Northville, Michigan

I make this dish often after the holidays when there's leftover turkey in the refrigerator or freezer. It's a hearty meal for the two of us and more simple to prepare than a traditional potpie.

> 1 package (3 ounces) cream cheese, softened
> 1 tablespoon milk
> 1/2 cup cubed cooked turkey
> 1/2 cup cooked peas *or* vegetable of your choice
> 4 teaspoons sliced almonds
> 1 tablespoon minced fresh parsley
> 1 tablespoon finely chopped onion
> 1-1/2 teaspoons diced pimientos
> Dash *each* salt, pepper and garlic powder
> 1 cup biscuit/baking mix
> 1/4 cup cold water
> 1 tablespoon butter *or* margarine, melted
> 1/2 to 3/4 cup condensed cream of chicken soup, undiluted *or* chicken gravy

In a mixing bowl, beat cream cheese and milk until smooth. Stir in the turkey, peas, almonds, parsley, onion, pimientos, salt, pepper and garlic powder; set aside. In a bowl, combine biscuit mix and water until a soft dough forms. On a floured surface, knead gently 5-6 times or until dough is no longer sticky. Gently roll into an 11-in. x 7-in. rectangle; cut in half.

Spoon half of the turkey mixture onto each. Carefully fold pastry over filling; seal edges tightly with a fork. Brush tops with butter. Place on a greased baking sheet. Bake at 350° for 30-35 minutes or until golden brown. Meanwhile, heat soup; serve with turnovers. **Yield:** 2 servings.

Red Pepper 'n' Corn Skillet

Barbara Marshall, Concord, California

This is an old recipe we used when I was growing up in Kentucky. We called it "fried corn" and made it as long as we could get corn on the cob. It's an attractive side dish and very tasty, flavored with bacon.

> 1 bacon strip, diced
> 3/4 cup fresh *or* frozen corn
> 1/3 cup chopped onion
> 1/2 cup chopped sweet red *or* green pepper
> 1/4 cup chicken broth
> 1/2 teaspoon salt
> 1/4 teaspoon pepper
> 1 tablespoon cider *or* red wine vinegar

> 2 teaspoons minced fresh sage *or* 1/4 teaspoon rubbed sage

In a skillet, cook bacon over medium heat until nearly crisp. Add the corn, onion and red pepper. Cook and stir over medium heat for 5 minutes or until vegetables are tender. Stir in the broth, salt and pepper. Cook for 5 minutes or until liquid is almost absorbed. Stir in the vinegar and sage. **Yield:** 2 servings.

Caramelized Apple Rings

Helen Steele, Polk City, Florida

When my children were little, they liked fruit, so I tried to make several dishes with different kinds. This recipe was one of their favorites. We lived close to an apple farm, so we always had apples on hand.

> 1 large tart apple, cored and sliced 1/2 inch thick
> 2 tablespoons butter or margarine
> 1/4 cup packed brown sugar

In a skillet, cook apples in butter until tender. Sprinkle with brown sugar. Cook until apples are golden brown and caramelized, about 5 minutes. **Yield:** 2 servings.

Oatmeal Apricot Squares

Veronica Roza, Bayport, New York

Easy to prepare and designed to make a small amount, these fruity oatmeal squares are a marvelous blend of flavors. It's a dessert that can be stirred up in no time to satisfy a sweet tooth...warm from the oven or as a treat later.

> 1 cup all-purpose flour
> 1 cup quick-cooking oats
> 1/2 cup packed brown sugar
> 1/4 teaspoon salt
> 1/4 teaspoon baking soda
> 1/2 cup cold butter *or* margarine
> 3/4 cup apricot preserves

In a bowl, combine the first five ingredients. Cut in butter until the mixture resembles coarse crumbs. Press half of the mixture into a greased 8-in. square baking pan. Spread with preserves. Sprinkle with remaining oat mixture; gently press down. Bake at 350° for 38-42 minutes or until golden brown. Cool on a wire rack. Cut into squares. **Yield:** 16 servings.

General Recipe Index

A

APPETIZERS & SNACKS
Cold Appetizers
Chicken Salad Puffs, 12
Cucumber Canapes, 5
Ham Pickle Pinwheels, 14
Marinated Shrimp, 5
Sweet-Sour Deviled Eggs, 12
Dips and Spreads
Ham Salad Spread, 150
Onions and Cream Appetizer, 14
Shrimp Appetizer Spread, 7
Sweet Potato Cheese Ball, 14
Taco Joe Dip, 6
Tropical Fruit Dip, 167
Zippy Cheese Dip, 150
Hot Appetizers
Catch Some "Z's", 8
Fried Jalapenos, 13
Ham 'n' Cheese Tortillas, 8
Hawaiian Egg Rolls, 6
Party Franks, 15
Speedy Pizza Rings, 6
Starry Night Taco Cups, 8
Snacks
Apricot Burritos, 13
Confetti Caramel Corn, 12
Slumber Party Cookie Pizza, 9

APPLES
Apple Crisp for Two, 171
✓Apple Delight Salad, 59
Apple Graham Dessert, 163
Apple Ham Steak, 30
Apple Rhubarb Crumble, 117
Apple Snack Cake, 108
Caramelized Apple Rings, 175
Harvest Apple Cheesecake, 126
Pear Apple Crisp, 135

APRICOTS
Apricot Burritos, 13
Apricot-Filled Pork Tenderloin, 38
Apricot Peach Cobbler, 118
✓Apricot-Stuffed Turkey Breast, 40
✓Apricot Turkey and Rice, 48
Oatmeal Apricot Squares, 175

ARTICHOKES
Antipasto Sub, 20
Artichoke Steak Salad, 63
Artichoke Tossed Salad, 68

ASPARAGUS
Asparagus Onion Casserole, 80
Chilled Asparagus Soup, 75
Creamy Dressing Over Asparagus, 66

B

BACON
BLT Macaroni Salad, 70
Bacon Veggie Roll-Ups, 27
Deluxe Bacon Burgers, 146
Warm Bacon Spinach Salad, 173

BANANAS
Banana Delight, 139
Banana Split Shortcake, 133
Carrot Banana Bread, 97
Orange Banana Salad, 163
Strawberry-Banana Gelatin Salad, 63

BARS & BROWNIES
Almond Coconut Brownies, 105
Caramel Cashew Brownies, 104
Cashew Blondies, 111
Coconut Pecan Blondies, 101
Fast Fudgy Brownies, 111
Frosted Fudge Brownies, 100
Fudgy Nut Brownies, 104
Glazed Chocolate Chip Brownies, 104
Holiday Brownies, 114
Holstein Brownies, 113
Macadamia Chip Brownies, 105
Macaroon Brownies, 99
Microwave Brownies, 110
Mint Brownie Cupcakes, 108
Mocha Truffle Brownies, 109
✓No-Guilt Brownies, 102
Oatmeal Apricot Squares, 175
Out-of-This-World Brownies, 99
Peanut Butter Brownies, 110
Pecan Brownies, 111
Treasured Brownies, 108

BEANS
Bean Tossed Salad, 139
Beef 'n' Green Bean Pie, 47
Big-Batch Baked Beans, 87
Black Bean Rice Bake, 24
Chicken Bean Stew, 23
✓Chili Non Carne, 58
Fit-for-a-King Baked Beans, 82
Green Beans with Cherry Tomatoes, 142
Hearty Bean Soup, 60
Meaty Bean Casserole, 22
Navy Bean Squash Soup, 59
Roasted Vegetable Soup, 66
Taco Joe Dip, 6
Tex-Mex Bean Salad, 133
Tomato Bean Salad, 137
Two-Bean Turkey Salad, 67
Vegetable Bean Soup, 77

BEEF (*also see Ground Beef*)
Artichoke Steak Salad, 63

Barbecue Sandwiches, 28
Beef Stew with Herb Dumplings, 50
Braised Beef Rolls, 144
Cajun Pepper Steak, 46
Cube Steak Skillet Supper, 163
Easy Beef and Noodles, 35
Herb-Crusted Chuck Roast, 32
Mom's Vegetable Soup, 61
Old-Fashioned Swiss Steak, 33
Prime Rib and Potatoes, 173
✓Sesame Flank Steak, 20
Sirloin with Bernaise Sauce, 54
Stir-Fried Steak and Veggies, 39
Stovetop Pot Roast, 18
Swiss Steak with Dumplings, 148

BEVERAGES
Almond Tea, 7
Citrus Frost, 171
Halloween Punch, 7
Hot Raspberry-Lemonade Drink Mix, 15
Peach Smoothies, 9
Rosy Fruit Punch, 150
Sleepy-Time Shakes, 8
Summertime Strawberry Punch, 5

BISCUITS
Butter-Dipped Biscuit Squares, 94
Whole Wheat Biscuits, 159

BLUE-RIBBON RECIPES
Appetizers
Hawaiian Egg Rolls, 6
Marinated Shrimp, 5
Sweet Potato Cheese Ball, 14
Taco Joe Dip, 6
Bars and Brownies
Coconut Pecan Blondies, 101
Frosted Fudge Brownies, 100
Macaroon Brownies, 99
Out-of-This-World Brownies, 99
Breads, Muffins and Rolls
Cardamom Braids, 92
Mashed Potato Rolls, 92
Orange Swirl Coffee Cake, 91
✓Tangerine Muffins, 96
Desserts
Chocolate Cookie Torte, 112
Macaroon Cherry Pie, 125
Northern Cherry Puffs, 118
Old-Fashioned Chess Pie, 124
Pretty Plum Parfaits, 118
Main Dishes
Almond Turkey Casserole, 45
Apricot-Filled Pork Tenderloin, 38
Au Gratin Peas and Potatoes, 17
Baked Chicken and Acorn Squash, 32
Baked Cod, 52
Barbecued Turkey Sandwiches, 38

Cranberry Pork Chops, 20
Deluxe Ham Balls, 48
Grilled Chicken with Peach Sauce, 49
Grilled Pork and Poblano Peppers, 37
Herb-Roasted Turkey, 46
Italian Sausage Stew, 19
Sliced Ham with Roasted Vegetables, 24
Spinach Swiss Pie, 53
Stovetop Pot Roast, 18
Sweet 'n' Sour Meatballs, 17
Teriyaki Glazed Chicken, 52

Side Dishes
Asparagus Onion Casserole, 80
Cheesy Zucchini Saute, 79
Creamed Cauliflower, 84
Scalloped Potatoes and Carrots, 79
Zucchini Supreme, 88

Soups and Salads
Cauliflower Ham Chowder, 68
✓Festive Fruit Salad, 74
Navy Bean Squash Soup, 59
Nectarine Chicken Salad, 73
Old-Fashioned Potato Salad, 75
Sesame Cucumber Salad, 69
Turkey Dumpling Soup, 62

BREADS (see Biscuits; Coffee Cakes & Doughnuts; Corn Bread & Cornmeal; Muffins; Quick Breads; Rolls; Yeast Breads)

BROCCOLI
Broccoli Squash Bake, 169
Broccoli-Stuffed Chicken, 155
Carrot Broccoli Salad, 77
Crumb-Topped Broccoli Bake, 86
Raisin Broccoli Toss, 76
Sweet Floret Salad, 72

C

CABBAGE & SAUERKRAUT
Bavarian Bratwurst Supper, 42
Cabbage-Tomato Pasta Toss, 85
Citrus Pineapple Coleslaw, 58
Colorful Cabbage Skillet, 153
Fruit Slaw in a Cabbage Bowl, 71

CAKES & CUPCAKES (also see Cheesecakes)
Apple Snack Cake, 108
Chocolate Cookie Torte, 112
Chocolate Snack Cake, 161
Chocolate Sweet Potato Cake, 149
Lemon Cake Roll, 102
Lime Angel Food Cake, 101
Maple Carrot Cupcakes, 142
Mint Brownie Cupcakes, 108
Old-Fashioned Raisin Cake, 100
Orange Date Pound Cake, 114
Potluck Chocolate Cake, 112
Saucy Chocolate Cake, 137

CARROTS
Almond-Topped Carrots, 84
Carrot Banana Bread, 97

Carrot Broccoli Salad, 77
Golden Gelatin Salad, 148
Maple Carrot Cupcakes, 142
Maple-Glazed Carrots, 173
Scalloped Potatoes and Carrots, 79

CASSEROLES (also see Meatballs & Meat Loaves; Meat Pies & Pizza; Oven Entrees)
Main Dishes
Almond Turkey Casserole, 45
Barbecue Chicken Casserole, 41
Black Bean Rice Bake, 24
Cheddar Chicken Spaghetti, 31
Ham and Swiss Strata, 42
Meaty Bean Casserole, 22
Mini Tuna Casseroles, 153
Mother's Ham Casserole, 40
Potato Ham Bake, 21
Sausage Spinach Bake, 171
Swiss Steak with Dumplings, 148
Where's the Squash Lasagna, 25
Side Dishes
Asparagus Onion Casserole, 80
✓Autumn Squash Bake, 81
Big-Batch Baked Beans, 87
Broccoli Squash Bake, 169
Corn Bread Casserole, 88
Creamy Corn Casserole, 81
Creamy Potato Casserole, 87
Crumb-Topped Broccoli Bake, 86
Grandpa's Party Potatoes, 80
Macaroni and Cheese Casserole, 79
Party Potatoes Au Gratin, 84
Scalloped Potatoes and Carrots, 79
Six-Veggie Casserole, 89
Spinach Pecan Bake, 140
Zucchini Supreme, 88

CAULIFLOWER
Cauliflower Ham Chowder, 68
Cauliflower Tomato Soup, 59
Creamed Cauliflower, 84
Sweet Floret Salad, 72

CHEESE
Au Gratin Peas and Potatoes, 17
Cheddar Chicken Spaghetti, 31
Cheese-Stuffed Burgers, 50
Cheesy Zucchini Saute, 79
Ham 'n' Cheese Tortillas, 8
Ham 'n' Egg Pizza, 45
Ham and Swiss Strata, 42
Ham Pickle Pinwheels, 14
Hash Brown Ham Quiche, 44
Lettuce with Blue Cheese Dressing, 66
Macaroni and Cheese Casserole, 79
Olive-Cheese Zucchini Boats, 165
Parmesan Ham Pasta, 39
Party Potatoes Au Gratin, 84
Quick Cheese Puffs, 171
Shrimp Appetizer Spread, 7
Spinach Swiss Pie, 53
Sweet Potato Cheese Ball, 14
Zippy Cheese Dip, 150

CHEESECAKES
Harvest Apple Cheesecake, 126
Mocha Cheesecake, 120

CHERRIES
Cherry Berry Pie, 126
George Washington Cherry Cobbler, 145
Holiday Brownies, 114
Macaroon Cherry Pie, 125
Northern Cherry Puffs, 118
Turkey with Cherry Stuffing, 38

CHICKEN
Avocado Malibu Salad, 57
Baked Chicken and Acorn Squash, 32
Baked Lemon Chicken, 142
Barbecue Chicken Casserole, 41
Black Bean Rice Bake, 24
Broccoli-Stuffed Chicken, 155
Broiled Chicken Slices, 133
Cheddar Chicken Spaghetti, 31
Chicken Bean Stew, 23
Chicken Caesar Salad, 62
Chicken Fajitas, 36
Chicken Salad Puffs, 12
Chicken Sausage Skillet, 28
Chicken Vegetable Potpie, 159
Chicken Veggie Saute, 34
Chicken with Fettuccine, 137
Creamy Mushroom Chicken, 21
Fruity Chicken Salad, 61
Grilled Chicken with Peach Sauce, 49
Meaty Bean Casserole, 22
Nectarine Chicken Salad, 73
Southern Fried Chicken, 23
✓Sunflower Chicken, 24
Teriyaki Glazed Chicken, 52

CHOCOLATE
Almond Coconut Brownies, 105
Brownie Baked Alaska, 109
Brownie Mocha Trifle, 131
Candy Bar Pie, 122
Cashew Blondies, 111
Chocolate Cookie Torte, 112
Chocolate Maple Cookies, 100
Chocolate Snack Cake, 161
Chocolate Sweet Potato Cake, 149
Coconut Chocolate Chip Cookies, 169
Coconut Pecan Blondies, 101
Creamy Chocolate Pudding, 157
Fast Fudgy Brownies, 111
Frosted Fudge Brownies, 100
Fudgy Nut Brownies, 104
Glazed Chocolate Chip Brownies, 104
Holiday Brownies, 114
Holstein Brownies, 113
Macadamia Chip Brownies, 105
Macaroon Brownies, 99
Microwave Brownies, 110

✓*Recipe includes Nutritional Analysis and Diabetic Exchanges*

✓Recipe includes Nutritional Analysis and Diabetic Exchanges

✓*Recipe includes Nutritional Analysis and Diabetic Exchanges*

Alphabetical Recipe Index

C

Cabbage-Tomato Pasta Toss, 85
Cajun Corn and Shrimp, 74
Cajun Pepper Steak, 46
Candy Bar Pie, 122
Caramel Cashew Brownies, 104
Caramelized Apple Rings, 175
Cardamom Braids, 92
Carrot Banana Bread, 97
Carrot Broccoli Salad, 77
Cashew Blondies, 111
Cashew Rice Pilaf, 86
Catch Some "Z's", 8
Cauliflower Ham Chowder, 68
Cauliflower Tomato Soup, 59
Cheddar Chicken Spaghetti, 31
Cheese-Stuffed Burgers, 50
Cheesy Zucchini Saute, 79
Cherry Berry Pie, 126
Chewy Ginger Drop Cookies, 141
Chewy Oatmeal Cookies, 114
Chicken Bean Stew, 23
Chicken Caesar Salad, 62
Chicken Fajitas, 36
Chicken Salad Puffs, 12
Chicken Sausage Skillet, 28
Chicken Vegetable Potpie, 159
Chicken Veggie Saute, 34
Chicken with Fettuccine, 137
✓Chili Non Carne, 58
Chilled Asparagus Soup, 75
Chocolate Cookie Torte, 112
Chocolate Maple Cookies, 100
Chocolate Snack Cake, 161
Chocolate Sweet Potato Cake, 149
Christmas Sandwich Cookies, 102
Chuck Wagon Tortilla Stack, 51
Cinnamon Raisin Bread, 95
Citrus Frost, 171
Citrus Pineapple Coleslaw, 58
Coconut Chocolate Chip Cookies, 169
Coconut Cream Meringue Pie, 122
Coconut Ice Cream, 119
Coconut Pecan Blondies, 101
Coffee Ice Cream, 147
Coffee Mallow Dessert, 167
Colorful Cabbage Skillet, 153
Colorful Vegetable Salad, 146
Colorful Vegetable Saute, 89
Confetti Caramel Corn, 12
Cookie Checkerboard, 103
Corn Bread Casserole, 88
Cornmeal Yeast Bread, 94
Country Ham Bread, 93
Crab Melt Loaf, 131
Cranberry Meatballs, 150
Cranberry Pear Salad, 155
Cranberry Pork Chops, 20
Cream of Mushroom Soup, 144
Creamed Cauliflower, 84
✓Creamy Basil Dressing, 161
Creamy Chocolate Pudding, 157

Creamy Corn Casserole, 81
Creamy Dressing Over Asparagus, 66
Creamy Mushroom Chicken, 21
Creamy Potato Casserole, 87
Creamy Seafood Enchiladas, 31
Crumb-Coated Tomatoes, 169
Crumb-Topped Broccoli Bake, 86
Crunchy Macaroni Salad, 159
Cube Steak Skillet Supper, 163
Cucumber Canapes, 5
Cucumber Potato Salad, 165
Curried Ham and Fruit, 42
Curried Leek Soup, 75

D

Deep-Dish Blackberry Pie, 165
Deluxe Bacon Burgers, 146
Deluxe Ham Balls, 48
Dilled Noodles, 153

E

Easy Beef and Noodles, 35
Egg Rice Salad, 157
Egg Salad Pitas, 54

F

Fast Fudgy Brownies, 111
✓Festive Fruit Salad, 74
Fit-for-a-King Baked Beans, 82
French Dressing Over Iceberg Wedges, 62
French Onion Soup, 163
Fresh Fruit Medley, 142
Fried Jalapenos, 13
Frosted Fudge Brownies, 100
✓Fruit Crepes, 26
Fruit Slaw in a Cabbage Bowl, 71
Fruited Fish, 121
Fruity Chicken Salad, 61
Fruity Cranberry Relish, 82
Fudgy Nut Brownies, 104

G

Garden Tossed Salad, 148
George Washington Cherry Cobbler, 145
Glazed Chocolate Chip Brownies, 104
Golden Corn Puff, 86
Golden Gelatin Salad, 148
Golden Peach Pie, 117
Grandpa's Party Potatoes, 80
Granny's Rhubarb Pie, 120
Green Beans with Cherry Tomatoes, 142
Grilled Chicken with Peach Sauce, 49
Grilled Dijon Summer Squash, 82
Grilled Pork and Poblano Peppers, 37

H

Halloween Punch, 7
Ham a la King, 46
Ham 'n' Cheese Tortillas, 8
✓Ham and Corn Chowder, 76

Ham 'n' Egg Pizza, 45
Ham and Swiss Strata, 42
✓Ham Pasta Salad, 60
Ham Pickle Pinwheels, 14
Ham Salad Puff, 60
Ham Salad Spread, 150
Ham Stew for Two, 157
✓Ham with Orange Sauce, 36
Harvest Apple Cheesecake, 126
Hash Brown Ham Quiche, 44
Hawaiian Egg Rolls, 6
Hearty Bean Soup, 60
✓Hearty Squash Skillet, 49
Herb-Crusted Chuck Roast, 32
Herb-Roasted Turkey, 46
Herbed Pork Roast, 140
Holiday Brownies, 114
Holstein Brownies, 113
Homemade Potato Salad, 146
Honey Fruit Dessert, 123
Hoppin' Good Salad, 58
Horseradish Honey Ham, 27
Hot Ham Salad, 68
Hot Raspberry-Lemonade Drink Mix, 15
Hot Turkey Salad Pitas, 53

I

Italian Ribs and Rice, 52
Italian Sausage Stew, 19

L

Lemon Cake Roll, 102
Lemon-Cranberry Mini Loaves, 91
Lemony Tossed Salad, 135
Lettuce with Blue Cheese Dressing, 66
Lime Angel Food Cake, 101

M

Macadamia Chip Brownies, 105
Macaroni and Cheese Casserole, 79
Macaroon Brownies, 99
Macaroon Cherry Pie, 125
Mango Nut Bread, 96
Maple Carrot Cupcakes, 142
Maple-Glazed Carrots, 173
Maple-Glazed Pork Chops, 26
Maple Squash Soup, 73
✓Marinated Citrus Salad, 70
Marinated Italian Pasta, 74
Marinated Shrimp, 5
Marinated Tomatoes, 69
Marshmallow Cream with Custard Sauce, 123
Mashed Potato Rolls, 92
Meat Loaf Pattie, 165
Meat Loaf Pie, 135

✓*Recipe includes Nutritional Analysis*
and Diabetic Exchanges

✓*Recipe includes Nutritional Analysis*
and Diabetic Exchanges